Globalization and Development

Globalization and Development

A LATIN AMERICAN AND CARIBBEAN PERSPECTIVE

Edited by

José Antonio Ocampo
Juan Martin

ECONOMIC COMMISSION FOR LATIN AMERICA AND THE CARIBBEAN

A COPUBLICATION OF STANFORD SOCIAL SCIENCES, AN IMPRINT OF
STANFORD UNIVERSITY PRESS, AND THE WORLD BANK

#5321/9032

© 2003 ECLAC   United Nations
Economic Commission for Latin America
and the Caribbean
Casilla 179-D
Santiago, Chile

1 2 3 4 06 05 04 03

A copublication of Stanford Social Sciences, an imprint of Stanford
University Press, and the World Bank.

Stanford University Press   The World Bank
1450 Page Mill Road   1818 H Street, NW
Palo Alto, Calif. 94304   Washington, DC 20433

The views and opinions expressed here are those of the authors and do not
necessarily reflect the official position of ECLAC.

ISBN 0-8213-5501-5 (World Rights except North America)
ISBN 0-8047-4956-6 (North America)

Library of Congress Cataloging-in-Publication Data has been applied for.

Latin American Development Forum Series

This series was created in 2003 to promote debate, disseminate information and analysis, and convey the excitement and complexity of the most topical issues in economic and social development in Latin America and the Caribbean. It is sponsored by the Inter-American Development Bank, the United Nations Economic Commission for Latin America and the Caribbean, and the World Bank. The manuscripts chosen for publication represent the highest quality in each institution's research and activity output, and have been selected for their relevance to the academic community, policymakers, researchers, and interested readers.

Advisory Committee Members

Inés Bustillo, Director, Washington Office, Economic Commission for Latin America and the Caribbean, United Nations

Guillermo Calvo, Chief Economist, Inter-American Development Bank

José Luis Guasch, Regional Adviser, Latin America and Caribbean Region, World Bank

Stephen Haber, A. A. and Jeanne Welch Milligan Professor, Department of Political Science, Stanford University; Peter and Helen Bing Senior Fellow, the Hoover Institution

Eduardo Lora, Principal Adviser, Research Department, Inter-American Development Bank

José Antonio Ocampo, Executive Secretary, Economic Commission for Latin America and the Caribbean, United Nations

Guillermo E. Perry, Chief Economist, Latin America and Caribbean Region, World Bank

Luis Servén, Lead Economist, Latin America and Caribbean Region, World Bank

About ECLAC

THE ECONOMIC COMMISSION FOR Latin America and the Caribbean (ECLAC), headquartered in Santiago, Chile, is one of the five regional commissions of the United Nations. It was founded for the purpose of contributing to the economic development of Latin America and the Caribbean, coordinating actions directed towards this end, and reinforcing economic relationships among these countries and with other nations of the world. The promotion of the region's social development was later included among its primary objectives.

Acknowledgments

The preparation of this document was coordinated by José Antonio Ocampo, Executive Secretary of ECLAC, and Juan Martin, Special Advisor to the Executive Secretary, with the collaboration of Reynaldo Bajraj, Deputy Executive Secretary, and María Elisa Bernal, Special Assistant to the Secretary of the Commission.

Contributions to individual chapters were prepared by Alicia Bárcena, Director of the Sustainable Development and Human Settlements Division; Juan Carlos Ramírez, Chief of ECLAC's Bogotá office; Vivianne Ventura-Dias, Director of the Division of International Trade and Integration; and Eugenio Lahera, Consultant.

Rudolf Buitelaar, Inés Bustillo, Mario Cimoli, Ricardo Ffrench-Davis, Manuel Marfán, María Angela Parra, Wilson Peres, Andrés Solimano, Miguel Villa, and consultants Armando Di Fillipo, Edmund V. FitzGerald, Stephany Griffith-Jones, Gabriel Palma, and Jaime Ros also provided valuable contributions.

Contents

Preface

IT HAS BEEN SAID THAT LATIN AMERICAN thought is the history of a quest to harmonize modernization and identity. Ever since its founding, the Economic Commission for Latin America and the Caribbean (ECLAC) has sought to contribute to this undertaking by highlighting the specific nature of regional situations, while at the same time advocating efforts to change the region's production patterns in conjunction with the promotion of social equity and, more recently, environmental sustainability. Globalization shapes the context in which this task must be undertaken. Precisely for this reason, the countries of Latin America and the Caribbean asked ECLAC's Secretariat to prepare a document on globalization and development (ECLAC 2002a) that was discussed in the 29th Session of the Commission (Brasilia, Brazil, May 2002).

The main motivation to produce this book lies in our perception of a sharp contrast between problems that are increasingly global in scope and international institution building, which lags behind. This uneven advance jeopardizes the balance of opportunities and risks of globalization. Thus, this book presents an analysis of the opportunities that are open to the developing world, but it also examines the asymmetries and risks entailed in this process, which may hinder development unless suitable institutional frameworks are put in place at the national, regional, and global levels. Although the conceptual considerations explored in this volume are based on one particular region of the developing world, Latin America and the Caribbean, the analysis is undertaken in a broader spirit and may therefore be relevant for other regions as well.

Economic globalization has deep historical roots. The current phase of globalization shares certain features with previous stages, but it also has a number of characteristics that set it apart, such as mass real-time access to information; the global planning of production by transnational corporations; the expansion of free trade, albeit still limited by multiple forms of protectionism in the industrial world; the contradictory combination of a high degree of mobility of capital and tight restrictions on the migration of labor; evidence of growing environmental vulnerability and interdependence; and an unprecedented trend toward the homogenization of institutions. This standardization of the applicable rules is biased, however, because only the most powerful international actors have succeeded in safeguarding their interests. The outcome of this bias is an incomplete international agenda. Both of these features—namely the bias and incompleteness of the current order—have profound implications for analysis and for public policy.

The vision of globalization set out in this analysis highlights the multidimensional nature of the process and, by extension, underscores the fact that it is not determined by economic forces alone. One of the dimensions of globalization, which ECLAC has termed the "globalization of values," consists of the gradual spread of common ethical principles, including those embodied in declarations of human rights and the principles enshrined in summits held by the United Nations. These processes have their roots in international civil society's long struggle to instill respect for human rights, social equity, gender equality, and environmental protection and, more recently, the globalization of solidarity and the right to be different.

Given the forcefulness of these processes, the lack of any true internationalization of politics is undoubtedly the greatest paradox of the current phase of globalization. The mismatch between problems that are worldwide in scope and national political processes has translated into a "governance deficit" at the global level, which has made it harder to balance the opportunities and risks inherent in globalization. The fact that the political arena continues to be essentially national in scope also has profound implications for the international order. In particular, it implies that the promotion of democracy as a universal value makes sense only insofar as national processes of representation and participation are allowed to shape strategies of economic and social development and to mediate effectively among sectors that are affected differentially by globalization.

Various aspects of globalization offer significant opportunities for developing countries. Potentially, developing nations stand to gain from broader market access and the availability of capital and technology from the rest of the world, but the globalization process also holds out an opportunity for championing human rights and other universal values. In light of these opportunities, the greatest risk of all may lie in exclusion from the process. At the same time, however, globalization carries the risks associated with new sources of instability (in the spheres of trade and, particularly, finance), the risk of exclusion for countries that are ill-prepared for the modern world's relentless demand for competitiveness, and the risk of heightened structural heterogeneity among social sectors and regions in countries whose integration into the world economy has been segmented. How successful the countries will be in taking advantage of the opportunities of globalization and mitigating its risks will depend upon the effectiveness of their national and regional strategies for participating in this process and upon the global institutions that establish the framework for those strategies.

The most reasonable response to the complex situation created by globalization is to pursue a positive agenda. Experience has shown, moreover, that in the long run mere resistance to such deeply rooted processes inevitably proves futile. We should not, however, view globalization as a natural, unalterable phenomenon that we have no alternative but to decry or embrace. The existence of various possible global orders is borne out not only by the history of the globalization process itself, but also by the range of different modalities of development and integration into the global economy pursued by industrial and developing countries alike.

The first of this book's five chapters focuses on the multidimensional nature of globalization; describes the current phase of the process within its historical context of global economic internationalization; and briefly examines its social, political, and cultural dimensions. Chapters 2 and 3 look at how the economic facets of the globalization process have evolved. Chapter 2 explores trends in international trade and in the new global production structure, and chapter 3 analyzes the international mobility of capital—within the framework of the various macroeconomic regimes of the world economy—and of labor. Income disparity trends and the underlying asymmetries of the current global order are discussed in chapter 4. The fifth and final chapter proposes an agenda for the global era. As part of this proposal—and on the basis of certain fundamental principles, such as global institutions that respect diversity; complementarity among global, regional, and national institutions; and equitable participation by the countries based on suitable rules of governance—this chapter outlines the national, regional, and global measures that are needed to achieve the three foremost objectives of a new international order: a supply of global public goods, the gradual correction of international asymmetries, and the progressive construction of a rights-based international social agenda.

1

Globalization: A Historical, Multidimensional Perspective

IN THE 1990s THE CONCEPT OF globalization was widely employed in academic and political debates, but the meanings attributed to this term are far from consistent. In this volume *globalization* will be used to refer to the growing influence exerted at the local, national, and regional levels by financial, economic, environmental, political, social, and cultural processes that are global in scope. This definition of the term highlights the multidimensional nature of globalization. Indeed, although the economic dimensions of globalization are spoken about the most, they are concomitant with noneconomic processes, which have a dynamic of their own and are therefore not determined by economic factors. In addition, the tension that is generated between the different dimensions of globalization is a pivotal element of the process. In the economic sphere, but also—and especially—in the broadest sense of the term, the current globalization process is incomplete and asymmetric and is marked by major shortcomings in terms of governance.

The dynamics of globalization are shaped, to a large extent, by the fact that the actors involved in this process are on an unequal footing. Industrial-country governments, together with transnational corporations, exert the strongest influence, whereas developing-country governments and civil society organizations hold much less sway. Moreover, some of these actors—particularly industrial-country governments—reserve and exercise the right to take unilateral and bilateral action and to participate in regional processes while continuing to engage in global debates and negotiations.

The meaning of the term *globalization* as used in this book is couched in positive terms and is intended to serve the purposes of analysis. It does not embrace the normative use of the concept, which is based on the idea that there is only one possible road to the full liberalization and integration of world markets and that this path traces the inevitable and desirable fate of all humankind.[1] The history of the 20th century refutes such a view; the period between the world wars was marked by a long and conflictive reversal of the internationalization process. The development of multilateral institutions that has accompanied the globalization process and the current debate on global governance show that there is not just one possible international order, nor is there a single way of dividing responsibilities among global, regional, and national institutions and agencies. Moreover, the course of events in industrial and developing countries has revealed that there are many ways to establish a position in the global economy (Albert 1993; Economic Commission for Latin America and the Caribbean [ECLAC] 2000a; Rodrik 2001b). The differences are a reflection of each country's history and of how each one weighs the opportunities and risks involved in becoming integrated into the world economy.

This chapter presents an initial approach to the globalization process as a whole. The first section gives a general description of the history and economic dimensions of the process, and the following section analyzes the main noneconomic factors (ethical, cultural, and political principles). The chapter concludes with an analysis of the opportunities and risks inherent in globalization.

Economic Globalization

The contemporary process of internationalization dates back to the emergence of capitalism in Europe in the late Middle Ages, the new scientific and cultural thinking embodied by the Renaissance, and the establishment of the great European nations and their empires. The expansion of capitalism is the only historical phenomenon to have been truly global (albeit incomplete) in scope. To a greater extent than other parts of the developing world, the history of Latin America and the Caribbean has been strongly influenced by the development of capitalism ever since the late 15th century.

Modern historians distinguish a number of stages in the last 130 years of globalization; with a few adaptations, three stages will be used in this volume.[2] The first stage, from 1870 to 1913, was marked by a high degree of capital and labor mobility, together with a trade boom that was the result of reduced transport costs rather than of free trade. This stage of globalization was cut short by the First World War, which gave way to a period that was characterized first (in the 1920s) by the impossibility of resuming the trend of previous years and then (in the 1930s) by an open reversal of the globalization process.

After the Second World War, there was a new impulse toward global integration. This period consisted of the second and third stages of globalization. The watershed events of the early 1970s marked the changeover from the second to the third stage. These events included the disintegration of the macroeconomic regulation regime established in 1944 in Bretton Woods, the first oil crisis, the increasing mobility of private capital, intensified by the first two events, and the end of the "golden age" of growth in the industrialized countries (1950–73) (Marglin and Schor 1990). If 1973 is taken as the turning point, then the second stage of globalization can be circumscribed to the period 1945–73. This period was marked by a major effort to develop international institutions for financial and trade cooperation and by a significant expansion of trade in manufactures among industrial countries. It was also characterized by widely varying models of economic organization and limitations on the mobility of capital and labor. The final quarter of the 20th century (1973 onward) ushered in a third stage of globalization, with the gradual spread of free trade, the growing presence on the international scene of transnational corporations operating as internationally integrated production systems, the expansion and notable mobility of capital, and a shift toward the standardization of development models. At the same time, selective trade protection mechanisms and tight restrictions on the movement of labor persisted.

This long process has been fueled by successive technological revolutions and, most importantly, by advances that have cut the costs of transportation, information, and communications.[3] The shortening of distances, in the economic sense, is a cumulative effect of cost reductions and of the development of new means of transport, in combination with the capacity for the real-time transmission of information, which started with the invention of the telegraph and expanded with the advent of the telephone and television. Access to information on a mass scale, however, became possible only with the development of information and communication technologies in recent years. These technologies have drastically reduced the cost of access to information, though not, obviously, the cost of processing it or of making effective use of it.

Advances in transportation, information, and communications are part of a wider range of technological innovations that have resulted in unprecedented advances in productivity, economic growth, and international trade. In the European countries, the major capital cities have been engaged in international trade ever since the inception of modern capitalism (Braudel 1994). The internationalization of corporate production dates back to the late 19th century, when it emerged as a by-product of economic concentration in the industrialized countries. In fact, this phenomenon marked the birth of transnational corporations. From the 1970s on, the increasingly common practice of outsourcing labor-intensive tasks, such as assembly or maquiladora activities, to other countries was facilitated by the reduction in transport costs and the trade regulations established by the industrial countries. This was the first step toward the development of internationally integrated production systems, in which production can be divided into various stages (a process known as "the dismemberment of the value chain"). In such systems, the outsourcers in different countries can then specialize in the production of certain components, in particular phases of the production process, or in the assembly of specific models.

These changes in the structure of production and trade have enabled large corporations and business conglomerates to come to the fore. In fact, the development of internationally integrated production systems and increased flows of trade and foreign direct investment go hand in hand with the growing influence of transnational corporations. The key factor has undoubtedly been the liberalization of trade, financial flows, and investment in developing countries, and the pace of liberalization has been increasing over the last two decades. These phenomena are some of the factors behind the huge wave of foreign investment and the marked concentration of production at the world level that were hallmarks of the final decade of the 20th century.

As in the case of trade, international financial transactions originated in Europe at about the same time as modern capitalism (Braudel 1994; Kindleberger 1984). In the 19th century, London was the main international financial center and presided over the consolidation of the gold standard as a system of international payments and macroeconomic regulation. Paris and, by the early 20th century, New York were its closest competitors. The subscription of capital for large-scale projects, especially in infrastructure and natural resources, and the creation of an international market in public bonds were the predominant sources of long-term international capital movements during the first stage of globalization. These developments were complemented by the emergence of an incipient international banking network that began to create instruments for financing international trade. Long-term financing arrangements were then hit by a series of crises, however, and nearly disappeared altogether as a result of the worldwide depression of the 1930s, the collapse of the gold standard, and the massive defaults that ensued. In response to this situation, the Bretton Woods agreements were adopted in 1944 with a view to creating a multilateral system of macroeconomic regulation based on fixed but adjustable exchange rates and on financial support for countries threatened with balance-of-payments crises. Another response was the establishment of an official international banking system at both the national level (export and import banks) and the multilateral level (the World Bank and, later, the Inter-American Development Bank and other regional banks).

In the 1960s, private long-term international flows reappeared, thanks in part to a new phase of global economic stability but also to other factors: the surplus of dollars that built up in the 1960s and of petrodollars in the 1970s; the abandonment of the Bretton Woods system of fixed rates and the flotation of the main currencies in the early 1970s; the rapid development of institutional saving in the 1980s, led by the United Kingdom and the United States; and the emergence of an increasingly large financial derivatives market in the last decade of the 20th century, which made it possible to hedge the risks associated with different financial assets and liabilities.

Globalization has proceeded at a faster pace in the financial sphere than in trade and production, and it can plausibly be argued that we live in an era in which the financial sphere holds sway over the real sector of the economy (ECLAC 2001b). Both processes are taking place within a framework of thoroughgoing institutional restructuring at the global level, the essence of which has been the liberalization of international current and capital transactions. The progress made in designing new global economic rules continues to be inadequate, however, and this structure clearly suffers from institutional gaps.

On the other hand, there has been no corresponding liberalization of labor flows, which are subject to strict regulation by national authorities (except among the member countries of the European Union). This is one of the major differences between the first and current stages of globalization. The first was marked by two major migratory flows: of European labor to temperate zones and of primarily Asian labor to tropical areas. Together, these two migrations encompassed around 10 percent of the world population of the time (World Bank 2002b).

In addition, the regulation of migratory flows is biased against unskilled labor, which consequently tends to seek out irregular channels. This exposes immigrants to abusive practices by traffickers, heightens their defenselessness against the authorities, and generates further downward pressure on wages for unskilled labor in the receiving countries. Meanwhile, as a result of the preference for skilled labor, the most highly qualified—and relatively scarce—human resources are drained out of developing countries. The segmentation of labor mobility therefore exacerbates income disparities between workers with different skill levels in both their home and their host countries.

A number of other factors that are closely associated with economic activity have taken on great importance at the world level. One of these factors is the scope of global environmental problems. In the last three decades it has become clear—and has been scientifically documented—that the entire planet is being subjected to unprecedented impacts as a result of the increasing scale and cumulative effect of human activity. The consequences are being felt worldwide and include global warming, the thinning of the ozone layer, the decline in biodiversity, and the spread of desertification and drought, which have taken on the perverse dimension of "global public bads." By revealing the existence of a web of causes and effects that are generated by human activities having global environmental impacts, advances in scientific knowledge have highlighted the increasing ecological interdependence and vulnerability of countries, regardless of their level of development.

The need to reverse these global ecological processes has given rise to new imperatives and opportunities for international cooperation, which have been reflected in the various world summits and conferences held in the 1990s and in the multilateral environmental agreements concluded on those occasions. In the course of these processes, governments have adopted a proactive attitude toward cooperating in order to protect and manage global public goods on the basis of innovative multilateral arrangements. They have also adopted principles based on the need for an equitable sharing, between rich and poor states, of the responsibilities and costs of reversing environmental damage. Accordingly, the environmental dimension is taking on increasing significance as an arena for negotiations between developing and industrial countries. Because regions of the developing world that are rich in biodiversity or are extensively forested provide important global environmental services by, for example, serving as carbon sinks (carbon dioxide is the primary cause of climate change through the greenhouse effect), the developing countries have both the potential and the opportunity to play a key role in solving global problems. The responses that have been developed thus far are clearly inadequate, however, given the magnitude of these problems, especially in view of the threat they pose to the sustainability of economic growth.

In the 1990s, great strides were made in this regard with the approval of new international legal principles concerning the environment and development, one of which is principle 7, on "common but differentiated responsibilities," of the Rio Declaration on Environment and Development, adopted at the Earth Summit held in Rio de Janeiro in 1992. Under this principle, industrial countries explicitly acknowledge the environmental debt they have accumulated vis-à-vis the rest of the international community as a result of the cumulative global externalities generated by their industrialization processes. This principle provides a political basis for industrial countries' assumption of greater environmental commitments than developing countries under multilateral agreements. It also reflects the express recognition that countries cannot and should not aspire to "level the playing field" in the environmental sphere, in contrast to the principles currently governing efforts to change the economic aspects of the international order.

Another variety of global public bads that is also linked to economic activity is the spread of international crime: the production, trade, and consumption of narcotics and their close linkage with terrorist financing, arms trafficking, and the international circulation of illicit capital generated by drug trafficking and by the different forms of corruption that transcend national borders. The system has been slow to recognize the need to control the circulation of illicit capital in both developing and industrial countries as well as in offshore financial centers, in large part because existing bank secrecy provisions will have to be scaled back to permit the operation of special mechanisms to monitor the circulation of illicit funds. Unfortunately, the systems that have been developed thus far do not include international measures to combat a number of forms of corruption that are particularly a problem for developing countries, such as tax evasion, illegal capital flight, bribery, and illicit enrichment.

Noneconomic Dimensions of Globalization

Ethical and Cultural Dimensions

Economic globalization is taking place alongside other processes that have a dynamic of their own. One of the most positive of these processes has been called the "globalization of values." This concept refers to the gradual spread of shared ethical principles (ECLAC 2000a) and is manifested most clearly in declarations on human rights. The two main dimensions of concern in this book are (a) civil and political rights, by virtue of which individuals have autonomy from the power of the state and are entitled to participate in public decision-making, and (b) economic, social, and cultural rights, which reflect the values of economic and social equality, solidarity, and nondiscrimination. This process has also found expression in the accession of a growing number of governments to U.N. human rights conventions (see figure 1.1). It is also reflected in the declarations issued by the participants in world summits held under U.N. auspices on the environment, social development, population, women, and the rights of

Figure 1.1 Ratification of Human Rights Conventions

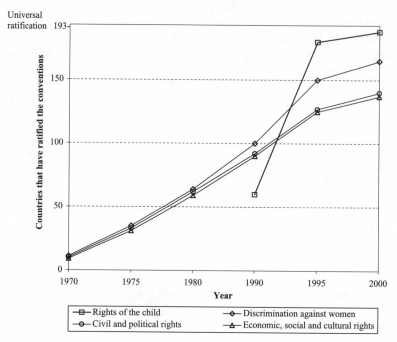

Source: United Nations (1999b).

children, among others. The Millennium Declaration (United Nations 2000) is one of the most comprehensive expressions of the principles agreed upon at these summits.

It is important to note that, like economic globalization, the globalization of values has a long history that is linked to the aspirations of international civil society. Its most recent manifestation is the formation of a "global civil society" whose capacity for mobilization and for information exchange has been multiplied by the new information and communication technologies. The history of this society dates back to the liberal internationalism that emerged in the wake of the American and French revolutions in the late 18th century, which was expressed most clearly in the French revolution's Declaration of the Rights of Man and of the Citizen. As is well known, these values strongly influenced the independence movements in Latin America and the Caribbean, which began with the outbreak of the Haitian revolution in 1791 as a direct consequence of the French revolution.

Whereas the civil and political rights enshrined in the Universal Declaration of Human Rights adopted by the United Nations (1948) are rooted in the liberal movements of the late 18th century, the International Covenant on Economic, Social and Cultural Rights (United Nations 1966) is a product of the social movements of the 19th and 20th centuries, whose chief political manifestation has been the International Socialist Organization in its successive forms. In addition, throughout the 20th century, feminist internationalism had a decisive influence in winning the recognition of women's equal rights, and environmental internationalism has played a major role since the 1960s in incorporating sustainable development principles into national and international agendas. Beginning at the Stockholm summit in 1972 and extending to the U.N. Conference on Environment and Development (Rio de Janeiro, 1992) and the World Summit on Sustainable Development (Johannesburg, 2002), global environmental conventions have been aimed at implementing some of the mandates of environmental internationalism.

At the same time, it is important to note that this globalization of values sometimes comes into conflict with a diametrically opposed type of globalization that reflects the penetration of market economy values into social relations (in the areas of production, culture, and even the family). The tension generated between these shared ethical principles and the extension of market relations into the sphere of values, which is implicit in the concept of a market society, is another hallmark of the globalization process. This tension sometimes generates conflicts because the international market lacks the mediation mechanisms that the political sphere has traditionally provided at the national level.

In recent years, the long history of social movements has taken on a new dimension: the effort to preserve the identity of peoples and social groups that feel threatened by the tendency toward cultural homogeneity that globalization engenders. This "right to be different" is interrelated in various ways with human rights in the traditional sense, which highlight the equality of citizens, both among themselves and before the state. Thus, at the global level, equality and identity are interrelated in complex ways.

Globalization simultaneously undermines cultural diversity and affords new opportunities for its expression. Indeed, large segments of the world population feel that their unique histories and the values that govern their communities are in jeopardy. At the same time, however, globalization builds closer relationships among different cultural traditions and ways of life, thereby increasing their visibility and the likelihood that they will be duly appreciated. This, in turn, promotes the emergence of myriad interpretations of the global order.

Nonetheless, the speed of this process poses unprecedented challenges. On the one hand, it threatens to turn the enriching dialogue of

---

Box 1.1 Inclusion and Identity: The Issue of Ethnicity

Latin America and the Caribbean comprise a melting pot of cultures in which diversity and universality are mixed and blended. The region is home to over 400 indigenous peoples who number 50 million individuals. These groups have gradually been strengthening their ability to organize politically, to assert their ethnic identities, and to defend their cultures. Five countries account for nearly 90 percent of the region's indigenous population: Peru (27 percent), Mexico (26 percent), Guatemala (15 percent), Bolivia (12 percent), and Ecuador (8 percent). The Afro-Latin and Afro-Caribbean populations total almost 150 million people, most of whom live in Brazil (51 percent), Colombia (21 percent), the Caribbean subregion (16 percent), or the República Bolivariana de Venezuela (12 percent).

In these early years of the new millennium, the indigenous, Afro-Latin, and Afro-Caribbean peoples of the region have the worst economic and social indicators, enjoy very little cultural recognition, and lack access to public decisionmaking circles. The Latin American and Caribbean countries face a formidable challenge in this respect. Social integration requires the acknowledgement and appreciation of cultural diversity, and this means that states, governments, and societies must recognize the rights of the different ethnic groups, incorporate those rights into their legislation, and provide the necessary means of exercising those rights. Development policy must also provide opportunities for these populations to develop their potential and share in the basic codes of modern life without losing their identities.

Source: Hernández (2002).

---

cultures into a monologue. On the other, interaction opens up cultural opportunities, including those created by the mixture of different cultures, to new and varied groups and individuals (see box 1.1). This process of incorporation through participatory and exclusionary mechanisms has given rise to new forms of organization. New networks, including some virtual ones, are replacing the organizational channels traditionally used by protest movements, for example.

The remarkable development of the communications media has strongly influenced these processes and has also given rise to new problems. First, it has greatly widened the gap between the cultural norms most broadly disseminated through global channels of communication and the cultural and artistic roots of countries and regions. Second, control of the media at the national and international levels is concentrated in the hands of a few. This situation threatens the ideal of cultural diversity, because the control of symbolic exchanges influences identity building, opinions, and beliefs.[4] Third, the development of audiovisual media has led to greatly heightened personal expectations regarding material wealth. Access to information is not always in balance with opportunities for steady employment and incomes and, accordingly, for well-being and consumption. Today, more than ever before, the demonstration effect cuts across national boundaries. Finally, participation in or exclusion from the electronic exchange of information has become a crucial factor for the exercise of citizenship, thereby posing the basic problem of how to prevent the emergence of a gap between those with access to information technology and those who suffer from what has been called "electronic invisibility" or "electronic blindness."

Political Dimension

International political relations have also undergone far-reaching changes in recent decades. The end of the cold war brought a dramatic change in the climate of international relations among sovereign states, and the exacerbation and increased visibility of a number of localized conflicts generated international tensions of a very different nature than those seen before. These trends had been in evidence since the 1970s, but they strengthened in the closing decade of the 20th century, particularly as a result of the profound changes that took place after the fall of the Berlin Wall. The heightened predominance of the United States, European efforts to form a bloc capable of playing a leading role in global economic and political affairs, the setbacks suffered by Japan, the increased prominence of China and India, and the sudden transition experienced in the former socialist countries were the most salient features of this period.

These sweeping political changes have placed representative democracy in a position of unparalleled preponderance. Political discourse is being shaped by an acceptance of the principles of pluralism, alternation of power, division of the powers of the state, election of authorities as a basis for legitimacy, and recognition of the majority combined with respect for minorities, and these principles have begun to be applied much more widely.

Nevertheless, the transformations now under way have raised questions about how democratic institutions should function in societies where information, "image," and the power of money play a fundamental role. Criticism along these lines extends to political parties, legislatures, the relationship between voters and representatives, and even the very meaning of politics, especially—though not exclusively—in the parts of the developing world that suffer from exclusion and poverty. Although democracy is the choice of the majority, there is certainly no scarcity of negative views regarding its workings and its effectiveness in meeting the population's needs.[5] As with the peace dividend that countries expected to receive after the end of the cold war, which has failed to yield significant benefits, it has not yet been possible to cash in on the "democracy bonus" either.

Despite these difficulties, it is generally recognized that democracy is the best means of setting a development agenda (Sen 1999) and that good governance is characterized by a focus on improving the design, management, and evaluation of public policy, which serves as the analytical and operational tool of government (Lahera 2002). Nonetheless, government authorities and political leaders are under pressure to win broad local support and, at the same time, to abide by the rigid rules deriving from specific forms of globalization. In this connection, it may be categorically stated that the promotion of democracy as a universal value is meaningless if national processes to provide for representation and participation are not allowed to define economic and social development strategies or to mediate effectively among the various actors affected by the tensions inherent in the globalization process.

In addition, the reduced capacity of the state in the current context of globalization limits the role the public sector can play in lowering the cost of the "creative destruction" associated with rapid structural change and may exacerbate the difficulties involved in the modernization of the state itself. It is therefore less than realistic to sing the praises of both globalization and the disintegration of the state at the same time. The role of the social state as a generator of technological and institutional externalities is and will remain very important. In a world of global risks, the claim that economic forces can and should take the place of public policy and the state is less and less convincing. It is helpful, in this connection, to recall the categorical warning issued by Polanyi (1957) in his analysis of the collapse of the first stage of globalization: if the market seeks to subordinate society, it will end up destroying its own foundations.

Opportunities and Risks

In terms of access to new technologies, as in the area of trade and financing, globalization offers developing countries ample opportunity to integrate themselves more fully into the world economy. The sustained growth of international trade and the strengthening of multilateral rules and dispute settlement mechanisms within the framework of the World Trade Organization (WTO) are promising signs in this regard, as is regionalism when understood in the positive sense of open regionalism proposed by ECLAC (1994). However, although inroads are certainly being made in these directions, progress is being hindered by the incomplete liberalization of industrial economies. The partial nature of this process is itself a reflection of the protectionist practices that still predominate in the world, as well as the oversupply of certain goods in international trade, particularly raw materials. In addition, developing countries face the challenge of adapting their policies to the institutional mechanisms required by the WTO. This task has not been easy, and it may have consequences that are more restrictive than desired.

The explosive pace of global financial development has created opportunities for financing and for hedging financial risk, but it has also revealed the enormous problems caused by the asymmetry existing between the powerful market forces and the weak institutional structures that exist for regulating them (see ECLAC 2001a; UNCTAD 1998, 2001a; United Nations 1999a). The coexistence of financial globalization and national macroeconomic policies, which are still formulated on the basis of domestic interests and contexts, creates considerable tension for developing countries. Their governments are subject to the uncertainty generated by the macroeconomic policies of industrial countries, which do not adequately internalize their effects on the rest of the world and lack coordination mechanisms to ensure global coherence. These difficulties are compounded by the problems inherent in the financial market, particularly its volatility, which have had such a strong impact on the Latin American and Caribbean countries in recent decades. These phenomena are related to the market's inability to distinguish properly between different groups of borrowers, which produces contagion effects that influence the behavior of the financial market during both booms and busts. The developing countries are thus threatened by the globalization of financial volatility, which can have adverse effects on economic growth and social equity (Ffrench-Davis and Ocampo 2001; Rodrik 2001a).

Financial instability is the clearest, but not the only, manifestation of the increasing asymmetry between the power of the market and the lack of adequate economic governance. Other manifestations include the considerable economic concentration in evidence throughout the world and the multiple distributional tensions caused by the globalization process both between and within countries (see Bourguignon and Morrison 2002; Cornia 1999; Rodrik 1997; UNCTAD 1997; UNDP 1999b; see also chapter 4 of this book). These phenomena reflect, among other factors, the stringent educational and knowledge requirements of global technologies and markets, which threaten to marginalize those who are not fully prepared and to further confine the availability of these technologies and of new knowledge to just a few countries, social groups, and enterprises. This process is part of an array of old and new threats to the economic and social security of the population, whose position is being made all the more precarious by a progressive debilitation of the entire range of social safety nets, including both those provided by the family and those furnished by the state.

Globalization can also promote the emergence and valuation of environmental comparative advantages, including the sustainable use of natural capital that has economic value (forests, fisheries, tourist attractions); ecological value (genetic information afforded by biodiversity or the role of forests in absorbing carbon dioxide and other pollutants); or aesthetic, historical, or scientific value. These positive developments can serve as the basis for countless policies on the development of ecotourism, research on new medicines or agricultural products, the use of empirical knowledge concerning natural resources management and the economic properties of local biodiversity, the use of the regional ecological supply (such as biomass and natural resources), the productive utilization of unique ecological niches, and international negotiations on regional environmental services of global interest. In addition, new technologies for clean production, low-emissions transport, and energy efficiency and the use of renewable sources represent a new wave of technological innovation and market creation, and these processes will no doubt flourish in the coming decades. At the national level, globalization can promote the improvement of public policies by raising the cost of implementing unsustainable strategies that adversely affect long-term development. One of the risks that arise in this connection, however, is the possibility that traditional comparative advantages may be lost without necessarily being replaced by new ones.

By definition, global environmental processes affect all countries, but small tropical countries, particularly island states, are especially vulnerable to global environmental changes, as is demonstrated by the increasing frequency and violence of weather-related disasters. Indeed, unless specific national and international policies are adopted, the trend toward the overexploitation of certain natural resources, the underutilization of others, and the transfer of environmental costs from major polluting countries to the region can be expected to intensify.

Globalization also provides unprecedented opportunities in noneconomic areas. The spread of global values, the struggle for the right to be different, and the establishment of international mechanisms to defend the exercise of citizenship are notable advances that are reflected in the consolidation—insufficient though it may be at this point—of respect for human rights, democracy, gender equality, and ethnic diversity. The breakdown of archaic structures of domination and the control of abuses of power at the country level are some of the areas in which advances have been made during this new global era. Nonetheless, tensions continue to arise owing to the lack of channels for reducing the enormous imbalances of power existing at the global level and, in some cases, for legitimizing international actions. The globalization and concentration of the communications media also pose new problems. A particularly disturbing noneconomic aspect of globalization is the enormous distance existing between symbolic integration into the globalized world and the achievement of true integration; sharp inequalities militate against the latter.

In the term used in the financial debates of recent years, all of this underscores the need for a new "international architecture" for this era of globalization based on a wide-ranging agenda and a representative and pluralistic negotiation process. Such a global agenda should be aimed at correcting serious flaws in the existing international order. One of the flaws of the current international structure is the contrast between the rapid development of markets and the slow development of global governance, which has resulted in a suboptimal supply of global public goods (Kaul, Grunberg, and Stern 1999). A second category of problems are the asymmetries faced by developing countries in the global order in the areas of production and technology, finance and macroeconomics, and factor mobility (Ocampo 2001b). A third problem area has to do with the lack of effective international instruments for guaranteeing the achievement of the development goals that have been formulated on numerous occasions, most recently in the U.N. Millennium Declaration (United Nations 2000).

In the first decades following the Second World War, the need to correct the asymmetries of the international economic system was expressly acknowledged. The commitments entered into in relation to official development assistance and preferential treatment for developing countries in international trade were some of the partial results of this effort to build a "new international economic order," although they clearly fell short of what was required. This vision has been seriously undermined in recent decades and has been replaced with an alternative paradigm whereby the basic objective of changes in the international economic order should be to "level the playing field" in the regulatory sphere to allow market forces to operate freely. However, in the absence of genuine equality of opportunity, this "leveling" can actually lead to greater inequalities. The evidence that inequalities have worsened over the last half century (and especially in the last quarter of the 20th century), thereby prolonging more long-standing trends, makes it clear that neither approach has had the hoped-for results.

The lack of global governance, which is implicated in all these problems, reflects another deep-rooted conflict: the contrast between global issues and local political processes. The exercise of citizenship and democracy remains confined to the national and local spheres[6]; in fact, in today's world, this is still the most basic meaning attached to the concept of a nation. The lack of global governance means that there are no decision-making mechanisms at the global level to ensure that the interests of the least powerful countries and social sectors are adequately represented. These tensions are all the more significant because globalization has made it more difficult for countries to reconcile the demands of their citizens, which have increased with the advent of democracy, with the limitations that globalization itself has imposed on the ability of governments to take action.

Notes

1. Helleiner (2000a) presented a comparison of these two visions.

2. See Dowrich and DeLong (2001), Lindert and Williamson (2001), Maddison (1991, 1995, 2001), O'Rourke (2001), and O'Rourke and Williamson (1999). The starting point, set at around 1870, is somewhat arbitrary, but it reflects the incipient and still limited integration at the international level (and even at the domestic level, in large countries) of goods, capital, and labor markets up to that time, as well as the restricted scope of the industrialization process in most of the countries that formed the nucleus of the world economy.

3. In fact, globalization could not have come about without the railway, the steamship, and the telegraph in the 19th century; the construction of canals connecting oceans (Suez in 1869 and Panama in 1903); automobiles, airplanes, telephones, and television in the 20th century; and, of course, the revolution in information and communication technologies in the final decades of the 20th century.

4. None of the world's 20 largest multimedia groups is Latin American, and four of the five largest conglomerates are from the Anglo-Saxon world. In 1999, just four agencies controlled the international flow of news in print.

5. This is definitely the situation in Latin America, as shown by the results of successive Latinobarómetro polls. See *The Economist* (2002).

6. Certainly, there are areas in which a form of "global citizenship" is emerging, as manifested in the participation of civil society organizations in U.N. world summits and in global debates on the environment and trade. This was demonstrated very clearly by the civil society event that took place in parallel with the Ministerial Meeting on Trade of the Summit of the Americas (Toronto 1999) and by stand-alone events such as the World Social Forum in Porto Alegre (2001 and 2002). The clashes surrounding the WTO Ministerial Conference in Seattle (1999), the annual meeting of the International Monetary Fund and the World Bank in Prague (2000), and the meeting of the Group of Eight in Genoa (2001) are further examples of this kind of participation.

2

International Trade and the New Global Production Structure

ALTHOUGH THE GLOBALIZATION PROCESS is a multidimensional phenomenon, some of its most visible and influential aspects are economic in nature. This chapter analyzes major trends in international trade and the new global production structure; the mobility of capital and labor is considered in the next chapter. This analysis covers a long period in history, from the last quarter of the 19th century to the present, and is structured according to the successive stages of globalization identified in the preceding chapter. The first section focuses on the development of trade and investment flows among the major regions of the world, and on the main challenges faced by developing countries as a result of these global trends. The second section highlights the microeconomic foundations of the new forms of production and market organization, their impact on business decisions and strategies, and the corresponding dynamics of foreign direct investment.

International Trade

Contrary to what is often believed, there has been no clear association between the expansion of trade and economic growth throughout successive stages in the internationalization of the world economy.

International Trade and Economic Growth: A Variable Historical Relationship

During the 19th century world trade expanded rapidly, outpacing world gross domestic product (GDP), which also grew briskly (see figure 2.1). This expansion can be traced to a number of factors, including the early industrial revolutions and the consequent drop in transport costs, the "pax Britannica" imposed at the end of the

Figure 2.1 Trade and Global Output, 1870–1998

A. Growth in world output and exports of goods

B. Ratio of exports to world GDP

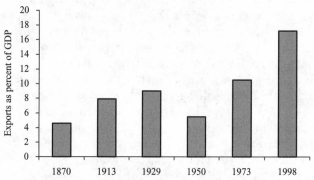

Note: GDP = gross domestic product.
Source: Economic Commission for Latin America and the Caribbean, on the basis of data from Maddison (2001).

Napoleonic wars, and the replacement of the principles of mercantilist regulation with those of free enterprise.

This period and, in particular, what was referred to in the preceding chapter as the first stage of globalization (1870–1913) were marked by a considerable degree of international capital and labor mobility and by the spread of the gold standard, from 1870 on, as a system of international payments and macroeconomic regulation. Contrary to what is widely believed, however, another notable feature of the period was the emergence of new forms of state regulation, not only in the economy (currency and financial system) and in social areas (principles of worker protection and social security), but also, most important, in the persistence of numerous trade restrictions.

In fact, except in the European powers committed to free trade (England and the Netherlands, in particular), in colonies whose economic relations with their ruling powers were governed by this system, and in some independent powers on which similar requirements were imposed (China, Japan, which did not regain tariff autonomy until 1911, and the Ottoman Empire, among others), and apart from a more widespread trend toward this form of trade in the 1860s and 1870s,[1] trade protectionism was the rule of the day in all nations that maintained tariff autonomy. Indeed, protectionism was the predominant practice in the self-governing territories of the British Empire that kept their autonomy (Australia and Canada), continental Europe, many Latin American countries, and the United States.[2] Bairoch (1993) rightly argued that it was economic growth that fueled the expansion of international trade during this period, not vice versa. This being the case, the idea that free trade was the primary engine of world economic growth between the mid-19th century and the First World War is one of the great myths of economic history.

The rapid growth of international trade was interrupted between the two world wars. Factors contributing to this break in the trend included global political instability, the deceleration of economic growth in the industrial countries, the inability to restore the gold standard, and in particular the frequent use of protectionist measures (exchange and import controls) and the widespread breakdown of the multilateral payments system during the depression of the 1930s. This combination of factors explains the importance that was attached, after the Second World War, to the establishment of standards and the founding of international organizations, which evidently were shaped by the unequal power structure of the players taking part in that process (discussed later in this chapter).

As a reflection of the manner in which the international trading system was structured in the postwar period, the most dynamic trade flows were originally centered in the two large European trading blocs. Subsequent developments in the two blocs were dissimilar because the European Community (now the European Union) succeeded in consolidating its position, whereas the Council for Mutual Economic Assistance—consisting of the socialist countries of Central and Eastern Europe—began to decline in importance and eventually disappeared altogether. Japan and the first generation of "Asian tigers" also began to increase their share of world trade shortly after the end of the war, thanks to their use of planning systems in which the conquest of foreign markets was a central component of development strategy. All the other regions of the world saw their shares of world trade shrink between 1950 and 1973 (see table 2.1).

Table 2.1 Global Exports, by Origin

(Percentage share at current exchange rate, 56 countries)

Region	1870	1913	1929	1950 Excluding Africa	1950 Including Africa	1973	1990	1998
Western Europe	65.7	56.3	47.4	40.8	38.6	50.3	51.9	47.4
United Kingdom	21.7	15.0	12.1	12.7	12.0	5.8	6.1	5.6
Continent	44.1	41.3	35.3	28.1	26.6	44.6	45.8	41.7
Central and Eastern Europe	5.8	6.0	6.6	8.3	7.8	9.2	5.4	4.9
North America[a]	10.3	16.4	21.4	26.7	25.3	19.1	17.0	18.6
Other industrial countries	2.8	4.7	6.2	6.0	5.7	9.6	11.0	9.5
Latin America and the Caribbean	4.9	7.2	7.9	9.8	9.3	3.9	3.5	5.0
Asian developing countries	10.6	9.3	10.5	8.4	7.9	5.1	9.5	13.1
Africa	—	—	—	—	5.4	2.9	1.7	1.5
World	100.0	100.0	100.0	100.0	100.0	100.0	100.0	100.0

— Not available.
a. Canada and the United States.
Source: Economic Commission for Latin America and the Caribbean, on the basis of data from Maddison (2001).

Beginning in the mid-1970s, the emergence of a highly dynamic trading bloc in East Asia ultimately came to be the most striking feature of world trading activity. Japan lost its lead in the last decade of the 20th century, and China emerged as a hub for the expansion of international trade. Other major changes that took place in the 1990s included an upsurge in exports from the United States.

This brief historical overview illustrates how the relationship between trade and economic growth has varied, not only in the course of the century that preceded the Second World War, but also during more recent stages of globalization. As shown in figure 2.1, world trade and world economic growth accelerated simultaneously between 1950 and 1973, but the upswing in world trade was largely a result of the reversal of the trend toward national isolationism observed between 1913 and 1950. The slowdown of the world economy between 1973 and 1990 also coincided with more sluggish growth in world trade, but the latter's great dynamism in the last decade of the 20th century was not accompanied by a commensurate global economic expansion.

This variable relationship is confirmed by the data shown in figure 2.2. The upswings in GDP growth seen in the various countries between 1950 and 1973 were associated with widely differing patterns of integration into the world economy. Thus, the second stage of globalization was not characterized by a strong positive correlation between export growth and GDP growth in the different countries, even though it is true that some of the fastest growing economies in that period—particularly Japan, the Republic of Korea, and Taiwan (China)—were also highly successful exporters. This correlation was, however, quite positive in the third stage of globalization. Thus, even though the liberalization and expansion of world trade did *not* translate into faster world economic growth in the period after 1973, the success achieved by individual countries has been closely linked to their effective integration into international trade flows.

In the developing world, the relationship among development strategy, external trade, and economic growth has undoubtedly varied since the end of the Second World War. Comparative analyses (see, for example, Helleiner 1994) categorically demonstrate that trade policy has played an important role in development strategies, but they also show that there is no simple correlation applicable to all countries in all time periods or to a given country in different periods. The import substitution strategy yielded benefits in terms of rapid economic growth at certain stages and was even a necessary factor in enabling many countries to begin exporting manufactures at a later stage, as noted by Chenery, Robinson, and Syrquin (1986). Nonetheless, the effects of protectionist policies tended to weaken over time.

Figure 2.2 Export Growth and GDP Growth in 35 Countries

A. 1950–1973

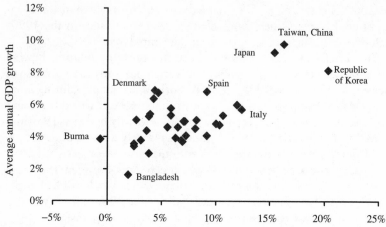

B. 1973–1998

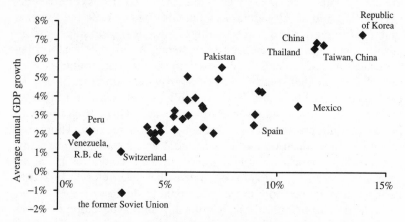

Average annual export growth

Note: The 35 countries are the following: Argentina, Australia, Austria, Bangladesh, Belgium, Brazil, Canada, Chile, China, Colombia, Denmark, Finland, France, Germany, India, Indonesia, Italy, Japan, Republic of Korea, Mexico, Myanmar, Netherlands, Norway, Pakistan, Peru, the Philippines, the former Soviet Union, Spain, Sweden, Switzerland, Taiwan (China), Thailand, the United Kingdom, the United States, and the República Bolivariana de Venezuela.

Source: Economic Commission for Latin America and the Caribbean, on the basis of data from Maddison (2001).

Furthermore, as noted earlier, in recent decades rapid economic growth has increasingly been linked to success as an exporter, but such success has been achieved under widely varying trade policy strategies. There is no close linkage between export growth and a liberal trade regime (Rodríguez and Rodrik 2001). Moreover, as indicated in the extensive literature on East Asia (see, for example, Akyüz 1998; Amsden 1989, 2001; Chang 1994; Wade 1990), cases of strong economic growth have been accompanied by mechanisms for state intervention in external trade, the financial sector, and technology. As noted by Rodrik (1999, 2001b), rapid growth in developing countries has coincided with various combinations of economic orthodoxy and "local heresies."

In the particular case of Latin America and the Caribbean, the region's share of world exports fell steeply between 1950 and 1973, stabilized between 1973 and 1990, and then began to increase. Admittedly, most of the increase is attributable to the upsurge in Mexican exports under the North American Free Trade Agreement (NAFTA). Nevertheless, swift growth in exports from small economies, as compared to the growth of aggregate output, can be observed starting as early as the mid-1950s, whereas exports from large and medium-size economies began to speed up shortly thereafter (see figure 2.3).[3] It was then that the countries of the region began to implement various combinations of import substitution and export promotion measures, including a number of subregional integration arrangements, the first of which was in Central America in the 1950s. It was this "mixed model"—rather than import substitution alone, as is often claimed—that was the most widely used arrangement in the region beginning in the 1960s (Cárdenas, Ocampo, and Thorp 2000b) and that had been advocated by the Economic Commission for Latin America and the Caribbean (ECLAC) since the late 1950s (Bielschowsky 1998; ECLAC 1998b; Rosenthal 2001). As early as the mid-1970s export growth began to surpass GDP growth in the region as a whole. This trend intensified during the "lost decade" of the 1980s, but more as a result of the slowdown in GDP growth than of an increase in exports and, in the last decade of the 20th century, as a consequence of export expansion.

Development of the Institutional Framework for International Trade

Such was the scale of the new international institutional framework that took shape after the Second World War that it marked a turning point in trade and financial history. Economic transactions had obviously begun to expand and bring about changes in international

Figure 2.3 Exports from Latin America

A. Percentages of GDP

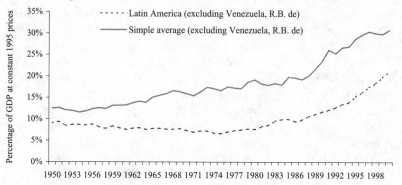

B. Percentages of GDP by size of countries (simple averages)

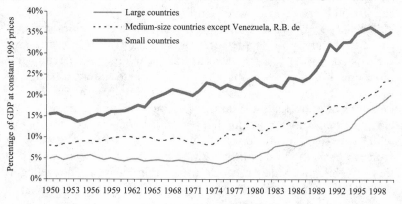

Note: GDP = gross domestic product. The large countries are Argentina, Brazil, and Mexico; the medium-size ones are Chile, Colombia, Peru, and the República Bolivariana de Venezuela; and the small ones are Bolivia, Costa Rica, Dominican Republic, Ecuador, El Salvador, Nicaragua, Panama, Paraguay, and Uruguay.

Source: Economic Commission for Latin America and the Caribbean, on the basis of official figures from the countries.

relations in the 19th century, two of which changes were the adoption of the "most favored nation" principle in trade agreements (although it was frequently contravened in the 1930s) and recourse to international arbitration to settle disputes between states. In addition, the gold standard came to be adopted by an increasing number of countries, although this primarily reflected a gradual acceptance of the monetary system employed by the leading international power of the time, rather than the implementation of principles of international co-operation. The application of this system was confined to weak forms of cooperation among the main central banks of the industrial countries during this period (Eichengreen 1996). In the 19th century, a number of conventions were signed and various specialized agencies were established, including the World Health Organization and the Pan American Health Organization, the Universal Postal Union, and the Paris Convention for the Protection of Industrial Property, but the most significant step in terms of international cooperation came later with the creation of the League of Nations in 1919. None of these processes, however, matched the scope of the international cooperation seen after the Second World War.

The period in which the international institutional framework developed most prolifically—the final years of the war and those immediately following it—was characterized by a vision whose first manifestation was the founding of the United Nations. In the economic domain, this vision led to the establishment of three key institutions: the International Monetary Fund (IMF), which was to restore multilateralism in current operations and provide financial support in times of crisis; the International Trade Organization, which was to oversee the development of multilateral trade principles; and the International Bank for Reconstruction and Development, or World Bank, which was to facilitate the reconstruction of countries devastated by war. When the effort to create the International Trade Organization failed following the Havana Conference of 1948, the role it was intended to perform passed to the General Agreement on Tariffs and Trade (GATT), which had fewer members.

There were two major counterweights to the strengthening of multilateralism in trading activity. The first was the formation of regional blocs, within whose borders trade expanded rapidly. The European Economic Community was the most striking example, and a number of agreements were established on a smaller scale, including several in Latin America and the Caribbean. The former Council for Mutual Economic Assistance also served to boost trade among the centrally planned economies.

The second counterweight to multilateralism was widespread recourse to protectionism in the developing world. This took the form not only of high tariffs, but also of quantitative restrictions, local content requirements for assembly industries, and minimum export requirements for firms and industrial sectors experiencing foreign exchange shortages. For newly independent countries, protectionism amounted to an expression of autonomy, as the colonial past was perceived as an era of economic failure that had to be overcome by means

Table 2.2 GDP Growth: World and Largest Regions,
1820–1998
(*Weighted average annual growth rates*)

Region	1820–1870	1870–1913	1913–1950	1950–1973	1973–1998
Western Europe	1.65	2.10	1.19	4.81	2.11
Australia, Canada, New Zealand, and United States	4.33	3.92	2.81	4.03	2.98
Japan	0.41	2.44	2.21	9.29	2.97
Asia (not including Japan)	0.03	0.94	0.90	5.18	5.46
Latin America	1.37	3.48	3.43	5.33	3.02
Eastern Europe and the former Soviet Union	1.52	2.37	1.84	4.84	–0.56
Africa	0.52	1.40	2.69	4.45	2.74
World	0.93	2.11	1.85	4.91	3.01

Source: Economic Commission for Latin America and the Caribbean, on the basis
of data from Maddison (2001).

of deliberate action on the part of the nation-state. In Latin America
and the Caribbean the increasing use of interventionism and protection represented what was perceived as a success. In fact, in the early
stages of the import substitution period, between the two world wars,
the region had achieved rapid economic growth, which facilitated a
relatively easy transition from export-based development to the "inward-looking" development model (see table 2.2).

In addition, during the period between the two world wars development and industrialization were considered to be one and the same,
and interventionism and state planning were standard practice worldwide, with very few exceptions. In several cases this represented an extension of the strict public controls imposed during periods of armed
conflict. Consequently, in the developing world the choice was seen as
being between central planning and the weaker forms of planning typical of mixed economies, rather than between state planning and a free
market.

There were also some notable departures from the move toward
trade liberalization within the framework of GATT. In fact, although
the first six rounds of negotiations promoted the liberalization of
intraindustrial trade in the industrial economies, the areas requiring
internal adjustments on the part of the industrial countries—including
the agricultural and textile sectors—remained outside the scope of
multilateral trade rules. These rounds reduced levies on imports of

nonagricultural products from industrial countries to a low average level.[4] From the late 1960s on, and in parallel with the lowering of tariffs, the multilateral trade agenda began to be focused on other public policies affecting competition between domestic and imported goods, such as administrative barriers, technical standards, contingency protection measures (safeguards), and trade protection (antidumping and subsidies), many of which came to be used for openly protectionist purposes. Voluntary export restraints, which became more widespread in the 1970s and 1980s, added to the use of protectionist instruments outside the GATT framework.

The Uruguay Round (1986–94) was unquestionably the most comprehensive of all the rounds of multilateral trade negotiations. The countries agreed to lower the effective average level of industrial tariffs even further. In addition, the number of duty-free tariff lines was increased, virtually all the tariff structures were bound, and stricter trade remedies (antidumping, countervailing, and safeguard measures) were adopted. With respect to issues that had previously remained outside the GATT framework, commitments were established for the agricultural sector not only to protect trade, but also to address export and production subsidies; agreement was reached on the gradual dismantling of the Multifibre Arrangement, voluntary export restraints were prohibited, and the signatories agreed to eliminate trade-related investment measures (local content or export requirements), which were used liberally by many developing countries. In addition, when the World Trade Organization (WTO) was given its mandate to take over the role formerly played by GATT, two new areas were included in its terms of reference: the liberalization of services and the development of international rules on the protection of intellectual property. In addition, a new dispute settlement mechanism was created.

More than seven years after the entry into force in 1995 of the Marrakesh Agreement establishing the World Trade Organization, the great majority of the member countries are well aware that the proper functioning of the WTO is important for the orderly conduct of international economic relations. WTO has fostered the settlement of trade disputes through mutually beneficial cooperation between countries and, as a result, has helped to create a framework of trade rules that are more reliable and predictable than those of the past. The fact that developing countries have made increasing use of the WTO dispute settlement mechanism demonstrates the importance of the organization's active role in upholding the system of standards in order to arbitrate trade disputes.

There is a serious imbalance, however, in the distribution of the benefits deriving from the Marrakesh Agreement. The industrial countries have continued to gain the most from the liberalization of trade in goods and services.[5] First, these countries were able to reduce the costs of adjusting their agricultural and textile sectors because they made sure they were given generous transition periods to make the changeover to more open and competitive markets. In addition, they introduced varying degrees of flexibility into the disciplines relating to their policies on agriculture and on certain industries. They also extended the GATT rules, which originally referred only to products, to cover the rights of private agents (firms) and brought into the multilateral trading system those areas in which they enjoy a solid technological predominance, including the protection of intellectual property rights. Although there are no specific agreements on investment or the safeguarding of competition, the industrial countries ensured that the commitments on investments, subsidies, and trade in services confer national treatment to transnational corporations (TNCs). Furthermore, they laid a firm legal foundation for the liberalization of some service delivery modes and sectors, such as financial services, basic telecommunications, electronic commerce, and information technologies. By contrast, despite the commitments undertaken, not only have the sectors that could be important markets for developing countries' exports been slow to open up, but their liberalization, such as it is, has been coupled with the introduction of measures that undermine existing obligations and new forms of selective protectionism, such as antidumping measures.

This asymmetry in the distribution of benefits and the slow progress made since the 1960s in terms of special and differential treatment prompted the developing countries to seek a new round of trade negotiations that would focus on areas of particular interest to them (chapter 4 analyzes this issue in greater depth). The commitment to develop measures to address this situation forms the basis of the Doha Declaration, which was adopted at the Fourth World Trade Organization Ministerial Conference (Qatar, November 2001), and lays out the work program of the WTO. This program covers several areas of interest to the multilateral trading system.[6] Deliberations and negotiations, to be completed by 2005, will be conducted to review, broaden, or alter the rules established at the Uruguay Round.

Recent Patterns of World Trade

In view of the increasing importance of export strength for countries' economic growth, it is important to pinpoint exactly what patterns have promoted an expansion of exports in recent decades. Table 2.3 illustrates the changes that have taken place in the international trade matrix, by geographic origin and destination, between 1985 and 2000. The most striking trend that can be discerned is the increase in the Asian developing countries' share of world trade. This was achieved largely at the expense of the relative volume of trade among industrial countries, which, in any case, still represents more than half of the world total. The share held by Canada and the United States grew as well, thanks to the considerable expansion of their exports to the developing world. Intraregional trade also rose steadily in Latin America and the Caribbean and, even more, within the Asian bloc. In contrast, the weighted share of Africa and the rest of the world (chiefly the countries of Central and Eastern Europe) continued to fall. The Latin American and Caribbean region's share of exports rose, but to a much lesser extent than its share of imports, with the result that the region's large trade surplus of 1985 had turned into a deficit by 2000, sharply contrasting with the Asian developing countries' hefty trade surplus.

The composition of world trade by category of goods has changed substantially over the last 15 years.[7] Table 2.4 classifies products as dynamic or nondynamic and indicates their importance relative to two categories of international trade: the category involving the intensive use of natural resources or technology, as identified by ECLAC,[8] and the Standard International Trade Classification (SITC). The slow growth of trade in commodities and natural resource–based manufactures is one of the most striking phenomena in this regard. Moreover, increasing market competition has resulted in a severe downturn in raw material prices, which constitutes a continuation of a more long-standing trend (see box 2.1). Among manufactures, those based on the use of advanced technology show a much higher growth rate than manufactures as a whole. The shares of agricultural products, nonfood raw materials, and especially fuel are declining. Finally, the largest increases are found in the category of machinery and equipment, especially electrical equipment and equipment related to the information and communications industry, whose share swelled by 9 percentage points.

An analysis of the growth of international trade can be combined with an analysis of the "revealed competitiveness" of various regions, as reflected in their share of different types of products. This gives rise to four categories: (a) dynamic products in which a given region's share of trade is increasing ("rising stars"), (b) dynamic products in which its share is falling ("missed opportunities"), (c) nondynamic products in which the region's market share is increasing ("falling stars"), and (d) products that combine low relative growth with a loss of market share ("retreat products").

Table 2.3 Structure of World Imports, by Origin and Destination, 1985 and 2000
(Percentages of total world imports)

Region of origin	Region of destination								
	Western Europe	United States	Other industrial	Total industrial	Latin America and the Caribbean	Asian developing	Africa	Total developing countries	Total by origin
1985									
Western Europe	30.0	5.2	1.6	36.8	0.8	2.5	1.2	4.6	41.4
Canada and United States	3.8	7.1	2.4	13.3	1.1	1.8	0.3	3.2	16.4
Other industrial	2.3	4.8	1.0	8.1	0.3	2.6	0.2	3.0	11.1
Total industrial	36.1	17.1	5.0	58.1	2.2	6.9	1.7	10.8	68.9
Latin America and the Caribbean	1.5	2.9	0.4	4.8	0.7	0.2	0.1	0.9	5.8
Asian developing countries	3.5	4.2	4.1	11.7	0.3	3.8	0.2	4.3	16.1
Africa	2.9	0.8	0.2	3.9	0.1	0.2	0.1	0.4	4.3
Total developing countries	7.9	7.9	4.7	20.5	1.1	4.3	0.4	5.7	26.2
Rest of world	3.3	0.2	0.3	3.8	0.1	0.8	0.3	1.1	4.9
Total by destination	47.3	25.2	10.0	82.4	3.4	12.0	2.3	17.6	100.0
2000									
Western Europe	25.5	4.6	1.5	31.7	1.0	2.9	0.6	4.5	36.1
Canada and United States	3.7	6.6	1.9	12.2	3.2	2.4	0.1	5.7	17.9
Other industrial	2.0	3.1	0.6	5.7	0.3	3.4	0.1	3.7	9.4
Total industrial	31.2	14.3	4.0	49.5	4.4	8.7	0.8	13.9	63.5

Latin America and the Caribbean	0.8	3.7	0.2	4.7	1.0	0.3	0.0	1.3	6.0
Asian developing countries	4.7	5.9	3.8	14.4	0.5	8.2	0.2	8.9	23.3
Africa	1.1	0.4	0.1	1.7	0.1	0.4	0.1	0.5	2.2
Total developing countries	6.6	10.0	4.1	20.7	1.6	8.8	0.3	10.7	31.4
Rest of world	3.7	0.5	0.2	4.4	0.1	0.5	0.1	0.7	5.1
Total by destination	41.6	24.8	8.3	74.7	6.1	18.0	1.2	25.3	100.0

Note: The data on world imports refer to the total imports of 82 reporting countries, corresponding to approximately 90 percent of world trade. "1985" figures are the annual averages for the period 1984–1986. "2000" figures are the annual averages for 1999–2000. The countries not included as reporting countries are primarily those with economies in transition. Western Europe = European Union plus Iceland, Norway, and Switzerland. Other industrial = Australia, Israel, Japan, and New Zealand. Rest of world is not included as a destination because of lack of information and, as an origin, it refers to economies in transition, Oceania except Australia and New Zealand, free zones, and so forth.

Source: Economic Commission for Latin America and the Caribbean, on the basis of data from UNSD (2002).

Table 2.4 Dynamic and Nondynamic Products in World Imports, 1985–2000
(Percentage of total imports)

Product	Dynamic products				Nondynamic products				Net increase or reduction (A – B)
	Number of items	1985 (1)	2000 (2)	Increase A = (2) – (1)	Number of items	1985 (3)	2000 (4)	Loss B = (4) – (3)	
By technological category									
Commodities	15	0.7	0.8	0.1	132	22.5	11.6	-10.9	-10.8
Natural resource-based manufactures	65	5.3	6.8	1.6	134	14.3	8.9	-5.4	-3.8
Low-technology manufactures	71	7.3	10.8	3.5	90	7.1	4.9	-2.2	1.3
Midlevel technology manufactures	91	16.7	21.1	4.4	111	11.8	8.6	-3.3	1.1
High-technology manufactures	45	9.5	21.6	12.2	21	2.2	1.3	-0.9	11.3
Unclassified products	4	1.4	2.8	1.4	7	1.4	0.9	-0.5	0.8
Total	291	40.8	63.9	23.1	495	59.2	36.1	-23.1	0.0
By SITC classification									
Food and live animals for food	17	1.1	1.4	0.3	77	7.5	4.3	-3.2	-2.9
Beverages and tobacco	4	0.3	0.3	0.1	7	0.7	0.6	-0.2	-0.1
Crude materials, inedible, except fuels	8	0.1	0.1	0.0	96	6.1	3.4	-2.7	-2.6
Mineral fuels, lubricants, and related materials	2	0.1	0.1	0.0	18	17.2	8.6	-8.6	-8.6
Animal and vegetable oils, fats, and waxes	3	0.0	0.1	0.0	15	0.6	0.3	-0.3	-0.3
Chemicals and related products	39	3.6	6.0	2.4	56	4.5	3.3	-1.2	1.3
Manufactured goods classified by material	76	6.5	7.9	1.4	115	9.1	6.1	-3.1	-1.6
Machinery and transport equipment	89	22.0	35.6	13.6	70	7.9	5.6	-2.3	11.3

Power-generating machinery and equipment	9	1.6	2.3	0.7	10	0.5	0.4	-0.2	0.5
Machinery specialized for particular industries	6	0.9	1.1	0.2	22	1.9	1.3	-0.6	-0.4
Metalworking machinery	4	0.3	0.3	0.0	4	0.4	0.3	-0.1	0.0
General industrial machinery and equipment	16	1.9	2.6	0.7	11	1.2	1.0	-0.2	0.6
Office machines and automatic data processing equipment	7	2.4	6.0	3.6	4	0.4	0.3	-0.2	3.4
Telecommunications and sound recording apparatus	6	1.6	3.7	2.1	6	1.2	0.8	-0.3	1.8
Electrical machinery, apparatus, and appliances	25	4.7	9.8	5.1	0	—	—	0.0	5.1
Road vehicles, including air cushion vehicles	8	7.6	8.1	0.6	5	1.5	1.1	-0.4	0.2
Other transport equipment	8	1.1	1.6	0.6	8	0.7	0.3	-0.3	0.2
Miscellaneous manufactured articles	52	5.8	9.6	3.9	36	4.7	3.6	-1.1	2.8
Commodities and transactions not elsewhere classified	2	1.3	2.7	1.3	4	1.0	0.5	-0.6	0.8

— Not available.

Note: SITC is the Standard International Trade Classification (Rev. 2) and it is used at the level of subgroup (four-digit level). Dynamic products are those whose rate of growth exceeded the average rate of growth of world imports, and nondynamic products are those whose rate of growth lagged behind the average rate of growth of world imports.

Source: Economic Commission for Latin America and the Caribbean, on the basis of data from UNSD (2002).

Box 2.1 The Long-Term Deterioration of Raw Material Prices

The terms of trade between commodities and manufactures have a crucial influence on both short-term macroeconomic performance and the developing countries' growth prospects, owing to the importance of commodities in these countries' export structures. In the 1950s Prebisch (1951) and Singer (1950) formulated the hypothesis of a secular trend toward a decline in the terms of trade for commodities. This hypothesis has been studied in depth since then, and both its theoretical and empirical bases have been called into question. Be that as it may, price data for 24 commodities in the period between 1900 and 2000 show that the terms of trade for nonfuel commodities have deteriorated to such an extent that they now represent less than one-third of their pre-1920 levels (see figure 2.4). This is equivalent to an annual decrease of 1.5 percent over the last 80 years, which is obviously a significant decline.

Figure 2.4 Real Commodity Price Indexes, 1900 = 100

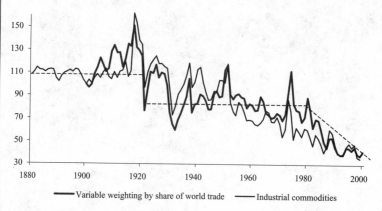

Source: *The Economist* (2002).

A time series analysis does not reveal a persistent downward trend, however, but rather two structural changes, one occurring around 1920 and the other around 1980. Historical analyses indicate that the First World War ushered in a period of slow economic expansion in the industrial countries, particularly the European countries, which interrupted the brisk growth that had characterized the first stage of globalization. The first structural change in the terms of trade coincided with the severe postwar crisis of 1920 and 1921, when real raw material prices plummeted by 45 percent. As a consequence of overproduction in both industrial and developing countries, the terms of trade improved over the rest

(Box continues on the following page.)

Box 2.1 (continued)

of the decade but never again reached their prewar levels, despite the fleeting growth spurt in the world economy and especially the U.S. economy. The global economic collapse of 1929 triggered another slide in the prices of raw materials, which remained low until the end of the 1940s.

Economic growth sped up sharply throughout the world after the Second World War, but commodity prices never regained the ground they had lost in earlier decades. The expansion of supply hindered their recovery, despite increased demand. The 1973 oil shock brought a strong upturn in commodity prices but also the onset of a new period of slower growth worldwide. The real turning point in commodity price trends, however, came in 1979, when the U.S. economic authorities decided to raise interest rates to curb inflation and protect the value of the dollar. Since then, despite the upswing in the U.S. economy in the 1990s, world economic growth has been sluggish, and the industrial countries have stepped up their policies of instituting protectionist measures and providing agricultural subsidies. The deterioration of the terms of trade for commodities, which accelerated during this period, has not been reversed. Currently, the oversupply of commodities and the slowdown in the world economy hold out little hope for a recovery in the near future.

Source: Ocampo and Parra (2003).

Export growth in the Asian developing countries and in Canada and the United States in the 1990s was associated with the first group of products (see table 2.5). In contrast, Europe's market reveals the increasing weight of low-growth products in which the region also is losing its market share. In the group of other industrial countries (dominated by Japan), dynamic products prevail, although with a loss of market share. The export position of Africa is marked by an overwhelming predominance of nondynamic products in which the region is losing its market share, and the export position of the rest of the world (basically Central and Eastern Europe) is characterized by a loss of market share in dynamic products.

Within these parameters the Latin American and Caribbean region has a large share of the less dynamic products, which, in fact, represent the largest proportion of its exports (more than three-fourths in the 1990s). However, there are actually two main patterns of specialization. In one, the relative share of exports of manufactures is on the rise (some Caribbean and Central American countries and Mexico); in the other, natural resource–intensive products—whose share of world trade is growing sluggishly—predominate (South America). The most notable change between the periods 1985–90 and 1990–2000 was the

Table 2.5 Export Structure, by Type of Competitive Situation
(*Percentage of exports*)

| Region and year | Dynamic products | | Nondynamic products | | Regional change in market share |
	Increasing regional share	Decreasing regional share	Increasing regional share	Decreasing regional share	
1985–1990					
Western Europe					
Base year	30.7	36.7	20.5	12.1	3.3
Final year	36.5	38.9	16.7	7.9	
North America[a]					
Base year	15.3	44.5	13.3	26.9	–0.6
Final year	22.9	47.2	11.8	18.0	
Other industrial					
Base year	21.0	47.0	11.2	20.9	–0.1
Final year	30.9	44.1	12.4	12.6	
Latin America and the Caribbean					
Base year	11.4	20.8	23.9	43.8	–1.1
Final year	22.6	24.3	24.5	28.6	
Africa					
Base year	5.2	11.0	14.3	69.5	–1.4
Final year	12.5	13.4	17.2	56.9	
Asian developing countries					
Base year	38.2	6.7	44.4	10.7	1.2
Final year	57.8	6.3	31.0	4.8	
Rest of world					
Base year	10.8	30.4	7.9	50.9	–1.3
Final year	21.9	34.4	14.2	29.5	
1990–2000					
Western Europe					
Base year	2.7	37.9	4.8	54.5	–8.6
Final year	5.7	44.8	5.7	43.8	
North America[a]					
Base year	31.3	13.3	32.3	23.2	2.1
Final year	43.2	14.7	28.9	13.2	
Other industrial					
Base year	6.4	48.8	19.5	25.3	–1.5
Final year	10.4	51.3	22.0	16.3	
Latin America and the Caribbean					
Base year	18.1	2.7	57.2	22.0	1.3
Final year	37.0	2.2	49.8	11.0	

Table 2.5 (continued)

Africa					
Base year	2.5	8.6	19.8	69.1	–0.8
Final year	6.6	9.1	23.9	60.4	
Asian developing countries					
Base year	31.4	3.9	37.0	27.6	6.0
Final year	50.1	3.0	31.7	15.2	
Rest of world					
Base year	24.3	2.0	44.1	29.6	1.5
Final year	49.8	1.2	39.0	9.9	

a. Canada and the United States.

Note: Dynamic products are those whose rate of growth exceeded the average rate of growth of world imports, and nondynamic products are those whose rate of growth lagged behind the average rate of growth of world imports.

Source: Economic Commission for Latin America and the Caribbean, on the basis of data from UNSD (2002).

expansion in the market share of nondynamic products (both raw materials and manufactures), as reflected in the increase in falling stars relative to retreat products. In addition, as the region upped its market share in dynamic products, the weight of the rising stars increased relative to the products classified as missed opportunities. In sum, the factor that has contributed most to the growth of regional exports has been not their reorientation toward the fastest growing products in international trade, but rather the enhancement of competitiveness within the existing export structure.

Two Challenges Posed by the Relationship between Trade and Economic Growth

In recent decades, the relationship between external trade and economic growth has raised two basic issues for developing countries, whose responses will have significant implications for the future. The first question is how to translate the opportunities provided by world markets into rapid economic growth. The second issue concerns the pattern of change in the structure of employment.

There is no simple answer to the first of these questions. As noted previously, countries' opportunities for advancement have been linked to their success as exporters, but the swift growth seen in international trade, especially over the 1990s, has not resulted in a commensurate expansion of world output. Figure 2.5 shows that this was clearly the case in Latin America; although export growth was faster in the 1990s

Figure 2.5 Trade and GDP in Latin America, 1870–1998

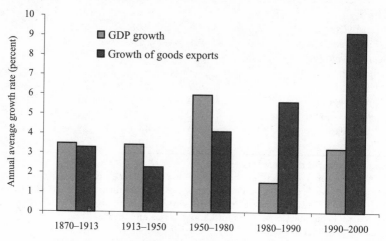

Note: GDP = gross domestic product.
Source: Economic Commission for Latin America and the Caribbean, on the basis of data from Maddison (2001).

than at any other time in the region's history, that decade was also a period of relatively slow economic expansion, with the growth rate unquestionably falling short of the rates recorded in the region in the period of state-led industrialization between the 1950s and the 1970s.

This situation can be explained in part by the dynamics of international trade itself. When more successful countries seize the few opportunities that arise in a sluggish international environment, they deprive other developing countries of potential markets, including their own domestic markets, or they cause export prices to fall, as happened with commodity prices over the last two decades.

In addition, trade liberalization has entailed a restructuring of the domestic macroeconomic framework and production sector, which has not been conducive to rapid economic growth. From a macroeconomic standpoint, increased openness to foreign trade has reduced the antiexport bias of protectionist regimes, but it has also led to a contraction in the sectors that compete with imports. Indeed, export success has been based in large part on the more intensive use of imported raw materials and capital goods. For most developing countries, the net result has been a structural deterioration in the correlation between economic growth and the trade balance (UNCTAD 1999). The case of Latin America and the Caribbean, as shown in figure 2.6A, illustrates this situation: The region's trade deficit in the 1990s was similar to that of the 1970s, but its growth rate was much lower than it was earlier. Furthermore, this

Figure 2.6 Relationships among Economic Growth, Trade, and the Technology Gap in Latin America, 1950–2000

A. Relationship between trade balances and economic growth

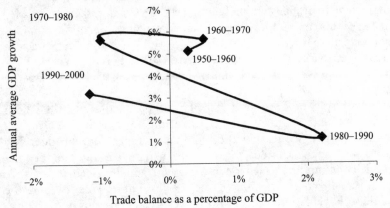

B. Relationship between the rate of reduction of the productivity gap and the income-elasticity of imports

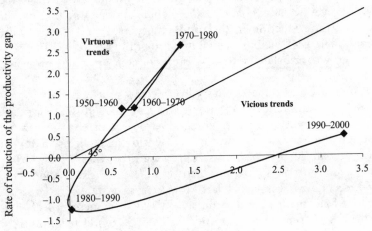

Source: Economic Commission for Latin America and the Caribbean, on the basis of data from Maddison (2001).

deficit increased the region's dependence on international financing, which, as will be discussed in the next chapter, has been volatile.

Another facet of this process is that certain features of the production structure have hindered the achievement of sustained high rates of economic growth.[9] Although a number of developing countries, especially those of Latin America and the Caribbean, have managed to increase their share of world markets and of foreign investment flows, the production linkages of these dynamic activities have been weak. In addition, the increasing use of imported intermediate and capital goods, which is characteristic of internationally integrated production systems, has led to a breakdown in pre-existing production chains and national innovation systems. Moreover, developing-country participation in the fastest-growing activities in international trade, especially those that are technology intensive, has been limited in most cases (UNCTAD 2001a, 2002a).

As a result, progress in narrowing the productivity gap has been slow. Figure 2.6B illustrates the relationship between the rate at which the gap separating the region's average labor productivity from that of the United States has been reduced, and the income-elasticity of imports, which is consistent with equilibrium in the balance of trade. From the 1950s to the 1970s, Latin America and the Caribbean were on the part of the curve characterized by a "virtuous" growth trend—that is, a trend in which GDP grew faster than exports. The increase in the income-elasticity of imports in the 1970s was thus accompanied by a still faster reduction in the productivity gap. In the 1990s, however, the increase in the income-elasticity of imports far outpaced the reduction in the productivity gap; consequently, the region entered a "vicious" economic growth cycle in which robust export growth translated into lackluster economic growth (Cimoli and Correa 2002).

It should be added that given the insufficient "pull" exerted by high-growth sectors and the low rate of overall economic growth, the structural heterogeneity (dualism) of production sectors has increased: although there are now many more "world-class" firms, many of which are subsidiaries of TNCs, a growing proportion of the workforce is concentrated in low-productivity informal sector activities.

The second basic issue is related to patterns of change in the structure of employment over the course of the development process and how this structure has been affected by worldwide technological change and the international specialization of different countries. As is well known, the primary sector of the economy is not a major source of new jobs, whereas the manufacturing sector tends to create a large number of jobs at first, then stabilizes and finally trends downward as per capita income rises, following the inverted U pattern propounded by Rowthorn (1999). The tertiary sector accounts for the remaining jobs. In view of the particular trend followed by job creation in the manufacturing sector, the tertiary sector will be considered in more detail.

Palma's (2002) analysis, which is based on a wide sample of countries, not only confirms the inverted U pattern of job creation in the manufacturing sector, but also introduces three striking considerations, two of which are illustrated in figure 2.7A. One of these is the continuous downward curve seen over the last four decades, which indicates a decrease in the share of manufacturing in total employment at all levels of per capita income. Palma attributed this trend to the fact that productivity has increased more rapidly than GDP, which implies that employment in manufacturing has expanded at a slower pace and, in some cases, has contracted in absolute terms.[10] The other is a shift in the peak rate to lower levels of per capita income from 1980 onward. This means that the point at which the manufacturing sector's share in total employment begins to decrease is located at progressively lower levels of per capita income. In 1990, more than 30 countries recorded per capita incomes that were higher than the level at which manufacturing employment begins to decrease. The services sector exhibits a very different trend, with productivity growing much more slowly than GDP; as a result, employment in the sector has increased as a proportion of the total.[11]

The third consideration points to the need to assess the phenomenon of "Dutch disease" from a fresh perspective.[12] First, the ratio between the share of manufacturing in total employment and per capita income is a function of the pattern of international trade. Both industrial- and developing-country exporters of raw materials or services—especially financial services and tourism—thus exhibit a lower ratio than exporters of manufactures at all levels of per capita income (see figure 2.7B).

Although these countries are usually less industrialized than exporters of manufactures, this does not alter the general trend toward deindustrialization in either group. In fact, as figure 2.7C shows, from 1960 to 1998 manufacturing employment as a proportion of the total decreased by half in both groups of countries: from 39 percent to 21 percent in exporters of manufactures and from 29 percent to 16 percent in exporters of natural resource–based goods or services. The peak rate on the respective curves also shifted to a level of per capita income equivalent to half as much as before (from US$18,000 to US$9,000 in that period).

Dutch disease should thus be understood as an excess of deindustrialization owing to a change in the reference group. This occurred in the Netherlands, Norway, and the United Kingdom, as well as in Cyprus, Greece, and Malta (tourism); and Hong Kong (China), Luxembourg, and Switzerland (financial services). None of these considerations give substance to the idea that what has been called the

Figure 2.7 Deindustrialization, Foreign Trade, Employment, and Income

A. Sources of deindustrialization, 1960–1998

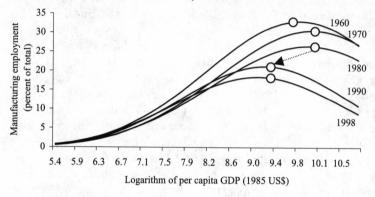

B. Foreign trade effect, 1998

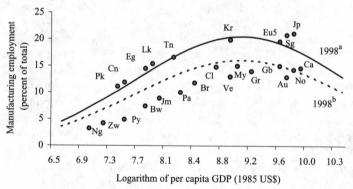

C. Changes in employment and income, 1960 and 1998

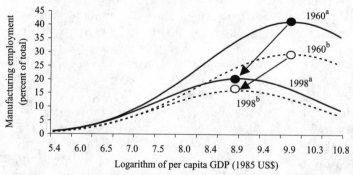

Figure 2.7 (continued)

D. Latin America and the Caribbean, 1998

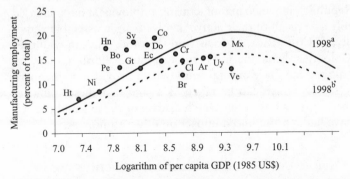

Note: Ar = Argentina; Au = Australia; Bo = Bolivia; Br = Brazil; Bw = Botswana; Ca = Canada; Cl = Chile; Cn = China; Co = Colombia; Cr = Costa Rica; Do = Dominican Republic; Ec = Ecuador; Eg = Arab Republic of Egypt; Eu5 = Austria, Germany, France, Italy, and Belgium; Gb = United Kingdom; Gr = Greece; Hn = Honduras; Ht = Haiti; Jm = Jamaica; Jp = Japan; Kr = Republic of Korea; Lk = Sri Lanka; Mx = Mexico; My = Malaysia; Ng = Nigeria; Ni = Nicaragua; No = Norway; Pa = Panama; Pe = Peru; Pk = Pakistan; Py = Paraguay; Sg = Singapore; Sv = El Salvador; Tn = Tunisia; Uy = Uruguay; Ve = República Bolivariana de Venezuela; Zw = Zimbabwe.

a. Specialization in manufactures.

b. Specialization in natural resources and services.

Source: Palma (2002).

"curse of natural resources" is at work here, however. In fact, in a number of well-known cases, such as those of Finland and of Malaysia and other Asian countries (all of which have a generous endowment of natural resources), the countries concerned have been able to avert this phenomenon, either by carrying forward the industrialization process using the resources available or by developing a complementary manufacturing industry for the domestic market and for export. This indicates that although opportunities do exist, few countries appear to be prepared to take advantage of them.

One of the striking features of Latin America and the Caribbean is that whereas the ratio of manufacturing employment to total employment was similar in most of the countries of the region before they embarked on economic reform programs, marked divergences have emerged since then (see figure 2.7D). Brazil and the three Southern Cone countries (Argentina, Chile, and Uruguay) have exhibited the greatest degree of deindustrialization following their economic reform efforts and now conform to the typical pattern of raw material exporters, of which the República Bolivariana de Venezuela is a classic example. The second pattern corresponds to a number of Central American (El Salvador, Honduras) and Caribbean countries (the Dominican Republic), in which manufacturing employment has increased considerably as a result of their active involvement in assembly activities. Finally, in Costa Rica, Mexico, and the other Andean countries (Bolivia, Colombia, Ecuador, and Peru), economic reform has not significantly altered the share of total employment provided by the manufacturing sector, which can be taken as a sign that these countries have not been affected by either Dutch disease or the assembly activities that have had a pronounced impact on other economies.

The New Global Production Structure

The technological revolution is at the heart of the forces driving the third stage of globalization. The emergence of new technologies and the ever-faster evolution of existing ones have significantly altered the ways in which production is organized in firms, production sectors, and ultimately the world economy. In fact, these changes are so far-reaching that they have been called one of the greatest transformations in history (Piore and Sabel 1984). Of all these new technologies, information and communication technologies (ICTs) have had the most direct impact on the globalization process.

Microeconomic Foundations

The effects of the microeconomic forces generated by the ongoing technological revolution are mediated by social and political variables, and particularly by the policy of opening up the countries' economies to international trade and foreign investment. These variables can either speed up or slow down the absorption of new technologies. To understand the implications of this premise, it is important to identify the features of new technologies and to determine how they affect production, the structure of markets, and business decisions.

Industrial organization in the digital age involves a complex network of markets (such as markets for equipment, fixed or cellular telephone services, fiber-optic cable, connectivity, and application services) that converge in the transmission of data, voice, and sound. Each of these markets has its own types of industrial organization, intellectual property rules, conditions for reaping the benefits of research and development (R&D) investment in new products and processes, regulatory frameworks and bodies, competition rules, and forms of interdependence among production agents. Some of these markets are highly competitive, and others are characterized by collusion among firms to set exclusionary prices that block new competitors' access to the market. Of particular significance is the nonrivalrous nature of many digital goods and services, which opens up virtually infinite possibilities for realizing economies of scale. The industrial countries' technological leadership accounts for the advantages they enjoy in the current stage of globalization, as well as the disadvantages faced by developing countries (Katz and Hilbert 2002).

The impact of ICTs on the structure of the economy can be seen in the digitization of information flows, communication processes, and coordination mechanisms. This, in turn, has altered variables relating to firms' cost structures, in many cases practically eliminating the importance of segments that, until a few decades ago, determined the conditions of supply. In particular, these technologies have reduced the cost of processing and transmitting information; lowered the cost associated with distance; led to smaller product sizes and miniaturization; and absorbed complexities in the organization of production that previously had been handled by management teams, thereby paving the way for flexible forms of production (Cairncross 1997; Turner and Hodges 1992). The new technologies have also made it possible to achieve higher quality, greater precision, and enhanced product compatibility, which have significantly reduced the unit cost of products of a given quality.

What is more, technological change has been a key component of the changes that have taken place in dynamic learning curves, in combination with changes in learning processes themselves and in economies of scale (Chesnais 1993), all of which affect business decisions, the structure of markets, and patterns of productive specialization. Firms respond to signals from their environment when they acquire, adapt, and refine technologies in order to build up their technological capacities and competitive advantages. Because these signals come from the incentive structure, from factor and resource markets (skills, capital, technology, suppliers), and from institutions (in the fields of education and training, technology, and finance, among others) with which the firm interacts, innovation is the outcome of an interactive process linking agents that respond to market incentives—such as firms—with other institutions that operate on the basis of strategies and rules that are independent of market mechanisms.[13]

The reduction in the cost of transporting goods and transmitting information made possible by the technological revolution has led to a broadening of markets, which in some cases have reached global proportions.[14] As markets increase in size, economies of scale become more important in firms' cost functions. Both processes have been reinforced by the trend toward the homogenization of the preferences of large groups of consumers. This has, in turn, expanded the market for products that can meet this type of demand on the basis of keen price competition. In this context, there has been a relative decline in the importance of economies of scope, especially because of the impossibility of preventing competitors capable of operating in the world market from reproducing product mixes that achieve these kinds of economies. As competition has come to focus on the variable of price, the tendency toward technological homogenization has strengthened. This, together with the homogenization of preferences, is leading to the emergence of a "global consumer" in a global market dominated by economies of scale (Levitt 1983). This stylized fact is a key element in the current stage of globalization, but the extent to which it can be generalized will be considered later in this chapter.

Forms of global consumption have been available to elite social groups for at least a century. The current stage stands out because it has made this pattern of consumption available on a massive scale, encompassing many more people and categories of goods and services than it did a few decades ago. In any case, this trend toward the homogenization of consumption patterns is only a trend and does not, therefore, imply that all markets have become globalized.

The trend toward the homogenization of production technologies and consumer preferences in many markets, as well as the consequent trend toward the homogenization of products, has changed the conditions of competition. In particular, it has prompted firms to move away from competition based on mechanisms for covering variable costs—an example of which was the "redeployment" of industrial activities to some developing countries that began in the 1970s—toward competition in covering fixed costs. Production, especially manufacturing, has tended to become an activity involving a very large proportion of fixed costs. This does not mean that competition to cover variable costs has disappeared, but only that it has become relatively less important. This is particularly true of cutting-edge activities and processes; it is far less applicable to the production of goods, which continue to be assembled in locations with low variable costs (particularly wages). By reducing labor costs, the increased flexibility of labor markets has hastened the reduction of the proportion of variable costs. This is illustrated by the fact that in some manufacturing segments, variable costs amounted to 10 percent of total costs or less in the 1990s, after having represented some 25 percent just two decades earlier (Oman 1994).

In particular, the development of global brands and the intensification of product and process R&D have raised firms' fixed costs, which they cannot meet without increasing the scale of production. Thus, economies of scale in R&D and in marketing are combined with economies of scale in production. This sets the stage for the emergence of global producers that vie for market shares that are large enough to cover their fixed costs. This process, in turn, reinforces the trend toward market expansion, and the organizational structure of those markets changes accordingly.

New Forms of Production and Market Organization

The technological revolution has changed the way in which production is organized. In the early and mid-20th century, firms responded to the emergence of new markets and the expansion of existing ones by organizing production according to the Taylor/Ford paradigm, which was based on a strict separation between design and planning activities, on the one hand, and direct production operations, on the other. Many firms adopted the organizational features of this mode of production: a very high, narrow hierarchical pyramid; specialization in narrowly defined activities and skills; and separation between thought and action. In sum, these were the well-known "principles of scientific management." The revolution in technology, and particularly in ICTs, has made this form of organization obsolete and shifted the emphasis to a new set of features that are summed up in the idea of "flexible production" (Dussel Peters 2000).

This new way of organizing production can be described on the basis of six activities, all of which make use of ICTs to break down the old paradigm's dichotomy between thought and action. Specifically, it involves techniques of (a) simultaneous engineering, which integrates the design and manufacturing stages into a single process; (b) continuous, incremental innovation, sometimes by means of quality circles; (c) teamwork involving multiskilled workers; (d) production and management of just-in-time and real-time inventories, which permit production to adjust more quickly to changes in demand; (e) incorporation of quality control into the production process itself in order to avoid the costs associated with the ex post facto correction of errors; and (f) increasing interaction between suppliers and users in the areas of innovation, design, and production, which gives rise to global production and marketing chains and networks (Oman 1994).

One particularly important form of interaction has been the development of horizontal links between firms that have led to the formation of strategic alliances. Because technical progress has involved the use of many basic technologies, which no single firm can master in their entirety, firms have had to develop networks of agreements to complement one another—while continuing to compete with each other—in the area of innovation.

The combination of operations under the flexible production paradigm and the expansion of markets has given rise to two of the traits of the current model of market organization: the trend toward economic concentration and the trend toward the consolidation of global production chains or internationally integrated production systems, which cover the whole range of design, production, and marketing activities for a given product (Gereffi 1994; Mortimore and Peres 2001). In more analytical terms, the new forms of business organization, such as outsourcing, virtual cooperation, and strong vertical integration, are contingent on the trend in transaction costs and their impact in setting the production frontier between hierarchical coordination and market coordination (Hilbert and Katz 2002). Depending on whether transaction costs are reduced further within firms or within markets, this frontier will move toward either the expansion of firms or a greater reliance on outsourcing.

Global oligopolies are not new in the world economy, having characterized the production and marketing of products such as petroleum, minerals, and even some types of machinery and equipment since the first stage of globalization in the late 19th century. What *is* new is the increase in the number of sectors where oligopoly is the typical form of productive organization, as it is now the predominant configuration of supply in most industries with a strong technological R&D component and in manufacturing segments with sizeable economies of scale (Chesnais 1993). The ubiquity of oligopolistic structures is a product of efforts to achieve economies of scale in production, marketing, and technological research and development, which have surpassed even the market expansion driven by the new technologies.

These oligopolistic structures and the trend toward concentration exhibit dissimilar features in two types of internationally integrated production systems, with these systems being defined according to whether they are led by producers or marketers. In producer-led systems, large manufacturers (generally TNCs) coordinate the entire production chain, including its backward and forward linkages. In these systems, profits are derived from economies of scale and technological advances, as in the case of the automotive, aeronautical, computer, semiconductor, and heavy machinery industries.

However, in systems led by wholesalers and other vendors, such as large retail chains, wholesalers, and own-brand producers, more decentralized networks are set up. This is true in the clothing, footwear, toy, appliance, consumer electronics, and even handicraft sectors. In these systems, profits are derived from value added in the areas of design, marketing, and financial services. Through these activities, leading firms link outsourced production with direct producers located anywhere in the world and carve out demand niches in the principal consumer markets (Gereffi 1994).

In both types of systems, coordination of the entire production chain is a key source of competitive advantage, and the network is therefore used as a strategic asset. Information flows are the basic means by which firms improve or consolidate their position in the production chain, whereas the appropriation of benefits depends on the influence that leading firms can exert on different segments of the chain, and this influence naturally changes over time (Gereffi 2000).

Also in both cases, as in the trend toward the formation of global oligopolies, the most dynamic economic players have been TNCs. The reduction in information costs—because the flow of information is vital in coordinating activities worldwide—and market expansion have added to the traditional advantages enjoyed by TNCs in terms of technology, management, and scale. Accordingly, TNCs have been able to respond faster to shifts in the organization of production toward flexible arrangements and have capitalized on their competitive advantages to organize internationally integrated production systems, positioning themselves in the links of the production chain that enable them to capture a significant share of the profits it generates. The expansion of TNCs has entailed a sharp upswing in foreign direct investment (FDI) flows and has taken the form of both new investment and acquisition of existing assets, although to different degrees.

Implications for Business Decisions and Strategies

In a context in which production technologies and preferences tend toward homogenization, economies of scale necessarily lead to greater concentration. In fact, when firms are able to differentiate their products on the basis of trade or technological development strategies, market expansion tends to increase the average size of such firms.

In some cases, product differentiation efforts are based on increases in variable production costs. For example, in furniture making, differentiation may be based on the use of better wood, higher quality paints, or more labor per unit produced. In such situations, when the size of the market increases, there is always the possibility that new and relatively small firms may enter the market and capture part of its growth (Hotelling 1929). In this case, an increase in market size does not result in a concomitant increase in concentration.

However, when differentiation is sought on the basis of sunk costs incurred in creating a brand image or publicity or in moving forward along the technology curve, these efforts result in escalation. Some firms will expand, and the market structure will become more concentrated. The essence of this mechanism is that differentiation efforts that are not profitable in smaller markets become profitable in larger ones. Strategies for creating and defending global brands and for competing on the basis of technological progress are typical not only of technology-intensive activities, but also of marketing-intensive ones, even when they involve low- or mid-level technologies. These processes account for the highly concentrated supply structure for products such as certain processed foods and beverages, in which technology intensiveness is low (Sutton 1991, 1998).

Thus, there are forces that lead to larger average firm size and greater concentration, both when supply is highly homogenized and when significant differentiation efforts are made. In principle, this seems to conflict with the flexible production features that make it possible to reduce the scale of production and offer customized products. In this regard, it is important to distinguish between two types of concentration: technical concentration, which results directly from the minimum size requirements for optimal plant operation, and economic concentration, which takes the firm, rather than plants or production lines, as the relevant unit. Although some evidence points to a reduction in the technical scale of production activities involving dissimilar products, this does not mean that there is a trend toward smaller-sized firms. Only large firms can directly produce a broad range of products or coordinate internationally integrated production systems capable of supplying them. In these cases, economies of scope are usually significant but can be achieved only by firms or systems with considerable economies of scale (mass customization).

This background explains why, despite the deverticalization and tertiarization of nonessential activities, large firms are the leading economic players in the current stage of globalization and why, within that group, TNCs play an especially significant role. TNCs are the ones that set up both producer-led and marketer-led internationally integrated production systems either through new investment or by means of mergers and acquisitions, as will be discussed later in this chapter.

The ways in which TNCs organize production have changed during the current stage of globalization as a result of the interaction between two types of variables: the international location of their production processes (dispersed or concentrated activities) and the intensity of their coordination activities (high or low). Under the old paradigm, firms usually followed a strategy of managing relatively similar activities in different locations and made little effort to coordinate them (Porter 1986). Then, however, the increasing importance of economies of scale led them to adopt a supply structure based on the provision of products to the global market from one or a few locations (Hamel and Prahalad 1985; Levitt 1983), and the coordination of the work being done at these locations was based on their physical proximity; a pioneering example of this was provided by Japanese automobile makers in the 1960s and 1970s. Then, the ICT revolution led to a second change: as the cost of long-distance coordination has fallen, business strategies have aimed at combining activities in several, although not many, locations while making major efforts to ensure their real-time coordination.

Since the 1980s, TNCs have experimented with various forms of organization. Some of the more noteworthy structures include elements of head office organization, or networks in which the components have different relative weights in order to allow the concentration of decisionmaking processes and operations between the parent company and its subsidiaries (Bartlett and Goshal 1989). The number of locations involved varies considerably depending on what economies of scale can be achieved in production, ranging from configurations that are highly concentrated in producer-led internationally integrated production systems to configurations that are much more widely dispersed in marketer-led systems. In both cases, however, coordination is more intensive than in the past. The number of locations is determined by the characteristics of the firms' learning curves and the economies of scale available to them, whereas the choice of locations is determined by the comparative advantages of each place and the coordination advantages to be derived from the geographic concentration of production, design, and technological R&D activities (Porter 1986).

Meanwhile, firms seeking agglomeration economies have become concentrated in areas where they have easy access to global markets and factors of production, as well as appropriate innovation capacity, suppliers, and institutions.[15] The mobility afforded by technological advances has turned TNC subsidiaries, which used to operate as geographically dispersed but self-contained production units, into integrated production and distribution networks at the regional and global levels. Within these networks, firms can purchase the inputs they need locally and produce for the local or regional market, or they can integrate economic activities scattered over different regions. From this standpoint, the regionalization of the world economy is, paradoxically, a corollary of globalization.[16]

The comparative and coordination advantages of different locations raise the question of how the global and local (including supranational or regional) dimensions are related in business strategies. The positions taken on this point have tended to illustrate the need to combine the two. In particular, Akio Morita of Sony highlighted the need to think globally while taking local culture and demand into account, in a process of so-called global localization (Turner and Hodges 1992). Kenichi Ohmae, meanwhile, extolled the advantages of replicating, in different markets, strategies that have proved successful in North American, Western European, or East Asian markets as a means whereby firms can become "global insiders" (Ohmae 1985).

The local dimension is particularly important for national firms that cannot become transnational players in the globalization process, either as leaders of internationally integrated production systems or as participants in more or less significant segments of such systems. The firms that fit this description are highly diverse in terms of both their size and their managerial and learning capacity. These firms' strategies revolve around the opportunities offered by niches that are generated or strengthened in global markets having a strong tendency toward homogenization. Rising income levels (which enable consumers to indulge their taste for variety, quality, and novelty), regional and local differences in taste (idiosyncratic goods), and the demand for specialized inputs and equipment on the part of certain types of users are some of the factors that ensure the survival of what are sometimes very profitable niches for nonglobal firms (Mariti 1993). Within these niches, such firms have advantages over their global competitors, particularly because of their superior ability to monitor changes in local markets and their capacity to operate more flexibly.

Niche-oriented strategies can fail over the long term if global firms decide that a niche is profitable enough to warrant their entry with identical or substitute products or even their acquisition of the local producer. Usually, local firms are unable to counter such moves, because their more limited scale leaves them no resources for effectively developing a defensive strategy. For more advanced nonglobal firms, a particularly serious risk is that of falling into the "R&D trap" or the "marketing trap": in other words, trying to defend their niche through ever-greater efforts in technological R&D and in marketing, which make mounting resource demands and cannot be sustained over the long term.

International experience has shown that small and medium-size enterprises (SMEs) not taking part in internationally integrated production systems are nonetheless capable of maintaining market niches as well. This is true not only of low-value-added activities that hold little attraction for global firms, but also of sectors in which "disadvantages of scale" are offset by the advantages of flexibility and interaction with networks of similar firms that are usually in the same location. Industrial districts are one of the best-known examples of this type of configuration. There is a wide diversity of markets and business strategies. Even in the face of the overall trend toward homogenization that has given rise to global firms and internationally integrated production systems, niche strategies are still viable for nonglobal firms as a group, though they may entail high risks for the individual firms.

In any event, competitiveness conditions in different locations have not become homogenized, and global players see clear advantages of configuration and coordination in maintaining their operations in a limited number of locations in the world (Porter 1990). In particular, globalization and the lower cost of processing and transmitting information have not been mirrored by similar developments in the area of knowledge and the capacity to generate it, which remain highly localized and confined to specific individuals and, especially, institutions. In this respect, globalization has not eliminated the national, local, or sectoral dimensions of innovation systems and may even have strengthened them (Dosi 1999).

The components of an innovation system are arranged in a three-tiered structure (Cimoli and Dosi 1995; Freeman 1987; Nelson 1993). First, firms and the production system are crucial (though not exclusive) recipients of knowledge, which to a large extent is incorporated into operational routines and changes over time in response to rules of conduct and higher-level strategies (such as research activities, vertical integration, and horizontal diversification). Second, firms link up with networks consisting of other firms, nonprofit institutions, public sector agencies, universities, and organizations devoted to the promotion of production activities. These networks, as well as policies for improving the environment in which scientific and technological activities are carried out, are key elements because they can either strengthen or constrain firms' opportunities to improve their technological capabilities. Finally, in the broader context of a given country, microeconomic behavior is influenced by a series of macroeconomic effects, social relations, rules, and political constraints.

The generation and absorption of technology—and the consequent achievement and improvement of international competitiveness—are thus systemic processes, because an innovation system's performance depends on synergies and externalities that transcend a firm's efforts to optimize its position in response to changes in incentives. Technological opportunities and obstacles and the experience and skills acquired by the different participants in an innovation system flow through the system from one economic activity to another and set up a specific context in each country or region, so that a given set of economic incentives will have widely varying effects in terms of stimulating and constraining innovation.

Patterns of FDI and TNC Strategies at the Global Level

Historically, TNCs have focused on the exploitation of natural resources (where they sometimes come into conflict with nationalist interests in developing countries), on the construction and management of key segments of the infrastructure for agriculture- and mining-based export complexes, on the provision of domestic services in rapidly growing urban areas, and on capturing protected industrial markets under national import substitution strategies while, in some cases, also taking advantage of incipient subregional integration arrangements.

As a result of the changes in technology, production, and marketing analyzed in this chapter, FDI has soared, and the share of international production in the world economy has grown along with it. In the 1990s, FDI flows grew remarkably, particularly in the second half of the decade, rising from an annual average of about US$225 billion between 1990 and 1995 to nearly US$1.5 trillion in 2000. Nonetheless, in 2001, for the first time since 1991, worldwide FDI flows declined significantly, dropping to around US$735 billion.[17] Even so, this level is still equivalent to more than three times the annual average for 1990–95 and exceeds the values for each year of the 1990s, with the exception of 1999 and 2000 (see table 2.6).

Thus, between 1982 and 1999, the percentage of worldwide gross fixed capital formation represented by FDI rose from 2 percent to 14 percent, and the value added by TNCs climbed from 5 percent to 10 percent of world GDP (UNCTAD 2000). Moreover, sales by TNC subsidiaries grew much faster than world exports.

This global expansion is driven by the operations of more than 60,000 TNCs with nearly 800,000 foreign subsidiaries. Industrial countries remain the primary source and destination of FDI flows; in 2000, 92.2 percent of total FDI came from such countries, and 82.3 percent was directed to them. FDI flows have also increased significantly in developing countries, however, more than tripling their average level for the period 1990–95 in the year 2000 (see table 2.6). The primary recipients were China, Hong Kong (China), and India in Asia and Argentina, Brazil, and Mexico in Latin America.

A comparison of the global distribution of inflows and outflows in 1985 and 2000 shows that FDI has become a very important variable for more countries than in the past. FDI inflows of over US$10 billion

Table 2.6 Foreign Direct Investment
(Billions of US$)

	Average 1990–1995	1996	1997	1998	1999	2000	2001
Regional distribution of inflows and outflows							
Total FDI inflows	225.3	386.1	478.1	694.5	1,088.3	1,491.9	735.1
Industrial countries	145.0	219.9	267.9	484.3	837.8	1,227.4	503.1
Developing countries	74.3	152.7	191.1	187.6	225.1	237.9	204.8
Economies in transition	6.0	13.5	19.1	22.6	25.4	26.6	27.2
Total FDI outflows	253.3	395.0	474.0	684.0	1,042.1	1,379.5	620.7
Industrial countries	221.0	332.4	395.0	631.2	966.1	1,271.3	580.6
Developing countries	32.0	61.3	74.8	50.3	73.6	104.2	36.6
Economies in transition	0.3	1.3	4.2	2.5	2.4	4.0	3.5
Cross-border mergers and acquisitions							
Total	117.9	227.0	304.8	531.6	766.1	1,143.8	593.9
Sales, by region of sale							
Industrial countries	103.1	187.7	232.1	443.1	679.5	1,056.1	496.3
Developing countries	12.7	35.7	67.1	82.7	74.0	70.6	85.9
Economies in transition	2.1	3.6	5.6	5.1	10.4	17.1	11.7
Multinational[a]	0.0	0.0	0.0	0.7	2.1	0.0	0.0
Purchases, by region of purchase							
Industrial countries	108.5	196.8	269.3	508.9	700.8	1,087.6	534.2
Developing countries	9.2	29.6	35.2	21.7	63.5	48.5	55.6
Economies in transition	0.1	0.5	0.3	1.0	1.5	1.7	2.2
Multinational[a]	0.1	0.1	0.0	0.0	0.3	6.0	1.9

a. Sales or purchases involving more than two countries.
Source: Economic Commission for Latin America and the Caribbean, on the basis of data from UNCTAD (2002b).

are now concentrated in more than 50 countries (including 24 developing countries), compared to only 17 countries (including 7 developing countries) 15 years ago. The pattern of investment abroad is similar: The number of countries with more than US$10 billion in investments abroad rose from 10 to 33 and currently include 12 developing countries, compared to 8 in 1985.

Cross-border mergers and acquisitions have been one of the chief mechanisms for the expansion of TNCs. These operations, which intensified in the second half of the 1990s (see table 2.6), enable firms to rapidly acquire a portfolio of localized assets, which are essential in strengthening their competitive positions in the local, regional, or world economy. In many cases, a firm's survival is the primary strategic incentive for engaging in these operations, especially because firms that hesitate to do so may run a serious risk of being absorbed or of being placed at a competitive disadvantage when rival firms merge.[18] The intense interplay between changes in the global economic environment and the factors that induce firms to engage in cross-border mergers and acquisitions accounts for the steady increase in such operations.[19]

Although FDI has expanded geographically, its distribution remains highly asymmetrical. The parent companies of 90 of the 100 largest nonfinancial TNCs (classified as such based on the value of their assets abroad) are located in the European Union, Japan, and the United States. In 1999, for the first time, three developing-country firms were among the world's 100 largest (Hutchison Whampoa of Hong Kong, China; CEMEX of Mexico; and Petróleos de Venezuela). The 50 largest developing-country firms—the biggest of which are just barely comparable to the smallest of the world's 100 largest—are scattered among 13 newly industrialized economies in Asia and Latin America. They include firms in Hong Kong (China), the Republic of Korea, Malaysia, Mexico, and the República Bolivariana de Venezuela.

In terms of major sectors of economic activity, the most striking feature is the significant expansion of services. The share of FDI inflows corresponding to services between 1988 and 1999 rose by more than 6 percentage points worldwide, thus representing over half of cumulative FDI by the end of that period (see table 2.7). In developing countries the share of services increased even more rapidly (by almost 17 percentage points). This important change is essentially attributable to two factors. First, the liberalization and privatization policies adopted by developing countries in the last decade have prompted a copious inflow of FDI in financial services, telecommunications, and other components of infrastructure. Second, the emergence of new marketable services (including software development, data processing, telephone

Table 2.7 Foreign Direct Investment Inflows
(*Millions of US$ and percentages*)

Sector	Industrial countries 1988	Industrial countries 1999	Developing countries 1988	Developing countries 1999	World 1988	World 1999
Primary	10.3	5.7	13.7	5.4	10.7	5.6
Secondary	39.4	36.4	65.0	54.5	42.4	41.6
Tertiary	46.9	55.5	20.7	37.3	43.9	50.3
Unspecified	3.4	2.4	0.6	2.8	3.0	2.5
Total	890,456	2,520,194	119,016	1,014,657	1,009,472	3,534,851

Note: The data are for 47 countries in 1988 and 57 countries in 1999, which represent more than 80 percent of foreign direct investment inflows in both years. Eastern Europe is excluded for both years.

Source: Economic Commission for Latin America and the Caribbean, on the basis of data from UNCTAD (2001b).

calling centers, and business support services) has enabled developing countries to benefit from localization advantages. Moreover, organizational innovations such as just-in-time production require logistical and inventory management solutions that are supplied largely by independent service firms.

This process of services expansion has taken place alongside the restructuring of the industrial economies; as a result the relative share of services has risen to more than two-thirds of total value added in the Organisation for Economic Co-operation and Development (OECD) countries (OECD 2000a). Meanwhile, the share of manufacturing activities as such has declined, and they now represent less than a quarter of the final price of goods; the rest is derived from the service activities that come into play all along the way, from the product's conception to its final marketing (Giarini 1999). A majority of the earnings of firms classified as manufacturers now come from sales of services, which has prompted some authors to speak of an "encapsulation" of services in manufactures.[20]

Alongside the growth in the share of the service sector and the decline in the relative share of the manufacturing sector, a pattern marked by a strong geographic concentration of technology-intensive industrial production has proliferated. Table 2.8 shows indicators of geographic concentration for a number of industries, grouped according to whether their technological level is high (semiconductors and biotechnology), intermediate (motor vehicles, radios, television sets), or low (food, beverages, textiles). The resulting picture is very clear: The more advanced the industry's technology, the greater its geographic concentration, both within a small number of countries and within a small number of locations in each country. This is the case of biotechnology, which is highly concentrated in certain areas of industrial countries, and of the semiconductors industry, which is concentrated in those same countries and in some Southeast Asian nations. The manufacture of radios and television sets is somewhat less concentrated geographically and also extends to some developing countries, and this pattern is stronger in the case of the automotive industry. Finally, textiles and, particularly, the food and beverage industries are less concentrated in industrial countries.

Industrial countries' predominance as recipients of FDI flows continues to be based on industries with high and intermediate levels of technological sophistication, but it has also increased in low-technology industries, which were more geographically dispersed in 1988 than they were in 1999. This trend shows that the availability of low-skilled, low-cost labor, as well as opportunities to gain access to protected markets, holds less attraction currently for manufacturing industries than in the past. In this sector, flows from some developing countries, especially in Asia but also in Latin America and the Caribbean, have increased significantly. In contrast, many countries rich in natural resources have only a marginal share in such flows, indicating that an abundance of natural resources is, by itself, an insufficient condition for the development of internationally competitive enterprises.

Another salient feature of recent decades has been the close relationship between international trade and FDI. Although the participation of industrial-country firms in international trade is hardly new—as mentioned earlier, it dates back at least as far as the 19th century—this phenomenon took on greater importance after the Second World War. Indeed, there is evidence that the growth of international trade in recent decades, the expansion of TNCs, and the emergence of internationally integrated production systems are closely related. As early as the mid-1990s, it was estimated that two-thirds of world trade in goods and nonfactor services was derived, in some way, from the international production structure of TNCs.[21] One especially significant phenomenon has been the increased trade in intermediate products and services as a result of the deepening of the international division of labor between industrial and developing countries (Baldwin and Martin 1999; Feenstra 1998; Feenstra and Hanson 2001).

The interaction between the growth strategies of TNCs and patterns of production and competition in specific sectors, combined with localization factors, determine the characteristics of trade flows in products, parts, and components (Dunning 1993). One OECD study (1996) concluded that trade in the most science-intensive sectors (such as the pharmaceuticals industry) tends to take place within an intrafirm framework, whereas trade in scale-intensive industries and

Table 2.8 Geographic Concentration of Foreign Subsidiaries in Selected Manufacturing Industries, by Technology Intensiveness, 1999
(Share of total number of subsidiaries)

	High technology		Mid-level technology		Low technology	
Share of total industry[a]	Semiconductors	Biotechnology	Automobiles	Radio and television receivers	Food and beverages	Textiles
First 3 recipient countries	0.496	0.627	0.294	0.356	0.237	0.287
First 5 recipient countries	0.629	0.71	0.44	0.502	0.353	0.401
First 10 recipient countries	0.787	0.852	0.71	0.696	0.561	0.601
First 20 recipient countries	0.945	0.953	0.884	0.893	0.747	0.795
Memorandum						
Total number of foreign subsidiaries[b]	272	169	1,296	253	2,250	1,445
Total number of recipient countries	31	28	55	36	101	77

a. Calculated as a proportion of the total number of each industry's foreign subsidiaries throughout the world.
b. Only subsidiaries identified as primarily foreign owned.
Source: Economic Commission for Latin America and the Caribbean, on the basis of data from UNCTAD (2001b).

those that use more mature technologies (motor vehicles and consumer electronics, among others) primarily reflects assembly operations and intraregional trade. Natural resource–intensive products show low levels of intrafirm trade, and international integration is usually horizontal, meaning that it involves trade in homogenous products. In the garment industry, trade flows may involve either products assembled in different parts of the world (vertical specialization) or finished products (horizontal specialization). Both types of specialization generate intraindustry trade flows, which may or may not also be intrafirm flows.[22] Thus, in trade based on the segmentation of the value chain (Krugman 1995), countries specialize, in line with their absolute advantages, in activities rather than production sectors (Feenstra 1998; Knetter and Slaughter 1999; Rayment 1983).

The links between FDI and free trade have also been facilitated by changes in the regulatory frameworks governing trade and investment[23] and by other factors related to the ongoing technological and managerial revolution. Furthermore, the increasing competition faced by business enterprises, the technological advances that have made it possible to establish real-time links over vast distances, and the liberalization of external trade policies have resulted in greater geographic dispersion of all business functions, even essential ones such as design, R&D, and financial management. Some important manifestations of this phenomenon are the establishment of subsidiaries catering to regional markets (such as those in Singapore for the Asian market) and the international division of labor among various regions (as in the automotive sector) and continents (as in the case of semiconductors). In these complex systems, the reassigned functions encompass a wide range of activities; the simplest tasks, such as assembly, are assigned to less industrialized areas, whereas functions requiring specialized expertise and technology are transferred to more industrially advanced areas.

Notes

1. The most notable exception was the United States, which adopted highly protectionist policies after the northern states won the Civil War.

2. The Latin American countries concerned include Brazil, Chile, Colombia, and Mexico (Bairoch 1993; Cárdenas, Ocampo, and Thorp 2000a; Coatsworth and Williamson 2002; Maddison 1989).

3. The República Bolivariana de Venezuela is not included in the figure because its trend diverges radically from the regional average and, in fact, alters it significantly. Venezuelan oil exports were very robust in terms of volume in the first decades after the Second World War, but this trend reversed

direction beginning in the 1970s, partly as a result of the commitments entered into within the Organization of Petroleum Exporting Countries (OPEC).

4. The Kennedy Round (1963–1967) was the first in which an agreement was reached on effective tariff reductions, covering nearly 35 percent of tariff items corresponding to nonagricultural products, which represented 80 percent of dutiable trade (Winham 1986).

5. See, among others, Finger and Schuknecht (1999), François, McDonald, and Nordström (1996), Thomas and Whalley (1998), and United Nations Conference on Trade and Development and World Trade Organization (1996).

6. This agreement was reached after the failure of the Third Ministerial Conference (Seattle, Wash., 1999). The work program is set forth in the "Ministerial Declaration" (WT/MIN(01)/DEC/1 of 14 November 2001). This text and other declarations and final decisions of the Fourth Conference are available for consultation on the WTO Web site at www.wto.org.

7. The most recent report of UNCTAD (2002a) contains a complementary analysis of recent trends in international trade.

8. ECLAC (1992a) presented a system of classification by technology intensiveness in line with the Standard International Trade Classification four-digit classification system.

9. See ECLAC (2001b), Katz (2001), and Mortimore and Peres (2001) for a more extensive analysis of these issues.

10. In the European Union, for example, manufacturing employment decreased by almost a third in just three decades (from 1970 to 2000), whereas in the United Kingdom it fell by half during the same period.

11. This is also true of the European Union, in which the productivity of the services sector has increased at less than half the rate of GDP growth (1.1 percent and 2.6 percent, respectively) since 1973.

12. *Dutch disease* usually refers to a sharp appreciation of the local currency as a result of the discovery of internationally tradable natural resources.

13. The combination of agents, institutions, and rules on which technological absorption processes are based is called an *innovation system*, generally a national innovation system. These systems determine the speed with which technological know-how is generated, adapted, acquired, and disseminated in all production activities (ECLAC 1996b; Nelson 1988).

14. Other technological revolutions, such as the one driven by the development of the railroad in the mid-19th century, had similar effects, breaking down local barriers to merchandise trade and creating national markets, even in countries of continental proportions such as the United States (Sylos Labini 1957). What sets the current revolution apart, however, is not the broadening of markets as such, but rather its scope, which has resulted in the emergence of truly global markets and the inclusion of services in this process, thereby considerably reducing the number of products that cannot be traded in world markets.

15. Agglomerations of innovative activities, such as Silicon Valley in California (United States), Silicon Fen in Cambridge (United Kingdom), Wireless Valley in Stockholm (Sweden), and Zhong Guancum in Beijing (China), have evident advantages for attracting high-value FDI. Bangalore, India, has become a magnet in the area of software development, as have Penang, Malaysia, in the electronics industry and Singapore and the Special Administrative Region of Hong Kong, China, in the financial services industry.

16. Feenstra (1998) referred to this as the "integration of trade and disintegration of production." See also Burda and Dulosch (2000).

17. The sudden drop that occurred in 2001, which then steepened in 2002, is attributable to a number of factors, including the smaller number of cross-border mergers and acquisitions, the slowdown in the world economy and the sharp decline in stock prices, the heightened macroeconomic uncertainty that prevailed, and the strong impact of the telecommunications sector, which was hurt by the less-than-successful introduction of third-generation mobile telephony in Europe.

18. One of the most interesting examples in this regard is the strategy adopted by Spanish firms to expand their operations in a number of Latin American countries.

19. Changes in the environment are associated with technological innovations, changes in the regulatory frameworks that influence a firm's operations, and the development of capital markets. The primary strategic objectives are access to new markets, an increased share of such markets or a dominant position in them, ownership of natural resources, particularly nonrenewable ones, the use of synergies to boost efficiency, achievement of economies of scale through the firm's enlargement, hedging of risks through the diversification of activities, and financial considerations (UNCTAD 2001b).

20. For example, according to the relevant data, more than 50 percent of the earnings of IBM and Siemens come from service activities (Howells 2000).

21. According to this estimate, one-third of world trade in goods and nonfactor services consisted of operations between the parent companies, subsidiaries, and associates of transnational conglomerates, valued at transfer prices, whereas another third consisted of exports by TNCs to nonassociated firms (UNCTAD 1995).

22. The practice of producing and assembling a product in one country for subsequent re-export to the country in which the firm is based began in the late 1960s as a strategy adopted by U.S. firms in Asian countries. In 1966 these operations represented about 10 percent of the sales of subsidiaries of U.S.–owned firms in those countries; in 1977, they represented 25 percent (Grunwald and Flamm 1985).

23. Between 1991 and 2000, a total of 1,185 changes were introduced into national laws on FDI; 1,121 (95 percent) of these changes were aimed at creating more favorable conditions for such investment.

3

The International Mobility of Capital and Labor

THE RELATIONSHIP BETWEEN CAPITAL mobility and the movement of labor has varied a great deal during the different phases of the globalization process. Whereas both factors were highly mobile in the first phase of this process (1870–1914), their movement was relatively limited in the period between the two world wars and in the second phase of globalization (1945–73). By contrast, one of the central features of the current phase is a marked asymmetry in this respect: Whereas capital has become more mobile than ever before, the movement of labor—particularly unskilled labor—is subject to tight restrictions.

This chapter begins by looking at the major historical developments and more recent changes in international finance and macroeconomic regimes. The second section presents an overview of international labor migration. The relative magnitude of migratory flows and the regulatory environments in which they have taken place during the different phases of globalization are compared, as are the various patterns to be found around the world in terms of migrants' points of origins and destinations.

International Finance and Macroeconomic Regimes

After discussing how the international financial system has evolved over the last century, this section focuses on the volatility and contagion that have characterized capital flows in the third stage of globalization. It then goes on to analyze the scale and composition of capital flows to developing countries.

History of the International Financial System

The growth of international trade in the 19th and early 20th centuries was accompanied by an expansion of international finance and the consolidation of the gold standard as a system of international payments and macroeconomic regulation. This expansion required the development of instruments for the settlement and financing of commercial transactions (e.g., bills of exchange), and an international network of branches of large European and U.S. banks grew up around this system. Long-term financing instruments, including both public bond issues and private financing mechanisms, were developed around the same time. One of the main sources of private financing was the sale of equities in financial centers to fund infrastructure projects, especially railways, mining operations, and other ventures in different countries and territories. The first transnational corporations, many of which operated in the natural resources sector, came a little later on, but they developed rapidly and by the early 20th century had become a well-established feature of the international scene.

The gold standard, which was based on pre-existing monetary systems that relied on other metals, became an established feature of the system in the last three decades of the 19th century. Its emergence was the result of voluntary adherence to the system that had been adopted by what was by then the world's major power—the United Kingdom. The stability of monetary units was reinforced by their convertibility into gold at fixed rates established by law, but the key factor in the expansion of the monetary base was the fiduciary money provided by banks of issue. These banks, which were generally privately owned or had been founded primarily by private agents, acquired monopolies over the issuance of currency (sometimes after a period of unrestricted issues) in exchange for services rendered to the state. The system therefore consisted of convertible bank notes backed only partially by gold reserves and, at locations further away from the financial centers, by holdings of foreign exchange; that is, the currency issued by these centers. Consequently, full confidence in the currencies' convertibility into gold played a vital role in ensuring the system's continued stability by averting a potential run on these banks' reserves, which would invariably be insufficient. In addition, this banking system operated with minimum legal reserve requirements that provided only partial backing for deposits and for notes issued by private banks in economies and periods in which free stipulation was permitted. These minimum requirements could pose the risk of a domestic financial crisis in the event that problems experienced by one institution were to trigger a loss of confidence in others, or even throughout the banking system.

The systemic effects of such "contagion" led to the belated assignment of another function to the banks of issue: that of serving as lenders of last resort to commercial banks (Eichengreen 1996).

In order to sustain confidence in convertibility, the gold standard's "rules of the game" required a procyclical approach to macroeconomic policy in times of crisis: in the event of a dislocation in the system of international payments, central banks were supposed to raise discount rates to generate contractionary pressures; if the misalignment persisted, the outflow of gold would erode the monetary base, which could be expected to translate into a decrease in the money supply and hence lower demand. Finally, fiscal deficits could not exceed the amount of financing available, and in times of crisis, when financing dwindled and tax receipts were also likely to shrink, governments therefore had no alternative but to respond with austerity policies. As indicated by Triffin (1968) and further substantiated by more recent studies (Aceña and Reis 2000), this system operated in an asymmetric manner to the detriment of countries on the periphery of the system, who were both exporters of raw materials, whose prices tended to fall in times of economic turmoil, and importers of capital, whose inflows behaved procyclically. The strong pressures thus generated by the "rules of the game" in these cases account for the frequent episodes of inconvertibility seen in the peripheral countries, including several Latin American economies, during the crises of the late 19th and early 20th centuries.

The European countries themselves abandoned the gold standard en masse during the First World War. Efforts to reinstate this system in the 1920s ran into difficulties, and it was finally abandoned altogether during the Great Depression of the 1930s. Thus, the dual tensions generated between belt-tightening policies and social pressures in the countries during crises, on the one hand, and between the central banks' responsibilities as monetary regulators and as lenders of last resort, on the other, ultimately spelled the end of this system in the industrial countries.

The demise of the gold standard was followed by an episode of macroeconomic anarchy at the international level whose hallmarks were exchange rate instability and, especially, widespread and discriminatory exchange controls. This was exacerbated by the collapse of international finance. The First World War had raised New York's profile as a new international financial center. The center's expansion in the 1920s and subsequent breakdown in 1929, in combination with widespread moratoria during the depression of the 1930s, led to the almost total disappearance of long-term international financing. This absence was later compounded by the economic impact of the Second

World War and, in particular, by sharp structural imbalances between the United States and Western Europe, which gave rise to a chronic dollar shortage.

This was the context in which the countries embarked upon the international cooperation efforts that ultimately led to the adoption of the Bretton Woods agreements in 1944. These efforts were channeled in two directions. First, even though Keynes's ambitious proposals were rejected, a new international system of macroeconomic regulation was established. This regulatory regime was intended to surmount the problems of both the gold standard and the chaotic period following its downfall. The new system was built on three pillars. The first was a system of fixed but adjustable parities with respect to an international standard (known as the gold–dollar, as the parity between the two was fixed). The second pillar was the provision of exceptional financing to countries that lapsed into deficit positions in times of crisis, on the condition that they make a commitment to carry out economic adjustments, which could include exchange rate variations. This unprecedented combination of adjustment and international support was intended to prevent economic turmoil from spreading to the rest of the world via weaker demand for imports, excessive devaluation, increased protectionism, and in particular restrictions on current payments. The third pillar was a return to the principle of convertibility and nondiscrimination in respect of current payments; no commitment to capital convertibility was made, however, and the control of capital movements was thus accepted as a legitimate international practice.[1] This element of the system released domestic policies, especially monetary policy, from the limitations that the free movement of capital could place on the pursuit of full employment. The resources used by the International Monetary Fund (IMF) to fund its exceptional financing programs initially came from the contributions of member countries, in addition to credit lines that some industrial countries began to extend from 1962 on (General Arrangements to Borrow) and issues of a strictly international reserve currency, special drawing rights (SDRs), in 1969; these issues have been repeated twice, the last time in 1981.

The second direction taken by the postwar financial reforms was the development of new forms of long-term international financing. In response to the scarcity of private financing, official banking institutions began to perform this role, first through the World Bank and later through regional development banks and domestic export-import banks as well. The Marshall Plan and, subsequently, official development assistance served as complementary sources of long-term financing.

Although official banks played a key role in providing trade financing, private banks also continued to perform this function even during periods when tension within the international payments system was at its height. The dollar surpluses generated by the United States's persistent external deficits in the 1960s—which succeeded the initial shortage of dollars more quickly than expected—and by the petrodollars of the 1970s were recycled to provide the resources for a new growth phase in private international financing. The privileged position that private banks had acquired enabled them to play a key role in this recycling process.

As is widely known, the dollar surplus also undermined the applicability of the Bretton Woods agreements. The abandonment of the dollar–gold parity in 1971 and the decision to allow the major currencies to float rendered the first pillar of the agreement (fixed but adjustable parities) obsolete and profoundly altered the third (principle of convertibility). These changes were simply a consequence of events as they unfolded, rather than the outcome of explicit international agreements, nor were they the subject of broad negotiations such as those that had led to the Bretton Woods accords. The first pillar was replaced by national autonomy in the definition of each country's exchange regime. The countries took widely varying approaches to managing the new risks posed by exchange rate instability. The European Community attempted to reduce fluctuations among its members' currencies, thereby giving priority to economic integration. This marked the beginning of a process that lasted a quarter of a century and culminated in the formation of a monetary union; the final stage of this process was the replacement of most of the members' national currencies with the euro on January 1, 2002. The developing countries espoused a number of strategies, including the adoption of one of the major currencies as a reference or the diversification of risks by linking their exchange rate to a currency basket.

The floating of the major currencies represented a genuine "privatization of exchange risk." This created a need for financial instruments to hedge against that risk and led to a steep increase in the volume of currency transactions. In fact, the ratio of currency transactions to the value of international trade soared from 2:1 in 1973 to 10:1 in 1980 and 70:1 in 1995 (Eatwell and Taylor 2000). This, in combination with the burgeoning growth of international banking, substantially altered the third pillar of the Bretton Woods accords. In practice, the liberalization of capital flows became the norm in the industrial countries, which one by one eliminated controls on capital transfers in the 1970s and 1980s. A number of developing countries followed suit. The convertibility of the capital account was, in fact, to be officially endorsed at the 1997 annual meeting of the IMF in Hong Kong. The formulation of this principle was then postponed, however, because of the series of financial crises that then began to erupt in a number of Asian countries and that have yet to come to an end. As actually applied by international financial institutions, the principle of capital account convertibility has given way to a gradual liberalization of the capital account and of domestic financial sectors. The aim has been to sequence this process properly and to align it with the development of a parallel institutional structure in order to ensure domestic financial stability. As will be discussed later in this chapter, this has resulted in the emergence of new responsibilities for the Bretton Woods institutions.

The second pillar of the Bretton Woods agreement (exceptional financing in times of crisis) also saw substantial changes for two reasons. First, in the late 1970s, the IMF stopped lending to industrial countries, which had been a very significant part of its financing activities up until that time (see figure 3.1). The Fund thus began to concentrate on developing countries and, increasingly, on countries in which its operations were likely to have "systemic effects." The second change was an upswing in the demand for resources because of the structural nature of certain types of balance-of-payments problems, the severity of the cyclical disturbances associated with fluctuations in raw materials prices, and especially the volatility of capital flows. The need for larger volumes of funding over longer periods of time led to the establishment of new lines of IMF financing in the final two decades of the 20th century. In a parallel development, in 1979 the World Bank launched its structural adjustment programs. These arrangements gradually came to take precedence over the traditional lines of project financing that had previously been the focus of its lending strategy.

New conditionalities grew up around these changes and gave rise to a new function that came to be performed jointly by the IMF and the World Bank from the 1980s on. This new duty, which was not contemplated in the Bretton Woods accords, was the promotion of economic liberalization in developing economies, based on the assumption that their structural rigidities were caused by excessive state intervention. Like others before it, this new shift in the responsibilities of the Bretton Woods agencies did not arise from explicit negotiations but was instead a response to changes in the ideologies and power relationships prevailing at the global level.

The growing internationalization of finance made it necessary to have new regulatory standards. An awareness of this need had existed since the start of the 1970s, and in 1975 the Basel Committee on Banking Supervision was established under the auspices of the Bank for

Figure 3.1 International Monetary Fund: Total Credits and Outstanding Loans, 1950–2001

A. Proportion of international reserves

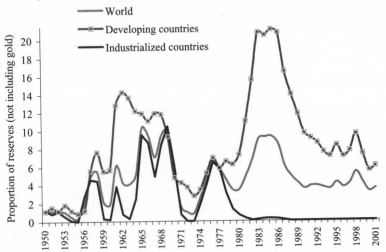

B. Proportion of exports

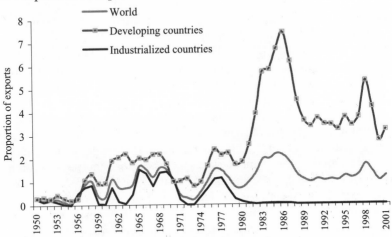

Source: Economic Commission for Latin America and the Caribbean, on the basis of data from IMF (2001b).

International Settlements (BIS). The most significant result of this initiative was the adoption of the Basel principles on the regulation and supervision of banks in 1988. A number of reform proposals have been made since 1999 with a view to bringing the Basel principles into line with recent developments in the global banking industry and rectifying the system's shortcomings.[2] The definition of minimum regulatory principles has extended to a growing range of issues, including rules on debt issues in financial markets, the insurance industry, and financial accounting. One of the elements of this reform movement that has received strong backing in recent years is the creation of a program to strengthen financial systems in developing countries. Such a program would include the adoption of these international standards, as well as a set of principles for the management of external and public debt and international reserves. This new function of the Bretton Woods institutions has not been clearly differentiated from the responsibilities of other agencies, however, particularly in the case of the BIS.

Recent Changes and Volatility in Financial Markets

Developments in the macroeconomic environment have been accompanied by far-reaching changes in industrial countries' financial systems. Broadly speaking, this process of change, which began in the 1980s and was consolidated in the 1990s,[3] has involved three basic trends. The first is the concentration of the industrial economies' financial systems.[4] During the 1990s the world's major private financial institutions embarked on an intensive process of mergers and acquisitions. This process, which became the hallmark of the decade, quickened its pace as the decade drew to a close.[5] As a result, the number of banking institutions declined in almost all countries, and banking concentration, calculated on the basis of the proportion of deposits controlled by the largest banks, tended to rise. In fact, this trend would be even more marked if operations off the balance sheet (particularly trading of financial derivatives) were included in the calculations.

Second, a widespread trend toward banking disintermediation and an institutionalization of savings has accompanied the emergence of nonbank financial intermediaries, such as mutual and pension funds, investment banks, and insurance companies (see table 3.1). Competition from these agents has eroded the predominant position in international financial intermediation enjoyed by the banks in the 1960s and 1970s. It has also obliged traditional banking institutions to form conglomerates that offer an ever-broader range of financial services. As a result, the dividing line between bank and nonbank activities has become increasingly blurred.

The operations of nonbank intermediaries were deregulated in the 1980s and this, in combination with the elimination of capital controls in industrial countries, allowed these institutions to play an increasingly important role in international financial markets and their

Table 3.1 Financial Holdings of Institutional Investors[a] in Selected OECD Countries
(Percentages of GDP)

Country	1992	1994	1996	1999	2000
Australia	61.6	65.9	92.4	127.9	131.2
Canada	68.6	80.2	92.1	112.7	111.3
France	61.9	71.8	86.6	125.4	133.3
Germany	34.0	41.3	50.6	76.8	79.7
Hungary	2.5	3.9	6.1	10.7	12.8
Iceland	55.3	66.7	79.6	111.3	110.1
Italy	21.8	32.2	39.0	96.9	—
Japan	78.0	81.6	89.3	100.5	—
Republic of Korea	51.8	53.7	57.3	88.5	72.6
Luxembourg	1,574.3	1,945.6	2,057.0	4,172.3	—
Netherlands	131.5	144.5	167.6	212.8	209.6[b]
Spain	21.9	32.3	44.3	65.4	62.1
United Kingdom	131.3	143.8	173.4	226.7	—
United States	127.2	135.9	162.9	207.3	195.2

— Not available.

Note: GDP = gross domestic product; OECD = Organisation for Economic Co-operation and Development.

a. Insurance companies, investment firms, pension funds, and other institutional savers.

b. Insurance companies include life insurance only.

Source: Economic Commission for Latin America and the Caribbean, on the basis of data from OECD (2001a).

expansion, which did a great deal to bolster the growth of secondary debt markets. In these markets, as in stock markets, the increased participation of institutional investors and of a large number of individual financial agents tended to push values higher, generating what was viewed by some as a virtuous circle and by others as a financial bubble. In any event, it paved the way for the development of new sources of financing. This process lasted for quite some time, until it was interrupted by the international crisis that began in 2000.

The expansion of secondary markets helped to deepen financial markets in industrial countries (Fornari and Levy 1999) and facilitated the emergence of new sources of corporate financing. One result was that the volume of bond issues in industrial-country markets, headed by Japan and the United States, more than doubled in the 1990s, and significant increases were seen in a number of Latin American countries as well. The depth and liquidity of this well-developed secondary market, particularly in the United States, helped to finance the new high technology sectors, which led the economic expansion of the

1990s. Another recent innovation, the creation of risk capital funds, contributed to the growth of these activities; both processes came to an abrupt halt with the outbreak of the recent crisis, however.

The development of these markets has also given credit rating agencies a considerably broader role than they had played before, as they provide information to investors and are consulted increasingly for regulatory purposes; for example, the Basel Committee on Banking Supervision recently put forward a proposal to use agency ratings in the regulation of the banking sector. There has been widespread criticism of the short-term horizon and procyclicality of agency ratings, however, particularly in terms of their impact on financing for developing countries (Reisen 2001, 2002).

Third, the rapid growth of institutional investors' financial holdings has boosted demand for new financial instruments and has encouraged risk diversification. Hence the development of specialized markets for particular instruments, such as high-yield bonds, bonds issued by emerging economies, and securitized assets (based on mortgages, automobile loans, and credit card receivables), as well as shares in foreign firms (American depository receipts and global depository receipts). This phenomenon, in combination with the privatization of exchange risk, is also behind the rapid expansion of the demand for financial derivatives designed to hedge specific kinds of risk (see figure 3.2). The Asian crisis has severely decreased the volume of exchange-risk hedging contracts that are being concluded, however.

These trends have had both positive and negative effects on industrial economies. On the positive side, financing opportunities for

Figure 3.2 Financial Derivatives Traded on Organized Exchanges
(*Millions of contracts at the end of each year*)

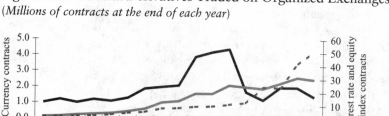

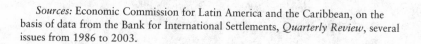

Sources: Economic Commission for Latin America and the Caribbean, on the basis of data from the Bank for International Settlements, *Quarterly Review*, several issues from 1986 to 2003.

production enterprises have increased substantially, with both high technology and medium-size firms reaping the benefits. On the negative side, however, these trends have heightened financial fragility, because many of the fastest growing activities are not covered by the regulatory mechanisms of traditional banking activities. In fact, the activities that entail the highest risks and the greatest degrees of leverage—those associated with the derivatives market—remain outside the existing regulatory frameworks, and there are as yet no proposals to extend regulatory standards to this domain. Even in the case of institutional investors, regulatory coverage is far from sufficient (D'Arista and Griffith-Jones 2001).

There is, of course, nothing new about the volatility of financial markets, as economic history amply demonstrates (Kindleberger 1978), even in recent times (BIS 2001). This volatility is clearly reflected in the remarkable frequency with which financial crises have broken out in both industrial and developing countries ever since the mid-1970s (IMF 1998). Because the transactions conducted on financial markets are essentially intertemporal operations, the lack of information about the future constitutes the prime "market failure" of financial markets (Keynes 1936; Eatwell and Taylor 2000). This volatility can thus be attributed to changes in agents' opinions and expectations, which continually shift back and forth between optimism and pessimism.[6] The impact of these shifts is magnified by the effects of the "contagion" of opinion and expectations from one market to another.[7] These externalities constitute another market failure, because they can give rise to multiple equilibria and to what amount to self-fulfilling prophecies when the expectations of a majority of agents point in the same direction.

Information asymmetries between debtors and creditors (Stiglitz 1994) are yet another market failure. These asymmetries translate into a bias in favor of borrowers that are considered low risk and generate a strong inclination to rely on creditors' flawed information about their borrowers, especially the highest-risk debtors. Because confidence varies over the course of the business cycle, the spreads on what are deemed to be the highest-risk loans on the market follow a strongly procyclical pattern, giving rise to alternating periods of investor appetite for high-risk activities and flights to quality. These variations in confidence also account for the fact that secondary markets display much greater liquidity in times of plenty, as they too depend on the market's confidence in the information available to buyers. For this same reason, derivatives markets also tend to behave procyclically, and the types of transactions considered to entail excessive risk may even dry up altogether during times of crisis.

Contemporary financial markets exhibit a number of features that have tended to exacerbate their volatility[8]:

• Inadequate regulation, as mentioned above, affects the activities of both institutional investors and agents in the derivatives market, and the existing regulations have a procyclical bias.[9]

• Problems of contagion to different markets are caused by the liquidity constraints faced by institutional investors. When the price of a given instrument falls, these investors may be obliged to sell other types of holdings—even assets that bear no relation to the first instrument—in order to restore their own liquidity. This pressure is even greater when funds are withdrawn from a market that generally operates on the basis of spot transactions or when these investors have to settle an account or make some other payment, including the collaterals required for certain types of derivatives transactions. accordingly, the larger the stake of highly leveraged institutions in the market, the more serious this problem becomes.

• Agents tend to use the same risk assessment systems, which heightens the correlation between the financial behavior of sometimes dissimilar instruments and exacerbates the effects of contagion.

• There is a tendency to evaluate the performance of institutional investors over short time horizons, which has a similar effect.

• The behavior of credit rating agencies is procyclical.

Figure 3.3A shows the correlation between two risk markets during the turbulent period that began with the crisis of 1997: the bond market in emerging economies and high-yield bonds in the United States. In both markets, spreads narrowed during the bond market boom and widened sharply in response to the Asian crisis and, especially, the Russian crisis, after which they moved part of the way back toward more normal levels. Throughout this cycle, the fluctuations were much sharper in emerging bond markets. By contrast, in the more recent crisis, which radiated from its epicenter in the United States, just the opposite occurred. During the period as a whole, there was a strong positive correlation between the two markets.[10] The changing nature of contagion is illustrated in figure 3.3B, which shows the increase in spreads in the main Latin American economies during the five most recent crisis periods. All the countries exhibited an upward trend at these times, but the impact was much more powerful during the Asian and especially the Russian crises than during episodes centered in Latin American countries. This suggests that crises in industrial countries have a much greater impact, especially when they affect highly leveraged agents, some of which have withdrawn from emerging markets in recent years.

Figure 3.3 Spreads in Emerging Markets

A. Merrill Lynch High-Yield Master Index and J.P. Morgan EMBI+

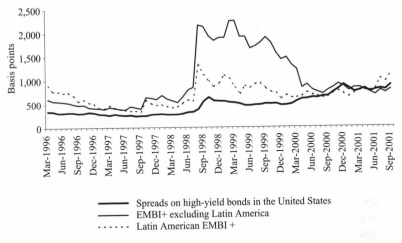

——— Spreads on high-yield bonds in the United States
——— EMBI+ excluding Latin America
· · · · · Latin American EMBI +

B. Increase in bond spreads (percentages)

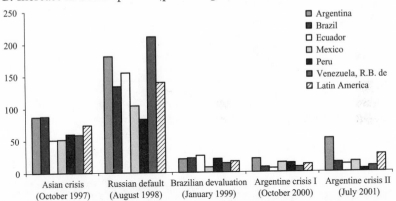

Note: EMBI+ = Emerging Markets Bond Index Plus.
Sources: Economic Commission for Latin America and the Caribbean, on the basis of data from Bloomberg 2002, electronic database, and J.P. Morgan Chase (2002).

State intervention to correct these market failures can easily give rise to "government failures" if adequate incentive systems are not in place. Regulation is the most important line of action, because it focuses on preventive measures aimed at ensuring that economic agents avoid assuming an excessive level of risk. The development of regulatory systems tends to lag behind that of the market, however, and can itself lead to evasion and avoidance (transactions conducted off the balance sheet, for example) or the use of suboptimal intermediation mechanisms. Supervision is also preventive, but it tends to be subject to information problems, and its discretionary nature can lead to abuses. Government intervention in response to systemic crises also offers incentives for excessive risk taking (moral hazard). Lastly, intervention intended to compensate for a market bias toward risk-seeking investors can create similar problems of moral hazard, such as the provision of guarantees to high-risk borrowers. The use of official financing to resolve the problem can generate dependence on the state ("graduation" problems) and can even oblige private creditors to take on higher risks owing to the preferred creditor status of official agencies. For this reason, all that the authorities can do is to offset volatility and risk discrimination partially using an appropriate combination of instruments.

Capital Flows to Developing Countries

Over the last three decades, the developments in international markets described in the preceding section have also been reflected in major changes in capital flows to developing countries.[11] The most striking aspect of these trends is the contrast between the slow growth of official financing flows and the increase in highly volatile private flows. As shown in figure 3.4, official financing has tended to decline as a proportion of developing-country gross domestic product (GDP), especially in the 1990s. This primarily reflects the scaling back of its main component, bilateral assistance, which, over a large part of that decade, declined both in real terms and as a proportion of industrial-country GDP (from 0.35 percent in the mid-1990s to an average of 0.22 percent in the period 1998–2000). The decrease in bilateral assistance has been most pronounced in the case of the largest industrial countries, although this has been partly offset by the rising proportion of grants vis-à-vis concessional credits. Moreover, unlike private flows, official financing has not been procyclical and, indeed, some components of it—particularly balance-of-payments support and multilateral development finance—have displayed countercyclical behavior.

Private external financing has fluctuated sharply owing to the effects of its most volatile components: short-term flows and long-term commercial bank lending (which, in figure 3.4, includes portfolio flows). During the most critical years, including both the debt crisis of the 1980s and the period since 1997, short-term flows have actually been negative at times. Together, these two sources of funding increased from 1.0 percent of developing-country GDP in 1971–74 to 2.3 percent in 1977–82, fell to 0.5 percent in 1983–90, peaked at 2.8

Figure 3.4 Net Flows to Developing Countries

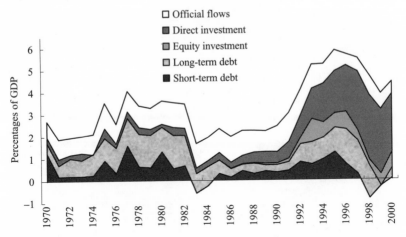

Note: GDP = gross domestic product.
Source: Economic Commission for Latin America and the Caribbean, on the basis of data from the World Bank (2001a).

percent in 1993–97, and dropped again to 0.7 percent in 1998–2000. A recovery began in 2000 but was interrupted in 2001. Foreign direct investment (FDI) has remained largely independent of this cycle and has tended to follow long-term trends instead, which were upward in the 1980s and reflected a significant upsurge in the 1990s. FDI was not affected by the series of crises that began in 1997 either, although it was affected in the 2001 crisis.

This cycle reflects only part of the instability that has characterized private financial markets. Since the Asian crisis, turbulence in these markets has taken various forms over shorter time spans: periodic interruptions in market access that have lasted varying amounts of time, simultaneous increases in risk spreads, and a shortening of maturities (see, in this regard, the preceding section).[12] In any event, it must be borne in mind that these short-term phenomena are compounded by the effects of contagion, which manifests itself over the medium term and affects access to financing for relatively long periods of time. In both cases, the essential characteristic of contagion is that it tends to have similar effects on countries regardless of whether they have sound or unsound economic fundamentals if the market classifies those countries in the same risk category.

The changes in the composition of financing that have occurred over the last three decades are detailed in table 3.2. The upsurge in the financing received by Latin America and the Caribbean in the 1970s

Table 3.2 Net Resource Flows, 1973–2001
(Annual averages, billions of US$ at 1995 constant prices)[a]

Resources	Developing countries	East Asia and Pacific	Europe and Central Asia	Latin America and Caribbean	Middle East and North Africa	South Asia	Sub-Saharan Africa
1973–81							
Total	143.2	23.2	10.5	62.6	21.1	8.4	17.3
Official flows	44.6	6.8	3.0	6.6	11.9	7.3	9.1
Direct investment	11.4	2.3	0.2	7.9	-0.9	0.2	1.8
Equity investment	0.0	0.0	0.0	0.0	0.0	0.0	0.0
Debt flows	87.1	14.2	7.4	48.1	10.1	0.9	6.3
Bonds	2.6	0.4	0.0	1.9	0.1	0.0	0.1
Commercial banks	44.1	5.9	4.7	28.3	2.2	0.4	2.6
Short-term	29.4	5.5	0.6	16.2	4.7	0.5	1.9
Other	11.0	2.3	2.1	1.7	3.0	0.1	1.8
1982–90							
Total	107.5	25.0	10.0	21.7	17.3	13.0	20.3
Official flows	51.8	8.0	2.4	9.1	9.5	8.0	14.9
Direct investment	17.9	6.6	0.4	7.3	1.8	0.4	1.5
Equity investment	1.3	0.8	0.0	0.2	0.0	0.1	0.0
Debt flows	36.5	9.7	7.1	5.1	6.0	4.7	4.0
Bonds	2.8	1.5	1.4	-0.6	0.2	0.3	0.0
Commercial banks	16.0	3.8	2.2	6.1	1.5	2.4	0.0
Short-term	7.5	3.1	1.1	-2.3	2.3	1.3	2.1
Other	10.1	1.3	2.4	1.9	2.0	0.6	1.9

1991–97							
Total	272.2	110.7	37.4	80.5	10.9	11.9	20.9
Official flows	50.2	10.3	11.6	3.5	4.4	5.8	14.6
Direct investment	93.1	43.3	11.1	29.9	2.8	2.2	3.7
Equity investment	32.2	12.3	2.7	12.6	0.6	2.7	1.3
Debt flows	96.6	44.7	12.0	34.4	3.1	1.2	1.2
Bonds	34.4	14.1	4.3	14.3	0.3	0.6	0.7
Commercial banks	20.4	7.3	2.0	10.7	0.2	0.9	-0.7
Short-term	36.9	20.0	3.2	10.8	2.5	-0.6	1.0
Other	5.0	3.3	2.5	-1.5	0.0	0.4	0.2
1998–2001							
Total	230.8	51.3	50.7	95.1	5.7	5.8	18.9
Official flows	40.1	10.9	7.7	5.5	1.2	4.3	10.5
Direct investment	161.5	50.9	25.7	71.0	2.7	3.2	7.9
Equity investment	27.6	17.5	3.0	4.0	0.6	1.1	1.4
Debt flows	1.6	-28.0	14.2	14.7	1.2	-2.8	-1.0
Bonds	22.6	0.4	7.9	10.1	1.7	1.7	0.8
Commercial banks	-1.7	-17.2	5.9	10.5	0.2	-0.2	-1.0
Short-term	-16.9	-12.7	2.0	-5.0	-0.1	-0.6	-0.4
Other	-2.4	1.5	-1.6	-0.9	-0.6	-3.7	-0.3

a. Original data at current prices were adjusted by the GDP deflator of the United States.
Source: Economic Commission for Latin America and the Caribbean, on the basis of data from the World Bank (2001a).

and its subsequent contraction were primarily a reflection of trends in both long- and short-term bank financing. Whereas long-term syndicated credits were the most common type of bank financing during the 1970s, in the 1990s short-term financing took on much greater importance. The Basel principles were undoubtedly a major factor in this respect, because they have resulted in a preference for lending short-term, low-risk credits. In the 1990s, the East Asia and Pacific region was the epicenter of the boom in short-term bank credit and of its subsequent contraction, which was much more severe and widespread in the developing world than the Latin American and Caribbean debt crisis of the 1980s. Reflecting the trend toward banking disintermediation and the institutionalization of savings, the 1990–97 boom was particularly evident in the bond market and in portfolio equity flows. Their performance during the financing crunch of 1998–99 varied widely from one region to another in relation to the averages for 1990–97: net bond issues turned negative in East Asia and the Pacific but rose in Latin America and the Caribbean and in Central Europe, whereas just the opposite occurred in the case of portfolio equity flows. FDI, meanwhile, tended to increase in all regions up to 1999.

The private credit boom of the 1990s was triggered not only by changes in financial intermediation, but also by monetary policy in the United States. Low interest rates were a decisive factor in the preference shown by institutional investors for emerging economies (Calvo, Leideman, and Reinhart 1992; D'Arista and Griffith-Jones 2001). Risk spreads were reduced in response to the greater supply of funds, strengthening the effects of low rates on these economies' financing terms. Rates in the United States and risk premiums in emerging markets developed in a diametrically opposite manner in the period of turbulence that began in 1997, demonstrating that varying perceptions of risk in emerging markets have been the predominant factor influencing the determination of those premiums and the size of capital flows (see box 3.1). What is more, U.S. interest rates have often responded endogenously to varying perceptions of risk, either because the flight to quality has raised the prices of U.S. government bonds, thereby reducing their yields, or because the Federal Reserve has responded to market uncertainty by lowering interest rates.

In the 1990s, private flows were concentrated in middle-income countries (see table 3.3). Conversely, the share of total private financing received by low-income countries not only has been smaller than their share of the total population, but also has been less than their contribution to the total GDP of the developing countries. This fact is particularly striking in bond issues, commercial banking, and equity flows (with the exception of India in the latter case). In all these

Box 3.1 Interest Rates and Emerging-Market Bond Spreads

One of the key external variables that influence emerging-market risk premiums are changes in U.S. interest rates (Calvo, Leideman, and Reinhart 1992). Theoretically, a rise in U.S. interest rates is supposed to lead, other things being equal, to an increase in the debt service to be paid by emerging-market borrowers, which will increase the likelihood of default and thus raise the corresponding risk premiums. Higher U.S. interest rates could also reduce investors' appetite for risk and, accordingly, their participation in risky markets (Kamin and von Kleist 1999). Similarly, a fall in U.S. interest rates ought to lead to a decrease in emerging-market risk premiums, both because of the positive impact lower rates will have on borrowers' ability to pay and because investors will tend to prefer emerging-market debt instruments whenever returns in mature markets fall.

Evidence for the 1990s indicates that prior to the Mexican financial crisis of December 1994, movements in emerging-market risk premiums and U.S. interest rates bore out this hypothesis. However, data for the second half of the decade indicate that emerging-market risk premiums and U.S. interest rates moved in opposite directions. From March 1996 to September 2001 there was a strong negative correlation (–0.6) between 10-year U.S. Treasury bond yields and the Emerging Markets Bond Index Plus (EMBI+) and Latin EMBI+ spreads estimated by J.P. Morgan. The correlation between risk premiums and the U.S. Federal Reserve's benchmark interest rate was also negative, albeit less so (–0.3 for the EMBI+ and –0.4 for its Latin American component).

One of the factors at work is that during this period, financial contagion became more intense than ever before and triggered a widespread increase in emerging-market risk premiums during the bouts of market turbulence set off by the Asian and Russian crises. Movements in risk premiums on U.S. high-yield corporate bonds were also strongly and positively correlated with movements in emerging-market risk premiums.

Moreover, flows to Latin America responded more to movements in risk premiums than to changes in U.S. interest rates during the period under analysis. Other things being equal, an increase in the latter should be associated with capital outflows from emerging markets, and a decrease should be associated with inflows to emerging markets. However, when periods of expansionary and contractionary U.S. monetary policy are isolated, the correlation between capital flows to Latin America and changes in U.S. interest rates does not show the expected negative sign. Instead, these flows (including debt paper issued abroad and Brady bonds) showed a positive correlation (0.6) with 10-year U.S. Treasury bond yields. This correlation was stronger in the periods corresponding to the Asian, Russian, and Brazilian crises.

Table 3.3 Net Resource Flows, 1990–99

(Annual averages, billions of US$ and percentages)

Countries	Direct investment		Equity investment		Grants		Bilateral financing		Multilateral financing (excluding IMF)		Bonds	
	Amount	Percentage	Amount	Percentage	Amount	Percentage	Amount	Percentage	Amount	Percentage	Amount	Percentage
Developing countries	103.7	100.0	27.7	100.0	29.8	100.0	4.1	100.0	15.8	100.0	30.6	100.0
Excluding China	75.4	72.7	24.8	89.4	29.5	99.0	2.6	62.4	13.9	88.0	29.4	96.0
Low-income countries	10.2	9.8	3.9	14.0	15.2	51.0	2.5	59.9	6.7	42.4	1.7	5.6
India	1.5	1.4	1.7	6.0	0.5	1.8	0.0	0.3	1.1	7.2	0.7	2.2
Other countries	8.7	8.4	2.2	8.0	14.7	49.2	2.5	59.6	5.6	35.2	1.0	3.4
China[a]	28.3	27.3	2.9	10.6	0.3	1.0	1.6	37.6	1.9	12.0	1.2	4.0
Middle-income countries	65.2	62.8	20.7	74.6	14.3	48.0	0.1	2.5	7.2	45.6	27.7	90.4
Argentina	6.6	6.4	1.1	4.1	0.0	0.1	-0.2	-5.6	1.1	6.9	4.9	15.9
Brazil	10.9	10.5	2.8	10.1	0.1	0.2	-0.8	-20.4	0.6	4.0	2.6	8.5
Indonesia	2.1	2.0	1.6	5.9	0.3	0.9	1.3	32.1	0.6	3.8	0.9	2.8
Republic of Korea[b]	2.6	2.5	3.7	13.5	0.0	0.0	0.4	9.2	0.8	5.1	4.9	15.9
Mexico	8.2	7.9	3.8	13.5	0.0	0.1	-0.4	-9.7	0.5	3.3	4.2	13.7
Russian Federation	1.8	1.7	0.8	2.7	0.8	2.7	1.1	27.0	0.7	4.3	1.6	5.4
Other countries	33.1	31.9	6.9	24.8	13.1	44.0	-1.2	-30.1	2.9	18.1	8.6	28.2

	Commercial bank credits		Other credits		Long-term debt flows		Short-term debt flows		Total net flows		Memo	
	Amount	Percentage	Amount	Percentage	Amount	Percentage	Amount	Percentage	Amount	Percentage	GDP Percentage	Population Percentage
Developing countries	17.1	100.0	4.0	100.0	232.8	100.0	22.5	100.0	255.4	100.0	100.0	100.0
Excluding China	16.6	97.1	1.1	26.6	193.2	83.0	21.7	96.2	214.9	84.2	88.2	74.8
Low-income countries	0.8	4.5	0.4	9.1	41.3	17.7	0.7	2.9	42.0	16.4	17.0	46.7
India	0.5	2.9	0.1	2.0	6.1	2.6	-0.4	-1.7	5.7	2.2	6.3	19.4
Other countries	0.3	1.6	0.3	7.1	35.2	15.1	15.1	67.1	50.3	19.7	10.8	27.3
China[a]	0.5	2.9	2.9	73.4	39.6	17.0	0.9	3.8	40.5	15.8	11.8	25.2
Middle-income countries	15.9	92.5	0.7	17.6	151.7	65.1	21.0	93.3	172.7	67.6	71.1	28.1
Argentina	0.6	3.7	-0.1	-1.3	14.1	6.0	3.4	15.1	17.5	6.8	4.5	0.7
Brazil	5.2	30.2	-0.4	-9.3	20.9	9.0	1.0	4.5	21.9	8.6	11.0	3.3
Indonesia	0.2	1.0	-0.1	-1.3	6.9	3.0	0.9	4.0	7.8	3.0	2.9	4.1
Republic of Korea[b]	-0.9	-5.5	-0.1	-3.6	11.3	4.9	5.9	26.4	17.2	6.8	7.0	0.9
Mexico	2.6	15.0	-0.3	-6.5	18.6	8.0	0.3	1.2	18.9	7.4	6.7	1.9
Russian Federation	0.2	1.1	2.0	51.1	9.0	3.9	-0.8	-3.4	8.2	3.2	7.6	3.1
Other countries	8.1	47.1	-0.5	-11.6	70.9	30.5	10.2	45.4	81.1	31.8	31.4	14.0

Source: Economic Commission on Latin America and the Caribbean, on the basis of data from the World Bank (2001a) and (2001b).

a. The Word Bank considers China a middle-income country; in this table, it is presented in a separate category.

b. The World Bank considers the Republic of Korea a high-income country; however, the World Bank (2001a) includes it in the middle-income group.

instances, flows of private financing to poor countries are minimal. The share of FDI received by low-income countries is also smaller than their contribution to the developing countries' GDP. For these reasons, the volatility of capital flows and issues of contagion have become particularly relevant to middle-income developing countries.

Accordingly, low-income countries have continued to depend on the dwindling supply of official funding. These countries rely heavily on official development assistance, particularly grants, most of which come in the form of bilateral aid. This is the only component of net resource flows to developing countries whose distribution is progressive. Multilateral financing has followed the same pattern, except in the case of IMF resources.

The volatility of private financial flows and their concentration in middle-income countries have created a strong demand for exceptional financing in a small number of emerging economies. As a result, IMF financing has exhibited a strongly countercyclical pattern and has been concentrated in the few countries where it could have systemic effects. However, exceptional financing has been lower than it was in the 1980s, whether measured in terms of the level of the recipient countries' international reserves or of their exports and also, in the case of international reserves, lower than it was in the 1960s (see figure 3.1). This is a clear sign that the level of IMF exceptional financing has tended to lag behind that of international economic transactions. Obviously, the comparison is even less favorable if the capital account shocks faced by the developing countries are taken as a point of reference, even though, in the view of the chairman of the U.S. Federal Reserve Board, "the size of the breakdowns and required official finance to counter them is of a different order of magnitude than in the past" (Greenspan 1998).

As shown in figure 3.5A, the countercyclical pattern of financing and its concentration in a small number of countries are closely related. The proportion of IMF financing directed to large borrowers[13] has trended sharply upward over the last two decades. Indeed, IMF financing data underestimate the provision of emergency funds to large borrowers, as they do not include bilateral contributions for the largest bailouts of recent years (Brazil, Indonesia, the Republic of Korea, Mexico, the Russian Federation, and Thailand, as well as the "financial armor" provided to Argentina in 2000).[14] These programs have been severely criticized in industrial countries as creating moral hazard, which has translated into a less favorable attitude toward exceptional financing. The outright renegotiation of external debts, on the other hand, has been supported, but the implementation of this type of process will nonetheless require the establishment of appropriate international institutions to address this problem.

Figure 3.5 Credits of International Financial Institutions

A. International Monetary Fund credits

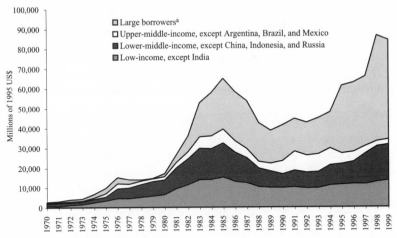

B. Development bank credits

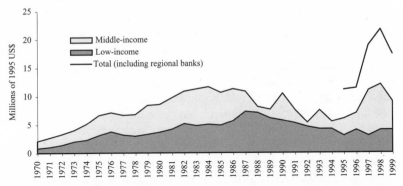

a. The Republic of Korea, which belongs to this group of countries, is classified as a high-income country by international financial institutions.

Source: Economic Commission for Latin America and the Caribbean, on the basis of data from the IMF (2001a).

Financing for middle-income countries provided by the World Bank and by multilateral development banks in general has displayed a similar countercyclical pattern (see figure 3.5B). This kind of financing complements the credit supplied by IMF, because it provides governments with long-term resources. In view of the volatility of private financing, these funds are usually the primary, and sometimes the only, source of long-term financing available in times of crisis.

The concentration of loans to middle-income countries has not completely crowded out low-income countries. Indeed, the flow of IMF resources to the latter has been fairly stable and has even increased slightly when they have needed additional balance-of-payments support. This occurred in Latin America and the Caribbean in the 1980s and in East Asia and the Pacific during the 1997–98 crisis. In the case of the World Bank, the flow of resources to low-income countries has followed an upward trend in recent decades.

Overall, the trend in developing countries' external debt positions has not been positive, although the patterns do vary considerably from one region to another. External debt-to-GDP ratios for all parts of the developing world are higher than they were in 1980 (i.e., prior to the Latin American debt crisis), but for certain developing regions (including Latin America and the Caribbean), these ratios have fallen in relation to the critical levels reached in the mid- or late 1980s (see figure 3.6A). External debt-to-exports ratios, meanwhile, have developed somewhat more favorably (see figure 3.6B). The problem appears more serious when both debt ratios are compared to certain benchmarks that reflect the sustainability of levels of indebtedness. On the basis of World Bank data on 84 developing nations for which information is available for the period 1980–2000, the number of countries with external debt-to-GDP ratios of less than 40 percent fell from 45 to 23 between the beginning and end of this period, whereas the number with external debt-to-exports ratios of less than 200 percent also fell, from 56 to 33.

Nonetheless, the risk of another interest rate spike such as the one seen in the early 1980s has declined as industrial countries have brought inflation under control. In any event, it should be remembered that real interest rates in these countries remained high in the last two decades of the 20th century (although they declined during the recent crisis) and, in particular, that the margins applying to developing countries in private capital markets are usually very high. In terms of the traditional sustainability criteria for debt ratios, calculated by comparing economic growth to real interest rates, the ratio continues to be unfavorable in most countries.

A final factor is that the banking system's tendency toward concentration at the international level has spread to developing countries. This process reflects both the expansion of large international banks and the strategy adopted by smaller ones to deal with international competition, as in the case of Spanish banks in Latin America. However, the degree to which banking is concentrated in foreign hands varies widely from one region to another and across countries within the same region. Central Europe and Latin America, for example,

Figure 3.6 External Debt

A. Percentage of GDP (in current US$)

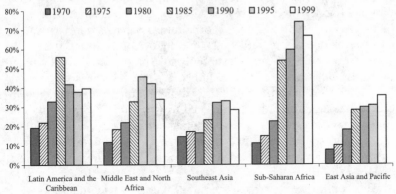

B. Percentage of exports

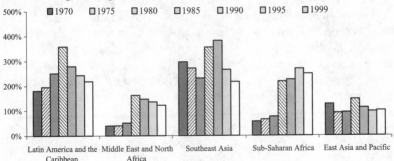

Note: GDP = gross domestic product.
Source: Economic Commission on Latin America and the Caribbean, on the basis of data from the World Bank (2001a).

exhibit much higher levels of concentration than the countries of East Asia and the Pacific (52 percent, 25 percent, and 6 percent, respectively, of total bank assets in 1999).

The share of foreign banks ranges from a high of between 42 percent and 54 percent in Argentina, Chile, and Venezuela to a low of around 18 percent in Brazil, Colombia, and Mexico. This process of concentration has been encouraged by the regulatory authorities of industrial countries as a means of reducing the banks' exchange rate risk (Hawkins 2001). The financial services annex to the World Trade Organization General Agreement on Trade in Services constitutes an international institutional framework that provides legal guarantees for this process.

The combination of financial liberalization, penetration by foreign banks, and new private sector external linkages has led to a profound restructuring of developing countries' financial systems. In many ways, national financial sectors are now more diversified in terms of services, but some of their traditional shortcomings persist. The bias toward short-term operations and high intermediation margins is still the norm, as is credit rationing, especially for small and medium-size enterprises and low-income households. Although local stock markets have expanded in some countries, primary equity issues have not increased, as large firms have preferred to issue their shares in international financial centers. Finally, despite major changes in banking regulation and supervision, the stability of local markets has shown no significant improvement, as demonstrated by the number and frequency of banking crises.

This confluence of strong external dependency and underdeveloped national financial systems has dimmed the expectations that prevailed in the early 1990s with regard to the preferred approach to developing countries' financial integration into the world market. It also reflects a rarely mentioned asymmetry in the globalization process. Essentially, the "one world, one financial system" approach has represented an attempt not only to level the playing field, but also to reorganize the developing countries' financial markets on the basis of the U.S. model by promoting convergence toward a financial structure based on the capital market.

The application of this approach has had negative consequences for the developing world. The most obvious one has been the aforementioned destabilizing effect of highly volatile capital flows. Another major adverse consequence, however, has been the imposition of a financial structure that is alien to the institutional traditions of developing countries and even to those of certain industrial countries.[15] This mismatch can have adverse repercussions if the process of dismantling existing institutions takes precedence over the construction of new ones, given the crucial importance of financial intermediation for economic development.[16]

International Migration

In the first stage of globalization, from the last quarter of the 19th century to the early 20th century, the expansion of trade and high capital mobility were accompanied by an increase in migratory flows, with the result that this period is also known as the "era of mass migration" (Castles and Miller 1993; Hatton and Williamson 1998). This wave of migration was directed toward a number of countries in the New World (Argentina, Australia, Brazil, Canada, and the United States). Between 1870 and 1920, the United States, which was the chief recipient of these migrants, took in more than 26 million people, primarily from Europe, who came to represent more than 10 percent of the country's total population (Solimano 2001).

Some of these migratory flows contributed to interregional and intraregional economic convergence (European emigration to the New World and to other European countries, respectively), whereas others accentuated the inequality of the international economic order, as in the case of the Chinese "coolies" and the Indians who were transported to tropical plantations and cities. Thus, two disparate trends prompted by these migratory flows emerged: a trend toward the convergence of wages at high levels in the industrial world and a trend toward their convergence at low levels in the developing world (Lewis 1978).

During that period, the countries of the New World adopted liberal immigration policies, and in a number of cases governments used various means to encourage foreigners to take up residence as they sought to increase the labor force and to populate their territories at a time of rapid economic expansion. In the early 20th century, governments began to apply increasingly restrictive policies, accompanied, in some countries (Australia, Canada, and the United States), by measures that discriminated against Asian immigrants, especially those from China (O'Rourke and Williamson 1999).

Then, after more than half a century, migratory movements once again began to gather momentum as part of the third stage of globalization during the last quarter of the 20th century. In that period, migration to nearly all the countries of the Organisation for Economic Cooperation and Development (OECD) was greater than it had been in previous decades, although these flows were still much smaller in volume than those of the late 19th century.[17] In some countries of destination (Canada, Germany, Japan, and the United States), this process peaked in the early 1990s, whereas in others (Australia and the United Kingdom) it had reached its high point some years earlier. Since that time, migratory flows have declined significantly, largely as a result of the widespread imposition of legal limits on immigration (see table 3.4).

Major changes also occurred with respect to the immigrants' regions and countries of origin (see table 3.5). Immigration to the United States during the third stage of globalization has consisted primarily of Latin Americans and Caribbeans (46 percent) and Asians (34 percent), in sharp contrast to the trend of the 19th century, when nearly 90 percent of the immigrants to the United States came from Europe

Table 3.4 Organisation for Economic Co-operation and Development: The 10 Main Countries of Destination of Immigrants

(Thousands of persons)

Recipient country	1990	1991	1992	1993	1994	1995	1996	1997	1998	1999	Average
United States[a]	1,537	1,827	974	904	804	721	916	798	661	647	979
Germany[b]	842	921	1,208	987	774	788	708	615	606	674	812
Japan[b]	224	258	267	235	238	210	225	275	266	282	265
United Kingdom[a]	—	—	204	190	194	206	216	237	258	277	223
Canada[a]	214	231	253	256	224	213	226	216	174	190	220
Italy[a]	—	—	—	—	—	—	—	—	111	268	190
France[a]	102	110	117	99	92	77	76	102	138	104	102
Australia[a]	121	122	107	76	70	87	99	86	77	84	93
Switzerland[b]	101	110	112	104	92	88	74	73	75	86	92
Netherlands[b]	81	84	83	88	68	67	77	77	82	78	79

— Not available.

a. Data based on residence permits or other sources.

b. Data based on population records.

Source: Economic Commission for Latin America and the Caribbean, on the basis of data from OECD (2000b), and SOPEMI (2001).

Table 3.5 Organisation for Economic Co-operation and Development: Nations of Origin of Persons Migrating to the Main Recipient Countries, 1999
(Percentages)

Recipient country	Primary countries of origin					Cumulative
	First	*Second*	*Third*	*Fourth*	*Fifth*	
United States	Mexico (19.9)	China (5.6)	India (5.5)	Philippines (5.2)	Dominican Republic (3.1)	39.3
Germany	Yugoslavia (13.1)	Poland (10.7)	Turkey (7.0)	Italy (5.2)	Russia (4.1)	40.1
Japan	China (21.0)	Philippines (20.3)	Brazil (9.3)	United States (8.8)	Korea (8.2)	67.6
United Kingdom	United States (16.2)	Australia (12.1)	South Africa (8.7)	India (7.1)	New Zealand (5.7)	49.8
Canada	China (20.2)	India (9.2)	Pakistan (4.9)	Philippines (4.8)	Korea (3.8)	42.9
Italy	Albania (13.9)	Morocco (9.3)	Yugoslavia (9.1)	Romania (7.8)	China (4.1)	44.2
France	Morocco (13.5)	Algeria (10.9)	Turkey (5.5)	Tunisia (3.8)	United States (2.6)	36.3
Australia	New Zealand (22.2)	China (11.4)	United Kingdom (10.5)	South Africa (5.9)	India (3.1)	53.1
Switzerland	Yugoslavia (14.7)	Germany (12.8)	France (7.2)	Italy (7.0)	Portugal (5.8)	47.5
Netherlands	United Kingdom (6.4)	Germany (5.7)	Morocco (5.6)	Turkey (5.4)	United States (4.2)	27.3

Source: Economic Commission for Latin America and the Caribbean, on the basis of data from OECD (2001b).

(Solimano 2001). In the European Union, internal migration predominates, representing two-thirds of the total (66.2 percent); other major regions of origin are Africa (16.2 percent) and Asia (10.6 percent) (Salt 1999). Almost three-fourths of Japan's immigrants come from Asia (53.3 percent), Latin America and the Caribbean (10.2 percent), and the United States (8.8 percent) (Salt 1999; OECD 2001b).[18] (The data in this paragraph correspond to 1997–98.)

The composition of these flows reflects the influence that factors such as distance, language, historical relations, and cultural affinity have on migrants' choices of destination. More than half of Japan's immigrants come from China, the Republic of Korea, and the Philippines, whereas nearly a quarter of the immigrants to the United States come from Canada, the Dominican Republic, and Mexico. The countries of origin of migrants to France and the United Kingdom reflect strong historical and cultural ties.

These ongoing migratory movements have taken place in the context of significant changes in the relevant legislation. In general, immigration laws are much more restrictive than in the past and are oriented toward achieving greater control over irregular immigration. In the United States, such legislation has been changed several times since the 1960s. The 1965 reform of the Immigration and Naturalization Act established a system of preferences based on family relationships with U.S. citizens, encouraged the immigration of individuals with the skills and training in greatest demand in the labor market, set quotas by country of origin, and introduced measures to eliminate ethnic discrimination. Further legislative changes were introduced in 1986 with the aim of controlling irregular immigration through increased vigilance at the country's borders and programs to regularize the status of undocumented immigrants. Another reform was introduced in 1996 with a view to strengthening the control of irregular immigration.

Since the early 1990s, the immigration policies of the European countries have been set by the European Union. The main feature of this legislation is the clear distinction laid down in the Treaty of Rome between immigrants from within the European Community and those of non-Community origin. Whereas the former have every right to reside and work in any country of the European Union, the latter are subject to strict limitations and are required to obtain a work visa before they can become residents. Australia, Canada, and Japan have also adopted restrictive immigration policies in recent years, particularly with respect to the issuance of permanent residence visas. To counterbalance this situation, special programs have been implemented to facilitate temporary residence, usually through the issuance of work permits in specific areas, as a means of either lending greater flexibility to the labor market or alleviating labor shortages in certain sectors (OECD 2001b).

One particularly disturbing issue is the selective "brain drain" of scientific researchers, engineers, and other qualified personnel engendered by the OECD countries' migration policies. This phenomenon is worsening the already sharp asymmetries between industrial and developing countries in terms of their capacity to carry out research and development activities (see chapter 4). In addition, as the literature on economic development has shown, although it is true that this can lead to virtuous circles, it may also create poverty traps (Easterly 2001a). Two factors have combined to trigger larger migratory flows of scientific researchers and engineers from developing to industrial countries. One is the fact that the creation of knowledge has generated growing returns and strong externalities that encourage the clustering of scientific communities. The other factor consists of the special migration policies adopted by the industrial countries in response to the rising demand for highly qualified personnel. The main magnet has been the United States, which in the 1990s received nearly a million specialists from the developing world in the field of information technology alone, under the special H1-B visa program. A number of other OECD countries (Australia, Germany, New Zealand, and the United Kingdom) have also implemented selective programs, such as Germany's "green card" scheme (Solimano 2002).

Thus, even though it has coincided with an increased tendency to reduce obstacles to capital mobility, the free movement of persons is limited to specific regions within the OECD countries and to workers who are highly or very highly qualified. Yet the persons having the greatest propensity to emigrate are relatively low-skilled workers wishing to move from South to North. In addition, since the disappearance of socialist governments, a strong trend toward emigration has been observed in the countries of Central and Eastern Europe, especially to European Union countries. Consequently, tighter controls over irregular migration and the employment of undocumented workers, along with limitations on the right to asylum on political and humanitarian grounds, have become another pillar of industrial countries' immigration policies (OECD 2001b).

In the 1990s this relationship between the propensity to migrate and restrictions on the free movement of labor resulted in a considerable increase in irregular migration to OECD countries, which, by its very nature, is impossible to measure with complete accuracy. The persistence of irregular migration has prompted nearly all the OECD countries to tighten controls on the entry, residence, and employment of foreigners. At the same time, various programs have been adopted to regularize the status of undocumented residents.

International migration has a far-reaching impact on the basic structures of the sending and receiving countries. It is widely acknowledged that inequalities in levels of development are the primary determinant of migration. Accordingly, if globalization results in the accentuation of these inequalities, the propensity to migrate will persist and may even increase. At the same time, growing interdependence among nations has heightened the transnationalization of communities and has led to the diversification of mobility patterns. Another factor that encourages migration is the wider dissemination of cultural models, modes of behavior, and aspirations, because potential migrants are more aware of existing global inequalities in levels of development. Moreover, advances in communications and transport have reduced the direct costs of migration.

In contrast to past trends, migration is not currently linked to the occupation of unpopulated areas. Because it is directed primarily from South to North, one of the challenges posed by migration is to incorporate immigrants into highly structured societies whose economic, social, and demographic conditions differ considerably from those of the immigrants' countries of origin. The integration of immigrants into the host societies and the definition of their rights and demands for citizenship have become a major political issue. Institutional responses to this situation have varied and have included both humanitarian and restrictive attitudes, with the latter based on the defense of sovereignty. In the countries of origin, ties with emigrants have become especially important, because they represent not only a source of funds (in the form of remittances), but also the potential for change and innovation. These links represent the reverse side of integration and, as shown by the emergence of immigrant communities and their social networks, one of the seeds of transnationalization.

Organizations of immigrants in the main recipient countries, such as those that have emerged in the United States, provide frames of reference for strengthening collective identity and facilitate the globalization of immigrants' cultural expressions and the spread of their products in the host societies. Such organizations help immigrants to maintain close bonds with their places of origin; one of the most important of these ties is the sending of remittances. The use and origin of remittances, the channels used for them, and their real and potential effects on the development of the recipient communities have been only partially assessed, and few policies have thus far been introduced in this area.

Although the debate on migration, its causes, and its consequences has awakened greater interest today than ever before, the controversial nature of these issues hinders the adoption of global agreements and specific courses of action on the subject. In recent years, it has become clear that international migration must be understood as a phenomenon requiring the adoption of multilateral measures based on cooperation among states. It is also clear that governments and civil society organizations in countries of origin, destination, and transit share a concern for the human rights of migrants, in relation both to the decision to emigrate or stay in the country of origin and to the possibility of exercising the rights of citizenship in the countries of origin and destination. These convictions have been strengthened by the need to join forces to mount a frontal attack on crime, which has grown to serious proportions: trafficking in immigrants is a source of illicit profits for organizations that operate on an international scale.

Notes

1. Article VI of the IMF Articles of Agreement provides that "Members may exercise such controls as are necessary to regulate international capital movements, but no member may exercise these controls in a manner which will restrict payments for current transactions."
2. There has been criticism of the procyclicality of regulation, which the new proposals would tend to accentuate, and of the adverse impact this can have on risk markets, including those of emerging countries. See Reisen (2001) and Griffith-Jones and Spratt (2001).
3. See, among others, Blommestein (1995), Culpeper (1995), D'Arista and Griffith-Jones (2001), Feeney (1994), Franklin (1993), and Group of Ten (2001) for a more detailed account of the changes that have occurred in the financial systems of the main industrialized economies.
4. The Group of Ten (2001) has offered a comprehensive analysis of the causes and consequences of this process.
5. Most of these mergers and acquisitions—70 percent, in fact—correspond to banking institutions. In addition, joint ventures and strategic alliances between institutions increased significantly.
6. There are many examples of the change of mood vis-à-vis emerging markets since the mid-1970s. One of the most outstanding recent examples is that of Argentina, which went from "irrational exuberance" up to the Asian crisis to "irrational panic" in 2001. Levels of external debt that were considered manageable up to the late 1990s suddenly became unsustainable to market analysts and the access to private financing was, in practice, closed off. As the financier George Soros has pointed out, the market has sometimes the capacity to impose its own views on reality, even when those expectations are irrational. It may be argued that, beyond the fundamental factors that determined it, the recent Argentinean crisis was not totally alien to such "self-fulfilling expectations."
7. As Bustillo and Velloso (2002) have pointed out, these contagion effects were stronger for Latin America during the Asian and Russian crisis of 1997 and 1998 than during the later events in Brazil and Argentina. Nonethe-

less the 2001 Argentinean crisis had strong effects on other Mercosur members and associates. Strong IMF support to Brazil and Uruguay was one of the factors that helped those countries avoid the meltdown that Argentina faced during the last months of 2001 and the first few months of 2002, when this country lacked IMF support and even faced open criticism from that institution.

8. An extensive range of literature has been produced on this subject. Among many other contributions, see Calvo, Arias, Rheinhart, and Talvi (2001), Dodd (2001), and Persaud (2000).

9. In the case of banking regulation, the rules on capital and loan loss reserves have this effect. In boom periods, increased earnings lead to credit expansion, which is further facilitated by the fact that debtors tend to make their payments on time, which permits creditors to reduce their reserves. During economic busts, however, defaults increase, which means that the reserve position must be strengthened, thereby reducing banks' profits and thus their lending capacity. A number of proposals have been put forward to mitigate this procyclical phenomenon (Ocampo 1999, 2002a).

10. The correlation of monthly spreads on Latin American instruments and high-yield bonds in the U.S. market was 0.56 in the period from March 1996 to September 2001 but rose to 0.79 between September 1997 and November 1999.

11. For a detailed analysis of these trends, see UNCTAD (1999) and World Bank (1999).

12. For detailed analyses of these trends, see the IMF's periodic reports on emerging markets and ECLAC (2001a).

13. This group consists of Argentina, Brazil, China, India, Indonesia, the Republic of Korea, Mexico, and the Russian Federation.

14. It is true, however, that a smaller proportion of the bilateral financing that is pledged for such bailout packages tends to be disbursed than in the case of the multilateral financing.

15. This is evident in the policies that the industrial countries adopted in an effort to build up their financial institutions after the Second World War. These policies varied considerably from one country to another, depending on each country's institutional features and the financial problems it had inherited. In Germany, which had long had a universal banking system closely linked to production activities, the authorities decided to reconstruct large private universal banks and introduce regulations and incentives so that these banks would provide intermediation between private saving and the financing needs of production firms. In France, on the other hand, efforts focused on reconstructing the state banks in view of the prominent role those banks had played prior to the war. Japan, too, reorganized its financial system according to a credit-based banking structure. It should be recalled that Japan had maintained a strong push toward industrialization since the last third of the 19th century, while at the same time establishing a financial system that was modern and sophisticated in terms of promoting development. The simultaneous development in these two areas was not spontaneous, but rather the result of deliberate public policies. In fact, Japan's big banks were of decisive importance in financing large-scale enterprises under a system based on high leverage and low, stable interest rates.

16. A great deal of the recent economic literature highlights the importance of financial development for economic growth (see, among others, King and Levine 1993; Demirgüç-Kunt and Maksimovic 1998; Rajan and Zingales

2001), which adds to the earlier analyses done more than half a century ago (such as Gerschenkron 1962; Keynes 1936; Schumpeter 1939). In these studies, economic development was normally associated with a significant demand for resources to finance the accumulation of capital, technological innovation, and growth and is linked to the fact that, in modern economies, these resources are mobilized through the creation of credit and financial intermediation. It is therefore not surprising that all the economies that have succeeded in achieving sustained growth have also developed financial structures that have enabled them to meet financing demands in the short, medium, and long terms (see Studart 1995).

17. In the case of the United States, the main country of destination, immigration rose to nearly 7.5 million people in the last two decades of the 20th century, compared to about 2.5 million in the 1950s and 1.0 million in the 1940s. However, measured as a proportion of the country's total population and in terms of annual averages, immigrants represented less than 3 percent of the population in the last third of the 20th century, which was much lower than the percentages recorded between 1870 and 1920 (over 10 percent).

4

Inequalities and Asymmetries in the Global Order

GLOBALIZATION HAS NOT ONLY engendered growing interdependence; it has also given rise to marked international inequalities. Expressed in terms of a metaphor widely used in recent debates, the world economy is essentially an *"uneven* playing field" (in contrast to a level playing field) whose distinctive characteristics are a concentration of capital and technological innovation in industrial countries and the strong influence of those countries on trade in goods and services. These asymmetries in the global order are at the root of profound international inequalities in income distribution.

This chapter analyzes those inequalities and asymmetries, whose accurate identification is essential in order to mitigate and, eventually, overcome these problems. The first section reviews the empirical evidence on the inequalities existing in global income distribution over the last two centuries. The second examines the asymmetries that exist between industrial and developing countries and the different ways in which these asymmetries have been addressed in the international debate since the Second World War.

Inequalities in Global Income Distribution

Per capita income disparities have been pervasive in the world economy both between regions and countries and among citizens in each society in more developed and less developed countries alike. Although there had been a few episodes of convergence in per capita income among some developed countries in the past, one of the central features of the third stage of globalization is the widening of inequality in both dimensions.

Long-Term Disparities between Regions and Countries

A widening income gap between different regions and countries has been a feature of the world economy for the last two centuries. Indeed, whereas per capita gross domestic product (GDP) in the more developed regions of the world was around three times that of the less developed regions in the early 19th century, this ratio has grown steadily and currently stands at just under 20:1 (see table 4.1). The only exception to this trend was the period 1950–73, in which the differential decreased slightly (Madisson 1995, 2001).[1]

Major interregional disparities in per capita GDP were already evident prior to the First World War, but they intensified rapidly between then and the mid-20th century[2] and have continued to increase ever since, although more slowly. These disparities follow a pattern that has been repeated by other indicators of inequality in global income distribution. The relatively slower increase in inequality after the Second World War coincided with the acceleration of economic growth in the developing world, which was one of the distinguishing characteristics of the second stage of globalization. This acceleration, however, was initially associated with protectionist policies that did not give way until much later—the trend began in the 1960s but did not really take hold until the 1980s and 1990s—to greater openness and participation in global trade (see chapter 2).

Latin America has exhibited a number of distinctive features in this connection. First, it was one of the first regions in the developing world to join in the trend toward globalization.[3] Ever since the initial phases of that process, this region, together with Central and Eastern Europe, has made up the group of middle-income countries, which has expanded to include several Asian nations in recent decades. Although no precise data are available on the subject, the gap in per capita output between this group and the industrial region of the world widened between 1820 and 1870 but then stabilized. In fact, the disparity between the per capita GDP of Latin America and that of the industrial region remained constant, hovering in the 27–29 percent range, for a little more than a century and began to decrease only in 1973, dropping to 23 percent in 1990 and to 22 percent by the end of the 20th century (see table 4.1). In terms of mean global GDP, the disparity increased from 1870 to 1950 and then began to decrease, slowly until 1973 and more rapidly from 1973 to 1990.

The Latin American countries' relatively good performance—in comparison with that of other developing countries—in the first stage of globalization (1870–1913) was followed by similar successes during the first phases of "inward-looking development," which took place at

Table 4.1 Patterns of Interregional Disparities

Area of Disparity	1820	1870	1913	1950	1973	1990	1998
Per capita GDP, by region[a]							
Western Europe	1,232	1,974	3,473	4,594	11,534	15,988	17,921
Australia, Canada, New Zealand, and United States	1,201	2,431	5,257	9,288	16,172	22,356	26,146
Japan	669	737	1,387	1,926	11,439	18,789	20,413
Asia (excluding Japan)	575	543	640	635	1,231	2,117	2,936
Latin America	665	698	1,511	2,554	4,531	5,055	5,795
Eastern Europe and former Soviet Union	667	917	1,501	2,601	5,729	6,445	4,354
Africa	418	444	585	852	1,365	1,385	1,368
World	667	867	1,510	2,114	4,104	5,154	5,709
Interregional disparities (percentages)							
Developing region/industrial region	33.9	18.3	11.1	6.8	7.6	6.2	5.2
Latin America/industrial region	54.0	28.7	28.7	27.5	28.0	22.6	22.2
Latin America/world	99.7	80.5	100.1	120.8	110.4	98.1	101.5
Latin America/developing region	159.1	157.2	258.3	402.2	368.1	365.0	423.6
Regional share of world production (percentages)							
Western Europe	23.6	33.6	33.5	26.3	25.7	22.3	20.6
Australia, Canada, New Zealand, and United States	1.9	10.2	21.7	30.6	25.3	24.6	25.1
Japan	3.0	2.3	2.6	3.0	7.7	8.6	7.7
Asia (excluding Japan)	56.2	36.0	21.9	15.5	16.4	23.3	29.5
Latin America	2.0	2.5	4.5	7.9	8.7	8.3	8.7
Eastern Europe and former Soviet Union	8.8	11.7	13.1	13.0	12.9	9.8	5.3
Africa	4.5	3.6	2.7	3.6	3.3	3.2	3.1
World	100.0	100.0	100.0	100.0	100.0	100.0	100.0

Note: GDP = gross domestic product.
a. In 1990 Geary-Khamis international US$.
Source: Economic Commission for Latin America and the Caribbean, on the basis of data from Maddison (2001).

a time when the globalization process was stalled at the international level. In the second stage of globalization (1945–73), the region experienced the highest rates of per capita GDP growth in its history, although they were nonetheless slightly slower than the global rate.[4] Thus, the most notable characteristic of the period between 1870 and 1973 was the region's inability to make steady progress in approaching industrial-country levels. Within this general pattern, some countries experienced periods of rapid expansion,[5] followed by periods of much slower growth or even declines. Over this long period, Latin America could be described as having stabilized at an intermediate position within the world context, with individual cases of "truncated convergence" rather than divergence from the industrial countries, although divergence did occur in some instances.

In reality, the region began to fall behind only during the third stage of globalization (which began in 1973) as it failed to achieve a sufficient degree of integration into the financial globalization process and was then overtaken by the ensuing debt crisis. Moreover, its recovery from the "lost decade" of the 1980s proved to be a hesitant one. As the Economic Commission for Latin America and the Caribbean (ECLAC) has shown in various studies, this has been reflected in the fairly disappointing growth rates attained by the region in the wake of its major economic reform effort, which began in the 1970s in some countries and spread throughout the region between the mid-1980s and the early 1990s.[6]

Variations in per capita GDP and differences in population dynamics between the different regions of the world have led to a significant skewing of the distribution of world production (see table 4.1). In the 19th century, the most notable event was the preeminence of Western Europe and the emergence of "Western offshoots"—as Maddison (1989) called them—in the Americas and Oceania (Canada, Australia, New Zealand, and the United States,) at the expense of Asia. This process led to an overwhelming concentration of the world's production of manufactured goods in the main bastions of capitalism. The trend reversed itself after the Second World War, but more than half of world output is still concentrated in the industrial countries (now including Japan), especially in the technology-intensive manufacturing and service sectors. Table 4.2 shows the differences in per capita GDP between groups of countries. As in the case of interregional disparities, the most striking characteristic is the pronounced and sustained increase in inequalities across countries. This process also accelerated until 1950 and then slowed, especially during the second stage of globalization.

The only apparent case of convergence in levels of per capita output occurred among industrial countries during this second stage, which

Table 4.2 Indexes of Per Capita Income Inequality in the World[a]

Index	1870	1913	1950	1973	1990	1998
Deviation index[b]						
Industrial OECD countries	0.43	0.45	0.50	0.24	0.22	0.22
34 countries	0.58	0.72				
48 countries		0.70	0.87			
141 countries			0.96	1.07	1.13	1.22
Developing countries			0.85	0.93	0.94	1.04
Latin America			0.51	0.56	0.60	0.70
Mean logarithmic deviation[c]						
Industrial OECD countries	0.08	0.09	0.11	0.03	0.02	0.02
34 countries	0.16	0.23				
48 countries		0.24	0.33			
141 countries			0.54	0.56	0.58	0.65
Developing countries			0.53	0.50	0.42	0.51
Latin America			0.14	0.14	0.16	0.21

Note: GDP = gross domestic product; OECD = Organisation for Economic Development and Co-operation.

a. In 1990 Geary-Khamis international US$.

b. Standard deviation of the logarithm of per capita GDP.

c. Average of the logarithms of the mean ratio of per capita GDP/per capita GDP of each country.

Source: Economic Commission for Latin America and the Caribbean, on the basis of data from Maddison (2001).

was their "golden age" (see table 4.2). This phenomenon has been the subject of several detailed studies (see, among others, Maddison 1991). The process proceeded steadily until 1990, albeit at a slower pace, but then came to a halt in the final decade of the 20th century. A historical period in which wage convergence was clearly occurring was the first stage of globalization in the second half of the 19th century. O'Rourke and Williamson (1999) have demonstrated that during this period, the United States and Europe witnessed a convergence of wage levels, basically as a result of the mass migration of European labor to the New World. Within Western Europe, this process of wage equalization also occurred between several of what were then peripheral countries (especially Austria, the Scandinavian countries, and to a lesser extent Ireland and Italy) and the most industrial countries (France, Germany, the Netherlands, and the United Kingdom). However, the same authors also note that the process did not encompass other countries of the European periphery (the countries of Central and Eastern Europe and the Mediterranean countries, with the exception of Italy) or other regions of the world. Hence, even within the group of countries that today make up the Organisation for Economic Co-operation and Development (OECD), there was a slight divergence in the trend of per capita GDP, and this divergence appears to have been greater when considered in the context of a wider group of countries (see table 4.2).

This subject has been examined thoroughly in the literature on economic growth in the last quarter century.[7] In general, these analyses confirm that there was no worldwide convergence of per capita income levels in the sense in which the term is used in this book. To use the terminology of the literature, there was no "unconditional convergence." However, various studies indicate that there is some statistical evidence of "conditional convergence," in which other factors that influence the growth of countries are taken into account, including the education level of the population; infrastructure; macroeconomic stability; and the level of development of political, social, and economic institutions. These determinants of economic growth are distributed just as unequally as per capita GDP, or even more so. This fact has led some authors to question the validity of the concept of "conditional convergence."

Table 4.3 illustrates another phenomenon that differs completely from those described above: the marked and growing dispersion of growth rates among the developing countries during the last quarter of the 20th century—in other words, the increasing number of "winners" and "losers" among developing nations. This dispersion increased just as much in the period 1973–90 as it did in the 1990s. This trend has been much more widespread than the trend toward greater international disparities in per capita GDP; indeed, it has affected all regions

Table 4.3 Standard Deviation of Per Capita GDP Growth[a]

Countries	1870–1913	1913–1950	1950–1973	1973–1990	1990–1998
OECD	0.37	0.62	1.53	0.59	1.16
34 countries	0.54	1.04			
48 countries		1.01	2.76		
141 countries			1.73	2.35	2.95
Developing countries			1.69	2.50	3.09
Latin America			1.50	1.43	2.15

Note: GDP = gross domestic product; OECD = Organisation for Economic Co-operation and Development.

a. In 1990 Geary-Khamis international US$.

Source: Economic Commission for Latin America and the Caribbean, on the basis of data from Maddison (2001).

and both low- and middle-income countries. Within countries, a similar differentiation has occurred across both different social sectors and different geographic regions.

Undoubtedly, all these factors contribute to the tremendous uncertainty about the future that exists in contemporary society. This insecurity places further demands on the international system and on the social safety nets of each country, in addition to the more traditional demands for a reversal of the trend toward greater distributional inequality.

Overall Effect of International and National Inequality

Several recent studies offer a much more detailed view of trends in international inequality. Figure 4.1 shows the results of Milanovic's (2002) study on disparities in population-weighted per capita GDP.

Figure 4.1 International Inequality, Weighted by Population, 1950–98

A. World

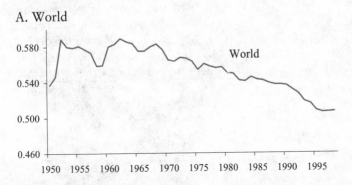

B. Excluding China and India

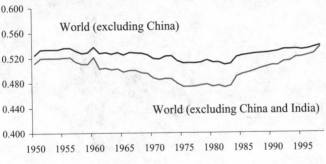

Source: Milanovic (2002).

The calculations are highly sensitive to the inclusion of China and India, given their extremely large populations. Both of these countries registered relatively little economic growth during the second stage of globalization (1945–73) but rank among the most successful countries during the third stage (1973 to the present). When these two countries are excluded, it appears that the international disparities between the mean values lessened substantially from the 1950s to the 1970s, although they widened considerably later, in the last two decades of the 20th century. However, when China and India are included in the analysis, the results are quite different. Indeed, their excellent performance in recent decades counterbalances the adverse distributional trend seen in the rest of the world.

The study by Bourguignon and Morrison (2002) examined the combined effect of trends in disparities between countries and inequalities within them.[8] This analysis uses a broader concept of world inequality, according to which the units of analysis are not countries, but their inhabitants. Based on this concept, the authors concluded that international inequalities increased significantly between 1820 and 1910, remained stable from 1910 to 1960, and grew again from 1960 to 1992 (see figure 4.2). Up to 1910, the dominant aspect of this process was the deepening of international disparities, which increased quite sharply until the mid-20th century. However, during the period associated with a reversal of the globalization process (1914–50), this trend coincided with an improvement in income distribution within countries, which curbed the further growth of international inequality.

Figure 4.2 Global Income Inequality, 1820–1992

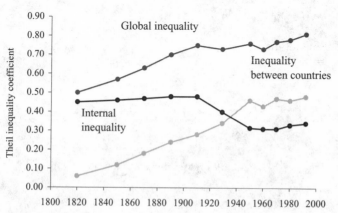

Source: Bourguignon and Morrison (2002).

This improvement was linked both to the emergence of the "welfare state" in the United States and Western Europe and to the socialist revolutions in Central and Eastern Europe. The trend toward an amplification of international inequalities in recent decades, on the other hand, can be attributed not only to moderate growth in international disparities, but also to a sharp increase in inequalities within countries.

The combination of these two trends is, in fact, one of the hallmarks of the third stage of globalization (see U.N. Conference on Trade and Development [UNCTAD] 1997; U.N. Development Programme [UNDP] 1999a; and Milanovic 1999). Indeed, several studies have shown that the relative stability of inequality within countries that marked the world economy in the decades after the Second World War (see Deininger and Squire 1996) was followed by a steady upward trend in inequality during the last quarter of the 20th century. Cornia's (1999) figures are very informative (see table 4.4). According to his analysis, 57 percent of the population included in a sample of 77 nations lived in countries that exhibited growing inequality in income distribution during the period 1975–95. Only 16 percent lived in nations where inequality decreased. The rest of the population lived in countries that had stable levels of inequality or in countries for which no trends could be discerned. These general trends were observed, with some variations, across the major regions of the industrial, transitional, and developing worlds.

In the case of the industrial countries, the trend toward an increasingly unequal distribution of income was more marked, because 72 percent of the population lived in countries where the gap was

Table 4.4 World Trend in Income Inequality, 1975–95
(Percentages of population)

Groups of countries	Growing inequality	Stable inequality	Decreasing inequality	No identifiable trend
Africa	31.6	11.9	7.7	48.8
East Asia	79.4	4.4	16.1	0.1
Eastern Europe	98.1	0.0	0.0	1.9
Industrial countries	71.8	1.2	27.0	0.0
Latin America	83.8	0.0	11.4	4.8
South Asia and Middle East	1.4	70.2	14.4	14.0
Former Soviet Union	100.0	0.0	0.0	0.0
World	56.6	22.1	15.6	5.7

Source: Economic Commission on Latin America and the Caribbean, on the basis of data from Cornia (1999).

widening. This relatively widespread deterioration in income distribution did not occur in the industrial world during the two earlier stages
of globalization.[9] According to several analyses (Atkinson 1996, 1999;
Cornia 1999), inequality rose because of an expanding wage gap,
caused mainly by the erosion of institutions for the protection of labor,
coupled with technical progress that favored more highly skilled workers, although trade liberalization may also have been a contributing
factor. Some authors (Wood 1998) have attached more importance to
this last element. Industrial countries in which centralized institutions
continued to be responsible for wage setting (e.g., Germany and Italy)
and those that placed greater emphasis on the role of labor organizations and on upholding the minimum wage (e.g., France) were able to
blunt these factors' tendency to heighten existing levels of inequality.
The greatest increases in the inequality of income distribution took
place in Australia, New Zealand, the United Kingdom, and the United
States, where wage negotiations are carried out in a decentralized manner and labor markets are more flexible.

The developing and transition countries displayed a more heterogeneous pattern. The greatest deterioration in these areas occurred in the
countries of Central and Eastern Europe, especially those of the former
Soviet Union (see also UNDP 1999b). East Asia also registered greater
degrees of inequality, mainly as a result of the widening gap between
levels of development in urban and coastal areas of China, on the one
hand, and rural areas and the interior, on the other. However, East
Asia was also the developing region in which the highest proportion of
the population lived in countries where inequality was on the decline.
In contrast, most of the population of Africa, the Middle East, and
southern Asia lived in countries where either indexes of inequality remained unchanged or there was no clearly identifiable pattern. In all
these regions, the existence of sharp inequalities was associated with
disparities between rural and urban areas.

In Latin America, the vast majority of the population lived in countries in which the inequality of income distribution increased in the last
quarter of the 20th century. In general, as indicated in several ECLAC
studies (1997, 2000b, 2001b, and 2001c), the upward trend in
inequality seen in the 1980s was not reversed in the 1990s. On the contrary, in the 1990s the number of countries that witnessed a deterioration in income distribution rose. One explanation for this trend is the
asymmetric nature of trends in poverty and income distribution in the
different phases of the business cycle: the debt crisis had a devastating
effect on the poorest sectors, but the subsequent resumption of growth
was not accompanied by a commensurate rise in income in these sectors (Cornia 1999; La Fuente and Sáinz 2001). The growing wage gap

between skilled and unskilled workers, and especially between workers with and without a university education, appears to be one of the main effects of the economic liberalization process (see Berry 1998; ECLAC 1997, 2000b, 2001b, 2001c; Morley 2000).

This global state of affairs suggests that new factors—in combination with more traditional ones, such as the distribution of assets and access to education—are strongly influencing income inequality. These new factors, which are associated with the third stage of globalization and with some of the national policy approaches that have accompanied it, are a reduction in earned income as a proportion of total income and a simultaneous increase in business profits and financial returns, growing skill-based wage differentials, and erosion of the state's redistributive capacity. The impact of these factors varies from region to region and even across countries within the same region.

Finally, national income distribution structures reflect very dissimilar regional situations. Latin America has the most unequal income distribution in the world (see figure 4.3), followed by the countries of Africa and the second generation of newly industrial countries in Eastern Asia. The next group consists of the countries of southern Asia, those of the former Soviet Union, those of North Africa, the first generation of newly industrial countries in Asia, and the Anglo-Saxon OECD countries. The last group, which has the best income distribution, comprises the other members of OECD and the countries of Central Europe (Palma 2001).

The existence of a highly unequal distribution of income is an important consideration not only because of the ethical and political problems it poses, but also because of its implications for economic growth (Solimano 2001). Although the reciprocal relationships between growth and equity have long been a subject of controversy, in recent years numerous studies have highlighted the negative effects of inequality on economic growth—the so-called inequality trap (see ECLAC 1992b; Ros 2000; Stewart 2000; and the review of recent literature by Aghion, Caroli, and García-Peñalosa 1999). The tremendous distributional inequalities found in several regions of the developing world, especially Latin America, may thus help account for international differentials in development levels or the blockage of convergence factors. Inequality as an obstacle to growth was a favorite topic of economic debate in the 1960s, and it has awakened new interest in recent years. However, unlike the debates of that earlier period (which focused on whether the concentration of income impeded the development of domestic markets or whether, on the contrary, it facilitated capital accumulation), the current analyses are

Figure 4.3 Inequality and Per Capita Income

A. Regional Gini indexes

B. Share of the richest decile in household income

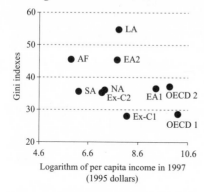

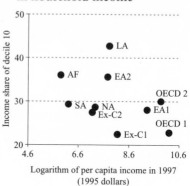

Note: LA = Bolivia, Brazil, Chile, Colombia, Costa Rica, Dominican Republic, Ecuador, El Salvador, Guatemala, Honduras, Mexico, Nicaragua, Panama, Paraguay, Peru, Uruguay, and República Bolivariana de Venezuela. AF = Burkina Faso, Burundi, Côte d'Ivoire, Gambia, Ghana, Guinea, Guinea Bissau, Kenya, Lesotho, Madagascar, Mali, Mauritania, Mozambique, Niger, Nigeria, Rwanda, Senegal, South Africa, Swaziland, Tanzania, Uganda, Zambia, and Zimbabwe. EA1 = Republic of Korea, Singapore, and Taiwan (China). EA2 = Malaysia, Philippines, and Thailand. NA = Algeria, Republic of Egypt, Jordan, Morocco, and Tunisia. SA = Bangladesh, Cambodia, China, India, Indonesia, Lao People's Democratic Republic, Pakistan, Sri Lanka, and Vietnam. OECD 1 = Austria, Belgium, Denmark, Finland, France, Germany, Greece, Italy, Japan, Luxembourg, the Netherlands, Norway, Portugal, Spain, Sweden, and Switzerland. OECD 2 = Australia, Canada, Ireland, New Zealand, United Kingdom, and United States. Ex-C1 = Bulgaria, Croatia, Czech Republic, Hungary, Poland, Romania, Slovakia, and Slovenia. Ex-C2 = Belarus, Estonia, Kazakhstan, Kyrgyz Republic, Latvia, Lithuania, Moldova, Russian Federation, Turkmenistan, Ukraine, and Uzbekistan.
Source: Palma (2001).

paying more attention to the implications of inequality in terms of political economy. The linkages between inequality and political economy encompass a number of different aspects, including the relationship between social cohesion and investment risk; the interaction between business and political cycles, which can undermine the sustainability of public decisions, particularly in the fiscal area; and the positive impact that a more equal distribution of production assets can have on human capital formation and the development of small and medium-size enterprises (SMEs). All of these processes are facilitated by a more smoothly operating capital market and by greater access to that market.

Taken together, the foregoing considerations leave no doubt as to the existence of a definite trend toward distributional inequality worldwide, both across and within countries. At the international level, there is no evidence whatsoever that income levels are converging. When convergence has occurred, it has done so only among industrial countries and only at specific stages in the evolution of the world economy. Trends toward divergence in development levels, truncated convergence, and stagnation in mean income levels have been much more common. By contrast, the deterioration of income distribution within countries has been widespread in recent decades.

These conclusions suggest the need for caution when examining recent analyses that downplay the second stage of globalization's favorable effects on the developing countries because of their belated and limited integration into the world economy, even as they emphasize the advantages some of them have gained through greater liberalization and integration in recent decades (World Bank 2002b). In fact, the relative isolation of the developing countries during the second stage of the globalization process coincided with a general acceleration in the rate of economic growth throughout the developing world—for the first time in history—as well as reductions in some indicators of international inequality (between regions and countries). As we noted in chapter 2, this positive assessment does not mean that the problems associated with the development process at that stage should be overlooked. Nonetheless, the fact remains that the most recent stage of globalization has been marked by increasing inequality at the international and national levels, even though, at the world level, this trend has been less pronounced than it was in the 19th century and the first half of the 20th (thanks, undoubtedly, to the economic success of China and India).

Basic Asymmetries in the Global Order

The persistence and exacerbation of international inequalities in development levels described in the preceding pages have been the subject of considerable debate ever since the Second World War. This debate arose at a time when the concept of economic development was gaining prominence on the international agenda as the world strove to build a new community of nations. From the very inception of the United Nations, economic and social development and peace have been considered vital and interrelated elements in the construction of a new world order. A third such element that serves as their ethical foundation is the defense of human rights (Emmerij, Jolly, and Weiss

2001). These elements characterize the prevailing vision in the United Nations to this day (Annan 2000, 2001).

Debates about development have revolved around two schools of thought: one that sees development or a lack thereof as essentially a consequence of national forces and another that, although it recognizes the importance of these factors, points to elements at the international level that tend to engender or perpetuate existing inequalities. This discussion is similar to the controversy about the determinants of social inequalities at the national level, which has been widely debated in the social sciences and in political circles. In this debate, one side views inequality as an effect of differences in individual effort, whereas the other side believes that a lack of true equality of opportunity has a decisive impact.

ECLAC has taken the second position in both of these debates. This stance is rooted in an awareness of the fact that true equality of opportunity does not exist in the real world, either at the national or the international level. Consequently, market mechanisms tend to reproduce, and sometimes exacerbate, existing inequalities. As noted earlier in reference to the international sphere, this acknowledgment of inequality should not be construed as an attempt to disregard the importance of national policies. On the contrary, a recognition of the fundamental role of national factors is entirely consistent with the idea that institution building, social cohesion, and the accumulation of human capital and technological capacity are essentially endogenous processes—an idea that is deeply ingrained in the thinking of ECLAC. This position is also consonant with the fundamental importance that ECLAC attaches to national efforts aimed at achieving a sound macroeconomy, dynamic productive development, greater equity, and environmental sustainability, together with the active involvement of society as a whole in shaping the public interest (ECLAC 2000a).

The fundamental role played by the international structure, however, has to do with the way it influences what opportunities will be available to countries and what risks they will face, as well as the effectiveness of national efforts to maximize the benefits of integration into the world economy. Just as the state must take redistributive action at the national level to ensure equality of opportunity, national efforts can fully succeed at the global level only if they are complemented by equitable and stable rules of the game, together with international cooperation designed to put an end to the basic asymmetries of the global order. These asymmetries fall into three basic categories: (a) extreme concentration of technical progress in industrial countries, (b) developing countries' greater macroeconomic vulnerability, and (c) high capital mobility and low labor mobility.

Extreme Concentration of Technical Progress in Industrial Countries

The first asymmetry is the extreme concentration of technical progress in industrial countries, which is the factor that all schools of economic thought identify as the primary source of economic growth in those countries. This concentration means that not only are research and development as such concentrated in those countries, but so are the production segments and activities that are most closely linked to technological change—sectors that are highly dynamic components of world trade flows and of the international production structure and that receive high innovation rents (see chapter 2). The growth impulses generated by technical progress originating in the countries of the "center" are transmitted to the "periphery" through four main channels: derived demand for raw materials; relocation to developing countries of production sectors considered to be "mature" in industrial countries; technology transfer per se, including technologies embedded in production equipment; and the possible participation of developing countries in the most dynamic production domains.

The main problems that arise in this area stem from the fact that, as Prebisch (1951, p. 3) affirmed in his classic work, "The spread of technical progress from the countries where it had its source to the rest of the world has . . . been relatively slow and irregular." This spread is slow because all of these mechanisms are subject to constraints or costs. In general, demand for raw materials is not income elastic, and because the entry cost associated with the corresponding activities is low, demand is often affected by downward pressure on prices, especially during periods of diminished global activity (see chapter 2, box 2.1). The mature industrial sectors have narrow margins and low entry costs. Their low entry costs may also lead to a sharp deterioration in profits and prices, much like what occurs in the case of raw materials during times of slow growth. The protectionist pressures generated by industrial countries are also concentrated in these two sets of sectors.

In addition, economies of scale and external economies, which have been the focus of the classic literature on urban and regional development and of more recent studies on international trade, may give rise to agglomeration economies that tend to lead to the polarization—rather than the convergence—of development levels.[10] This is one of the arguments highlighted by the various proponents of classical theories of economic development.[11]

In addition, technology transfers are subject to the payment of innovation rents, which are increasingly protected by the universalization of strict regulations concerning intellectual property rights.

Because of the "tacit" nature of technology—that is, the fact that it cannot be fully specified because it is so closely linked to the collective human capital accumulated by innovating companies—it may not be easy to transfer, or its transference may be attractive only if it occurs through transnational corporations' networks of subsidiaries. The production of knowledge is the epitome of an activity subject to strong agglomeration economies, as indicated by its overwhelming concentration at the world level. Developing countries therefore have very limited opportunities to participate in the most dynamic areas of activity, or else their participation is concentrated in low-skill areas (e.g., the assembly of electronic products in export assembly plants). What is more, the external economies linked to education and knowledge can, by themselves, hinder any trend toward convergence in productivity levels, as has been pointed out in the literature on endogenous growth.[12] Technological development also requires substantial government subsidies, a situation that rewards greater fiscal capacity as well as, perhaps, the less urgent nature of competing demands for the use of public resources in industrial countries.

The combined effect of these factors accounts for the trend toward the stagnation of mean income levels and the truncated convergence or outright divergence of income levels, in place of the convergence postulated by conventional theories of economic growth. In fact, the divergence of development levels has persisted despite the impressive industrialization process undertaken in many developing countries over the last half century and, in Latin America, even before that. Although this process has translated into a more diversified production structure in the developing world, except in the most backward regions, at the global level the production structure has continued to exhibit major asymmetries: an intensive and continuing concentration of technical progress in industrial countries (see box 4.1), their sustained predominance in intellectual property registrations[13] in the most dynamic segments and activities of international trade, and their preeminent position in the founding of large transnational corporations (see table 4.6).

Thus, the economic opportunities available to developing countries continue to be determined largely by their position in the international hierarchy. Certainly, "technical progress" has spread from the center through the aforementioned channels, but this transfer continues to be "relatively slow and irregular," and its fruits have been distributed unequally in the developing countries. Few countries—or sectors or companies within them—are able to move fast enough to catch up to the moving target represented by the world technological frontier (Pérez 2001); many others succeed only in advancing at the same rate as the frontier, and not a few are left behind altogether (Katz 2001).

Box 4.1 World Distribution of Research and
Development Activities

Empirical evidence shows that the richer a country (or region) is in both
absolute and relative terms (in per capita gross domestic product, or
GDP), the more likely it is to undertake research and development (R&D)
projects. In addition, as involvement in such activities increases, so does
the probability that the country or region will engage in more technolog-
ically sophisticated and capital-intensive projects, possibly in association
with other countries and regions.

And in fact, industrial countries account for 84.4 percent of gross
expenditure on research and development (GERD) and a somewhat
smaller percentage of scientific researchers and engineers (71.6 percent)
(see table 4.5). Other indicators paint a more dramatic picture of the existing asymmetries between industrial and developing countries: the ratio
of GERD per capita is 19:1, the ratio of the number of scientific researchers and engineers per capita is 7:1, and GERD per researcher is
more than double. This last indicator points not only to sharp differences
in remuneration (whose share of GERD ranges from one-half to two-
thirds), but also to a wide disparity in terms of the financial resources, instruments, and equipment available for these activities.

As noted in the Declaration on Science and the Use of Scientific Knowledge, "Most of the benefits of science are unevenly distributed, as a result
of structural asymmetries among countries, regions and social groups, and
between the sexes. As scientific knowledge has become a crucial factor in
the production of wealth, so its distribution has become more inequitable.
What distinguishes the poor (be it people or countries) from the rich is not
only that they have fewer assets, but also that they are largely excluded
from the creation and the benefits of scientific knowledge" (Declaration
adopted at the UNESCO World Conference on Science for the Twenty-
First Century, paragraph 5, Budapest, Hungary, 2001).

Developing Countries' Greater Macroeconomic Vulnerability

A second type of asymmetry is associated with the developing countries' greater macroeconomic vulnerability to external shocks, which
also strains these countries' lesser and very limited means of coping
with them. Vulnerability to such shocks has tended to increase with
the greater financial integration that has characterized the third stage
of globalization, as have trade vulnerabilities, which have persisted or
intensified as a result of fluctuations in demand and the terms of trade.
The increased instability of economic growth in developing countries

Table 4.5 World Distribution of Expenditures in R&D and Number of Researchers, 1996–97

Groups and countries	Gross expenditure on R&D (GERD)				Researchers			GERD per researcher ($PPP)
	Amount ($PPP)	% world GERD	% of GDP	Per capita	Number in thousands	% world total	Per million inhabitants	
World	547	100.0	1.8	100	5,189	100.0	946	105
Developing countries	86	15.6	0.6	20	1,476	28.4	347	58
Industrial countries	461	84.4	2.2	377	3,713	71.6	3,033	124
Memo								
Africa	4	0.7	0.3	6	132	2.5	211	29
Asian NIEs	27	4.9	1.1	66	241	4.6	595	111
Central and Eastern Europe	6	1.0	0.8	49	168	3.2	1,451	33
China	21	3.9	0.6	17	552	10.6	454	38
European Union	138	25.2	1.9	370	825	15.9	2,211	167
India	11	2.0	0.7	11	143	2.8	151	76
Japan	83	15.2	2.8	661	817	15.8	6,498	102
Latin America	17	3.1	0.5	34	348	6.7	715	48
Russian Federation	6	1.0	0.9	39	562	10.8	3,802	10
United States	199	36.4	2.6	750	981	18.9	3,697	203

Note: GERD = gross expenditure on research and development; NIEs = newly industrialized economies; $PPP = dollars with purchasing power parity; R&D = research and development.

Source: Economic Commission for Latin America and the Caribbean, on the basis of data from UNESCO (2001).

Figure 4.4 Instability of Economic Growth
(*Regional average standard deviation of growth, by country*)

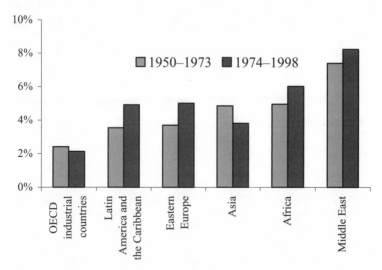

Note: OECD = Organisation for Economic Co-operation and Development.
Source: Economic Commission for Latin America and the Caribbean, on the basis of data from Maddison (2001).

during the third stage of globalization is a reflection of this fact (see figure 4.4).

The existing financial asymmetries stem from four characteristics of developing countries: (a) the currencies in which their foreign debt is denominated, (b) the maturity structures offered on financial markets, (c) the scope of secondary markets, and (d) the highly disadvantageous relationship between the size of developing-country financial markets and the speculative pressures they face. As a result of the first three of these features, agents that have access to international markets (governments and large firms) must contend with currency mismatches, whereas those that do not have access to international markets (SMEs) are affected by maturity mismatches, and it is generally impossible to have a financial structure that avoids both risks at the same time. These mismatches mean that developing-country financial markets are much more incomplete than international markets and, consequently, that some financial intermediation must necessarily take place in the international market. This state of affairs also points to the fact that international financial integration is an example of integration between unequal partners (ECLAC 2000a, 2001a; Studart 1996).

The existence of these macroeconomic asymmetries is attributable to the fact that the international currencies in use today are those of the industrial countries and to the procyclical nature of capital flows to developing countries. This pattern is linked to the perception that, with few exceptions, the developing countries are high-risk markets that are subject to sharp financial cycles in which phases marked by a greater appetite for risk alternate with droughts triggered by a flight to quality (see chapter 3).

The effect of all these factors is a very sharp macroeconomic asymmetry. Whereas the industrial countries have greater freedom to adopt countercyclical policies[14] that help stabilize financial markets, the developing economies have virtually no breathing space, because their financial markets tend to intensify cyclical fluctuations and market agents expect the authorities to behave procyclically.

From a historical perspective, the industrial countries have largely succeeded in exempting themselves from the rules of the game associated with the gold standard, but those rules have continued to determine the macroeconomic behavior of developing countries. The industrial countries' freedom from those restrictions came with the gold standard's abandonment in the 1930s. Since then, they have maintained a high degree of autonomy within the framework of the international macroeconomic agreements associated with the second and third stages of globalization. The developing countries, on the other hand, remained subject to strong external macroeconomic constraints during the second stage of globalization, whereas in the third they have become increasingly vulnerable to financial volatility. This vulnerability to fluctuations has translated into an increase in the center-periphery macroeconomic asymmetries already evident in the late 19th century during the heyday of the gold standard (Aceña and Reis 2000; Triffin 1968).

These asymmetries have become glaringly evident during the frequent crises suffered by developing countries in recent decades, when markets have pressured them to adopt "depression (macro)economics," as Krugman (1999) put it. More specifically, the developing economies' main response to global financial instability has been a tendency to alternate between phases of "boom macroeconomics" and "depression macroeconomics" (ECLAC 2000a, 2001a). Since the Second World War, multilateral macroeconomic and financial agreements have offered some temporary relief at critical junctures, but their scope has been relatively limited in comparison with the financial shocks that the developing countries have had to grapple with, and their application is invariably subject to the adoption of austerity measures. Moreover, they have not induced countries to take preventive measures during economic booms. This issue has been the focus of increasing attention in the international debate sparked by the Asian crisis.

High Capital Mobility and Low Labor Mobility

There is also a third type of asymmetry associated with the contrast between the current high degree of capital mobility and the restrictions placed on international movements of labor, especially among low-skilled workers. This asymmetry is a distinctive feature of the third stage of globalization; it was not observed in the first stage (when labor was highly mobile) or the second stage (when both factors showed little mobility). As Rodrik (1997) pointed out, the asymmetries existing in the international mobility of production factors skew the distribution of income, placing the less mobile factors at a disadvantage. In addition, these asymmetries have a disproportionate effect on developing countries owing to the relative abundance of low-skilled labor in those countries. The limited international mobility of low labor costs also tends to help create a glut on international markets for goods that are produced mainly by developing countries, which typically have low entry costs.

Leveling the playing field by regulatory means does not eliminate these asymmetries; on the contrary, it may end up making them worse, both because of the different countries' widely varying levels of institutional capacity for assimilating and enforcing such regulations and because of the differing effects that such regulations have on industrial and developing countries. Indeed, the high cost of building the national institutions needed to implement the Marrakesh Agreement, which established the World Trade Organization (WTO), has been regarded as one of its main flaws.

The distribution of the costs and benefits of leveling the playing field by regulatory means is also clearly unequal, especially because the policies and standards whose application is being extended to the global level are those of the industrial countries. Protection of intellectual property is the most conspicuous case. Regardless of its virtues in terms of creating incentives for world technological development, the benefits of protecting intellectual property rights accrue mainly to the industrial countries, where the bulk of new technology is generated (see table 4.6). The WTO subsidies code rewards the industrial countries for their greater fiscal capacity to allocate resources for authorized purposes while, on the other hand, prohibiting the use of alternative instruments that have no fiscal costs (tariffs, investment and export performance requirements, and free trade zones) and that have been used extensively

Table 4.6 International Asymmetries: Share of Developing
Countries in the World Economy
(Percentages of the world total)

Basic information	1990	1999
Population	84.0	85.0
Gross domestic product (current US$)	22.3	23.8
Gross domestic product (purchasing power parity)	43.6	46.9
Gross fixed capital formation (1995 US$)	23.9	24.0
Industrial value added, 1998 (1995 US$)		27.5
Rights granted to residents	**1995**	**1999**
Patents	6.1	8.7
Designs	15.3	11.0
Trademarks	33.9	21.9
Utility models	15.3	44.4
Plant varieties	7.0	17.8
500 largest firms		**1999**
Number of firms		5.0
Sales		4.6
Assets		3.6
Market value		5.8
Employees		12.0
Market quotas by categories of technology intensiveness	**1985**	**2000**
Primary products	62.0	59.6
Resource-based manufactures	31.3	31.8
Low-technology manufactures	33.6	50.3
Midlevel-technology manufactures	10.8	21.4
High-technology manufactures	16.8	36.6
Other transactions	28.8	41.6

Source: Economic Commission for Latin America and the Caribbean, on the basis
of data from the World Bank (2001a); *Fortune* magazine, "America's Largest Corporations, 2001"; and Patent Information Services in the World Intellectual Property
Organization (www.wipo.org).

by developing countries. The regulations on agriculture facilitate the
industrial countries' traditional forms of protection (tariffs and quotas)
and reward them for being the only countries with the fiscal capacity to
devote a considerable volume of resources to subsidizing agriculture.
Prohibiting the application of local content requirements to foreign
investors in developing countries runs counter to the general acceptance
of rules of origin, which constitute another form of local content
requirement because they force producers to use inputs of a specified
origin in order to qualify for a preferential tariff.

This situation has a parallel in the financial arena. As has been made
clear in the recent debate surrounding the Basel agreement on banking

regulation, the establishment of more rigorous standards or the application of internal bank standards to lender ratings may reduce the supply of funds on markets carrying high risk ratings, which include the developing countries as well as SMEs in all countries (Griffith-Jones and Spraat 2001; Reisen 2001). In addition, the establishment of mandatory debt workout mechanisms, unless accompanied by a sufficient supply of official emergency credits, may drive up these countries' borrowing costs.

It should be noted that this regulatory leveling of the playing field is unique to the current stage of globalization; no attempt was made to carry out this type of process in either of the prior stages. In fact, during those periods the industrial countries frequently relied on productive development instruments whose use is not permitted in the developing countries (see Chang 2001, 2002).

The Rise and Fall of International Cooperation for Development

The creation of international institutions to regulate the interdependent relations among states was one of the innovative developments in international law to occur in the 20th century. Indeed, until the beginning of that century, the purpose of the rules established under international law was to ensure the sovereignty of nations. States defended their full autonomy in the conduct of matters related to their national interests, and they ardently opposed any limitation of this principle. In reality, however, these principles of autonomy applied only to the imperial powers and to independent nations possessing considerable military power, because in many cases bilateral agreements between nations having unequal degrees of power limited the autonomy of the less powerful nation. Agreements in the 19th century that opened up China and Japan to international trade and imposed the principles of free trade on the Ottoman Empire were clear examples of this phenomenon, as were, in an even more extreme manner, colonial expansion and military occupation of foreign territories.

In any case, the increase in international trade and financial transactions called for the formulation of new rules and the creation of new institutions to ensure that international markets could operate efficiently and that nations could settle disputes without resorting to force. However, as pointed out earlier, these institutions were based on the existing balance of power among the major states. It was not until after the Second World War, with the creation of the United Nations and the adoption of the principle of decolonization, that developing countries begin to enjoy respect for their autonomy and their right to express their views in international forums. This recognition allowed them to begin to help build international institutions and to gain access to formal mechanisms for voicing their opinions about the asymmetries in the global order. This shift in international power relations, together with the bipolar confrontation that continued for several decades thereafter, formed the global political framework that shaped the evolution of international cooperation for development. The chief elements of this process were the emergence of official development assistance (ODA) and the introduction of the principle of special and differentiated treatment for developing countries in trade agreements.

This change was brought about through the efforts of economists, thinkers, and political figures to formulate the concept of economic development, which was then extended to include the sphere of international economic law. Legal experts recognized that, as at the domestic level, the application of the same conditions to vastly different economic and social situations resulted in greater inequalities. For a number of years, international economic law was conceived of as a compensatory mechanism for protecting weaker states from stronger ones by granting more rights to the former and imposing greater obligations on the latter. On the basis of this notion of international "affirmative action" for development, the governments of the developing countries endeavored to introduce and operationalize the development dimension in multilateral forums.

In the years following the Second World War, the reconstruction of Europe took clear priority, and international cooperation for development was relegated to a position of secondary importance. This emphasis was reflected both in the origins of the World Bank and, especially, in the priority attached to the Marshall Plan. The Latin American countries' failure to win approval for the implementation of a program in the region along the lines of the Marshall Plan was also a reflection of the priorities of that time. The region's interests did not, in fact, meet with a favorable response until the late 1950s, with the creation of the Inter-American Development Bank, and early 1960s, when the Alliance for Progress was launched.

This period in the region's history paralleled, to a certain extent, what was occurring at the international level. International development cooperation and the debates that surrounded it gathered considerable momentum in the 1950s and reached their zenith in the 1960s and 1970s, when UNCTAD was established, the generalized system of preferences was put in place, progress was made in promoting ODA, the United Nations introduced its international development strategy, and the dialogue on the new international economic order commenced. Nevertheless, the debates and activities that took place in those years did so within a context of international polarization, and the actual progress achieved was fairly modest.

The breakdown of the debate on the new international economic order in the early 1980s ushered in a radically different period. Those years were marked by waning interest in ODA; the "graduation" of the developing (especially middle-income) countries; a growing emphasis on regulatory standardization, to the detriment of the principles of special and differential treatment; and the promotion of uniform structural reforms within the framework of an excessive amplification of conditionality by the Bretton Woods institutions. Under this new paradigm, the chief objective of efforts to reorder the international economy was to guarantee equitable conditions (a level playing field) that would ensure the efficient operation of free market forces. In this context, the principal gains for the developing countries would be the possible dismantling of the protectionist measures used by industrial countries in "sensitive" sectors and the assurance of an export-led form of development within an international trading system based on clear and stable rules. According to this line of thinking, the correction of international asymmetries would be based exclusively on the recognition of the international community's responsibility to the developing countries. This was tantamount to a replication at the international level of the social policy strategy of targeting the poorest sectors as beneficiaries of state action. Here again, the developing countries' gains during this period were no more than moderate.

The evolution of trade relations between industrial and developing countries clearly illustrates this shift in the principles of international development cooperation. From 1948 to 1955—in the early years of the General Agreement on Tariffs and Trade (GATT)—the developing countries participated in the negotiations on an equal footing, with the same rights and obligations as the other parties. What is more, the first six rounds of GATT negotiations focused on intraindustry specialization within industrial economies, and the areas in which internal adjustments would be required in order to respond to possible competition from developing countries (liberalization of trade in agricultural products, textiles, and clothing, among others) were taken off the agenda and were not addressed by multilateral trade rules. As pointed out by Tussie (1987, 1988), intraindustry specialization made it possible for these countries to overcome some of the more painful aspects of their adjustment to changing patterns of international trade. Instead of causing production to contract and industries to emigrate to other countries, the change could be managed on an intrafirm basis or, at least, within each industry. None of the countries engaging in intraindustry specialization had to cease production or let its control slip from their hands.

In 1958, a decade after the inception of GATT, the Haberler report (GATT 1958) concluded that the barriers imposed by the industrial countries on imports from developing countries were the main cause of their trade problems.[15] This report served as the basis for the creation of Committee III of GATT, which was given responsibility for identifying trade measures that restricted exports from the developing countries and for devising a program to reduce those barriers. In 1963, after the committee had been working for five years without making any apparent progress, the developing countries succeeded in passing a resolution within GATT calling for an action program to freeze all new tariff and nontariff barriers, eliminate all duties on tropical commodities, and adopt a schedule for phasing out tariffs on semi-processed and processed products.[16] In reality, the developing countries were only seeking the application of GATT principles and greater consistency between the industrial countries' policies and their discourse in defense of trade liberalization (Dam 1970). Nevertheless, when the Uruguay Round negotiations began three decades later, the industrial countries were still applying most of the barriers identified by Committee III.

The first session of UNCTAD was held in 1964, and in November of that year part IV of GATT was adopted. Part IV provided the legal framework for the Committee on Trade and Development, whose work, however, remained largely symbolic. Later, in 1968, the developing countries succeeded in establishing the generalized system of preferences under the auspices of UNCTAD. At the Tokyo Round negotiations in the 1970s, a coordinated group of developing countries, in which Latin American diplomats played a prominent role, achieved the inclusion of an enabling clause that provided a more solid legal basis for special and differential treatment by industrial countries.[17] However, the industrial countries made sure that the generalized system of preferences was established on a voluntary basis and that the preferences did not become binding under GATT (Michalopoulos 2000). These concessions could therefore be annulled unilaterally, without conferring any right to retaliatory trade measures.

In retrospect, it can be seen that at no time in the history of GATT did the governments of the industrial countries balk at the developing countries' demands for special and differentiated treatment so long as such provisions did not require them to do more than take a tolerant view of the use of more closed trade regimes by developing countries (especially in cases where they were closed only in respect of goods, rather than capital or transnational corporations). However, the industrial countries have never acquiesced to demands for more secure and stable access to their markets. This refusal has gradually undermined the real significance of special and differential treatment, because preferential access for developing countries has never translated into contractual obligations.

Together with the international community's growing recognition of the specificities of development, new factors began to take on greater importance and to push the multilateral system in another direction. On the one hand, tariff reductions made the effects of trade and industrial policies more apparent, and the need to deal with non-tariff measures gradually eroded tolerance for diversity in national policies, which was the pivotal element of the international consensus to create and maintain the multilateral trading system. On the other hand, as a result of the slowdown in growth and the transformation of the industrial countries, these countries were less inclined to support affirmative action on behalf of developing countries within the framework of international development cooperation.

The context of the Uruguay Round negotiations proved particularly adverse for the developing countries. The preparations for that round marked a turning point in their negotiating capacity, because the 1982 GATT ministerial meeting (at which several industrial countries expressed their intention to deepen the liberalization process initiated at the Tokyo Round) preceded the announcement of Mexico's financial insolvency by just a few months. Large debtors, including Argentina and Brazil, recognized the frailty of their bargaining position, which remained quite weak throughout the 1980s.[18] The institutional problems confronting these governments hindered society as a whole from becoming more involved in the diplomatic trade debate. Furthermore, because these countries' decisionmakers lacked sufficient training in technical matters and negotiation skills, their tendency was to continue to pursue the traditional market access agenda and maintain a defensive stance in relation to the new issues that were being brought into the debate.

In response both to internal factors and to pressure from the structural reform programs being promoted by multilateral financial agencies, many developing countries embarked upon a unilateral liberalization of their economies.[19] By the end of the Uruguay Round, they had consolidated almost all their tariff structures and had, for the most part, given up their demands for greater autonomy in designing and executing policies on investment and productive diversification and even in using trade restrictions to cope with balance-of-payments crises.[20] The provisions on special and differential treatment contained in the Uruguay Round agreements were limited to the extension of deadlines for meeting commitments and the implementation of technical assistance programs.[21] To a certain extent, these agreements were a throwback to the early days of GATT, as they reflected the belief that the increase in trade brought about by liberalization would be enough to stimulate the growth and development of all the parties concerned.

More recent international debates and negotiations suggest that a new stage has begun, although its exact nature is not yet entirely clear. Many different factors have contributed to this situation, including the following:

- the adoption of the Heavily Indebted Poor Countries (HIPC) debt initiative, which began to function in the late 1990s;
- the commitment of some industrial countries to curb the downward trend in ODA;
- the debate surrounding the unbalanced results of the Uruguay Round and the difficulties encountered in implementing the WTO agreements;
- the priority attached to various development issues at the Doha round of WTO negotiations initiated in November 2001;
- criticism of excessive increases in conditionality as a result of the adoption of structural adjustment programs during the debt crisis;
- the transition being made by the economies of Central and Eastern Europe and the Asian crisis;
- formal acceptance of the principle of developing-country ownership of economic and social policies within the context of international cooperation policies and multilateral lending arrangements;
- rejection of policy standardization, which, in part, extends to the Bretton Woods institutions that promoted it in the past; and
- within the policy debate, widespread criticism of the Washington Consensus (for a recent discussion of the Washington Consensus, see Kuczynski and Williamson 2003).

In fact, many of these positions are formally shared by the principal international financial cooperation agencies (IMF 2001a; World Bank 2002b).

Thus, this is a particularly good time to engage in a constructive debate on development cooperation. Such cooperation should seek to correct the basic asymmetries of the international economic order within the framework of a world economy that is much more open today than it was during the debates on development cooperation of the 1960s and 1970s. It may well be that the U.N. Millennium Declaration (United Nations 2000) is the fullest expression of a new vision of the relationship between peace, democracy, and development that can serve as the foundation for a new era of international cooperation for development.

Notes

1. See also Bairoch (1981). However, this author's estimates of per capita income differentials in the late 18th and early 19th centuries are substantially lower than Maddison's (1995, 2001).

2. Because of Asia's relative weight in the world population, one of the basic reasons for these trends was that the Asian economies (except those of Japan and a handful of other countries) stagnated until the middle of the 20th century, but then grew rapidly in the period following the Second World War.

3. Bulmer-Thomas (1994); Cárdenas, Ocampo, and Thorp (2000a, 2000b); Hofman (2000); and Thorp (1998) present more detailed analyses of the region's performance since the mid-20th century.

4. If the figures are adjusted for the effects of the demographic transition, both the acceleration of the region's growth rate in 1950–73 and its later deceleration appear to have been even more pronounced. In fact, if GDP is calculated in relation to the working-age population instead of the total population, growth sped up from 1.4 percent in 1913–50 to 2.7 percent in 1950–73, then slowed to 0.4 percent in 1973–98. Furthermore, in the postwar period, the Eastern and Western European countries, as well as Japan and a number of developing nations, began to recover from the sharp contraction that immediately followed the Second World War, whereas the Latin American and Caribbean region was not comparably affected at either of these stages.

5. Among the most noteworthy are the periods of rapid growth experienced by three Southern Cone countries (Argentina, Chile, and Uruguay) in the late 19th and early 20th centuries; by Cuba in the first quarter of the 20th century; and by Brazil, Mexico, and Venezuela for several decades during the 20th century.

6. See, in particular, ECLAC (1996a, 2001b), Escaith and Morley (2001), and Stallings and Peres (2000).

7. See Barro (1997), Barro and Sala-i-Martin (1995), Easterly (2001a, 2001b), Kenny and Williams (2000), Pritchett (1997), Quah (1995), and Ros (2000), among many others.

8. Studies that paved the way for this type of analysis include the works of Berry, Bourguignon, and Morrison (1983, 1991).

9. The trends characteristic of the second stage of globalization have already been described. In the opinion of Lindert and Williamson (2001) and O'Rourke and Williamson (1999), during the first stage trends varied from one type of country to another, with a deterioration in distribution in countries rich in natural resources, improvements in European countries with a broad agrarian base (especially the large countries of continental Europe), and no clearly discernible trend in the most highly industrial European countries.

10. As examples of the copious literature on the subject, see Fujita, Krugman, and Venables (1999); Krugman (1990); and Rodrik (2001b).

11. See, among others, Hirschman (1958), Myrdal (1957), Nurkse (1953), Rosenstein-Rodan (1943), and, for a more contemporary perspective, Ros (2000).

12. See, for example, the now classic essays of Lucas (1988) and Romer (1990) and the extension of this analysis to international trade by Grossman and Helpman (1991).

13. The only exception is the registration of "utility models," which are granted only for "minor" improvements or adaptations of existing products. The World Intellectual Property Organization's legal definition of a utility model specifies that, although the requirement of novelty is always to be met, that of "inventive step" may be much lower or absent altogether. Moreover, the term of protection is much shorter than for patents, and the registration process is significantly simpler (www.wipo.org).

14. The degree of freedom enjoyed by the United States is certainly greater than it is for the rest of the industrial economies because the U.S. dollar carries the greatest weight internationally.

15. The panel of experts that produced this report was composed of Gottfried Haberler, James Meade, Jan Tinbergen, and Roberto Campos.

16. Srinivasan (1996) noted that some elements of this action program were still on the developing countries' negotiating agenda 20 years later at the 1982 GATT ministerial meeting.

17. This enabling clause, also known as the Decision on Differential and More Favourable Treatment, Reciprocity and Fuller Participation of Developing Countries, became the legal basis for the generalized system of preferences and the global system of trade preferences.

18. See Abreu (1993), Jara (1993), and Tussie (1993), which discuss the debtor countries' negotiating capacity and positions.

19. See Sáez (1999) for an analysis of the negotiations and Krueger and Rajapatirana (1999) for an examination of World Bank policies on the promotion of trade reforms.

20. Several countries (including Bolivia, Costa Rica, El Salvador, Mexico, and Venezuela) consolidated their tariffs before the end of the Uruguay Round, because this was one of the commitments required for their accession to GATT (Jara 1993). The provisions of the Understanding on the Balance-of-Payments Provisions of the General Agreement on Tariffs and Trade (1994) severely limit the use of quantitative restrictions for balance-of-payments purposes (GATT 1994). In 1995 the Committee on Balance-of-Payments Restrictions rejected Brazil's arguments for imposing tariff restrictions in order to contend with short-term balance-of-payments problems (see document WT/BOP/R/7 of 24 November 1995, available on the WTO Web site).

21. According to the WTO, the Uruguay Round agreements contain 97 provisions on special and differential treatment for developing countries, which may be grouped into the following six categories: (a) provisions aimed at increasing trade opportunities, (b) provisions that require WTO members to safeguard the interests of developing-country WTO members, (c) flexibility of commitments, (d) transition periods, (e) technical assistance, and (f) provisions relating to measures to assist the poorest developing countries (see the WTO Web site).

5

An Agenda for the Global Era

ON THE BASIS OF THE ANALYSIS IN chapters 1 through 4, this chapter will explore a number of elements that are considered essential for the development of a better international economic, social, and environmental order. The basic assumption underlying this proposal is that the developing countries, and particularly Latin America and the Caribbean, must adopt a positive agenda for the construction of a new international order and make a firm commitment to its implementation. This view is founded upon an essential lesson of history: that efforts to simply ignore or resist processes whose roots run as deep as those of the current globalization process, as well as the negative agendas that emerge out of such efforts, are doomed to failure. Finding ways to build a qualitatively better form of globalization and to achieve the best possible position within that process are, consequently, the best option.

The agenda to be proposed in this chapter seeks to overcome the shortcomings of existing institutions. These institutions have, first of all, exhibited a disturbing inability to provide a sufficient supply of global public goods. This failing is compounded by adverse distributive trends at the global level and the absence or weakness of institutional systems for ensuring international solidarity. All of this indicates that the globalization process requires a new institutional framework in which more efficient management of global interdependence can be combined with the introduction of firm, clearly defined principles of international solidarity. Only then will it be possible, as stated in the U.N. Millennium Declaration, "to ensure that globalization becomes a positive force for all the world's people" (United Nations 2000).

There are a number of major obstacles that will have to be surmounted in order to build a new global order. The first is the absence of a set of shared principles that are embraced by all the major stakeholders. The second is the fact that given the asymmetrical power relations found in global society, the various actors differ in their ability to influence this process. The third is the difficulty of forming international coalitions capable of offsetting those inequalities, whether through developing-country partnerships or international alliances of social sectors whose members feel that their interests are being harmed by the globalization process. In addition to these obstacles, there is the central paradox of the world of today, as discussed in chapter 1: the gap between global issues and what continue to be essentially national and local political processes.

The challenges involved in building a new institutional order are therefore enormous. The first section of this chapter sets out the basic principles for the creation of a better world order. The second section draws together the elements of various proposals regarding national strategies for dealing with globalization: macroeconomic stability in a broad sense, systemic competitiveness, environmental sustainability, and active social policies. The third section looks at the crucial role played by regional actors in a globalized world. The fourth and final section discusses some of the main issues that the Economic Commission for Latin America and the Caribbean (ECLAC) feels should figure on the world agenda: the provision of global public goods; the correction of the global order's asymmetries in the areas of finance and macroeconomics, production, technology, and factor mobility; and the consolidation of a rights-based international social agenda.

Fundamental Principles for Building a Better Global Order

The construction of a better world order calls for a determined effort to pursue the above key objectives, to establish rules and institutions that respect diversity, to develop complementarities among national, regional, and international institutions and, finally, to guarantee equitable participation coupled with appropriate standards of international governance.

Three Key Objectives

The globalization process has highlighted the importance of certain global public goods, such as the defense of democracy (and, hence, of civil and political rights), peace, security (including the war on terrorism), disarmament, international justice, the struggle to do away with international organized crime and corruption, environmental sustainability, the effort to combat and eventually eradicate pandemics and to increase cooperation in the field of health and sanitation in general, the worldwide war on drugs, the accumulation of human knowledge, cultural diversity, the defense of public spaces held in common by all, global macroeconomic and financial stability, and, more generally, the development of an appropriate institutional structure for the management of economic interdependence (Kaul, Grunberg, and Stern 1999).[1] There is a huge gap, however, between the recognition of these global public goods, on the one hand, and, on the other, the weakness of the existing international supply structures for these goods and the amount of resources allocated for them.

Support for the international institutions needed to supply or coordinate the provision of global public goods is therefore essential. The emphasis should be on the coordination of supply rather than on supply functions as such, because in many cases the regional level may be the most appropriate one for the provision of public goods. Another reason for focusing on the regional level is that the concerted efforts of nongovernmental organizations and the private sector must be brought to bear on this task. As a general rule, the provision of global public goods is accomplished through the efficient operation of networks of various types of institutions rather than by individual agencies.

The need to provide sufficient financing for the supply of global public goods has been underscored by a number of recent reports (United Nations 1999a; Zedillo and others 2001). It is important to differentiate between these kinds of contributions and official development assistance (ODA), because all countries should play a part in financing global public goods based on the principle of "common but differentiated responsibilities" laid down in the Rio Declaration on Environment and Development adopted at the 1992 U.N. Conference on Environment and Development.

The supply of global public goods is not the only item on the international agenda, of course. It must be backed up by the accomplishment of two complementary tasks: overcoming the asymmetries of the global order and formulating a rights-based international social agenda. These tasks might also be included on the global public goods agenda. Doing so would create confusion, however, because in the final analysis these two tasks are aimed at the equitable distribution of essentially private goods. Moreover, the elimination of international asymmetries and the formulation of a rights-based social agenda involve different spheres of activity; the former focuses on rectifying disparities between countries, whereas the latter focuses directly on individuals.

In order to surmount international asymmetries, the global agenda must include action on three different fronts. The first involves enhancing the transmission of growth impulses from industrial to developing countries via international trade and technology transfer. The second is to work through international lending agencies to give developing countries more breathing space for the adoption of countercyclical macroeconomic policies, help reverse the international concentration of credit, and expedite the financial development of these countries. The third concerns efforts to make sure that the global agenda places just as much emphasis on the international mobility of labor as it does on that of capital.

If an international social agenda is to be established, every member of the global society must be acknowledged as a citizen of the world and, hence, as possessing certain rights. The most cogent expressions of these rights are found in international declarations on civil, political, economic, social, cultural, and labor rights; on the rights of women, children, and different ethnic groups; and on the right to development.[2] The commitments made by countries at world summits, some of which are accorded special recognition in the U.N. Millennium Declaration, complement those instruments to a great extent. These instruments also reflect a recognition of the fact that states bear the primary responsibility for fulfilling their provisions. Because they represent international commitments, however, they will eventually have to become enforceable at the international level, because this is the only way they can help to build a true world citizenry.

These three key objectives of the global agenda reflect the fact that in an interdependent world, the rights of all ultimately depend on the existence of a global social covenant. Embracing this widely accepted principle of nation building is tantamount to an acknowledgment that economic affairs cannot be separated from the social and political fabric and that if nations are to survive and prosper, market forces must therefore function within the framework of an institutional order based on broader, more inclusive social values and aims.

The existing international order suffers from serious shortcomings in terms of its capacity to achieve these three objectives. The United Nations is the appropriate institutional framework for a dialogue about ways of ensuring the global coherence of the system and of filling the voids that exist in the area of international cooperation. Decisionmaking authority and executive capacity in certain fields are, however, held by a wide range of specialized agencies that work not only at the global level but in the regional and national arenas as well.

Global Rules and Institutions that Respect Diversity

The essentially national and local nature of policy making has profound implications for the international order. The globalization process notwithstanding, for a long time to come the primary setting for the exercise of democracy will continue to be nations and local communities. The focus for global institutions should therefore be on acknowledging interdependence and managing it proactively. Ultimately, however, these institutions rely on national responsibilities and policies, as sovereignty will continue to reside in communities of people organized into nations.

One of these principles' implications is that it is futile to promote democracy unless national representative and participatory processes give the people a say in the formulation of countries' economic and social development strategies (Ocampo 2001a). For this reason, respect for diversity—within the bounds of interdependence and, thus, of the common good of a "cosmopolitan society"—is a crucial element of any democratic international order.[3]

This view fits in with the idea that institution building (institutional capital), social consensus (social capital), the development of human capital, and technological capacity (knowledge capital) are essentially endogenous processes. It also reflects the belief that there is not just one "right" path to development and integration into the global economy. There are a range of different options depending on the political and institutional history of each country and the differing challenges and requirements to be met (Albert 1993; ECLAC 2000a; Rodrik 1999, 2001a).

This principle is embodied in the more recent thinking on cooperation for development, which emphasizes that its effectiveness will depend on there being a sense of national policy ownership. In fact, this principle has won formal acceptance as a basic guideline for the design of ODA and the policies of international lending agencies (Organisation for Economic Co-operation and Development [OECD] 1996; World Bank 1999; and, on conditionality, International Monetary Fund [IMF] 2001a). However, quite frequently, it is ignored in practice. Indeed, an effort is often made to "compel" ownership of the policies that international agencies feel are appropriate (Helleiner 2000b). Even so, the importance of ownership is one of the overarching rules governing the operations of international agencies. Their role is to support national decisionmaking, not take its place.

Complementarity of Global, Regional, and National Institution Building

In the absence of suitable institutions, globalization is proving to be a disintegrative force. At the national level, some regions, production sectors, and social groups are coming out as "winners" and others as

"losers" in the intense Schumpeterian process of "creative destruction" that is now being witnessed worldwide (ECLAC 2000a). This
process is not only increasing each country's internal heterogeneity,
but also undermining the state's ability to ensure its cohesiveness. The
powerful centripetal forces that the global economy has been generating for several centuries now (Prebisch 1984) impel developing countries to focus on carving out a foothold in industrial-country markets
and competing among themselves to attract footloose investments.
Under these circumstances, integration efforts aimed at forming larger
economic units are relegated to a position of secondary importance. A
virtuous circle of complementary global, regional, and national institution building is needed in order to cope with these forces.

International debate has gradually given rise to a broad consensus
as to the fundamental role of national strategies in determining how
successful a country will be in forming linkages with the world economy. Such strategies are also essential in order to handle the disintegrative forces being generated by globalization within each nation.
Moreover, as noted earlier, they continue to be the main vehicle for
democracy in the global era.

Without a suitable international framework, however, the supply of
global public goods will inevitably be insufficient, and this, in turn,
will hinder national development. What is more, unless a frontal attack is launched against the strong tendency toward inequality at the
international level, which has been in evidence for the past two centuries, national efforts may prove relatively ineffective. More specifically, within the context of a developing world whose overall growth
prospects continue to be a source of dissatisfaction, the heterogeneity
existing across countries and between winning and losing social
groups and production sectors may intensify.

Action at the regional and subregional levels plays a critical role as
a midway point between the global and national orders. This arena for
what ECLAC (1994) has termed "open regionalism" has, however,
been either ignored or regarded as a negative element in many of the
chief proposals being made regarding international economic and
social reform. But there are at least four arguments that attest to the
importance of this intermediate sphere.

The first is the complementarity existing between global and
regional institutions in a heterogeneous international community. Advocacy efforts toward democracy, peace, and disarmament are all examples of instances in which, given the existing degree of international
heterogeneity, it is best to base the provision of the corresponding
global public goods on a network of world and regional organizations.
The protection of strategic ecosystems and many spheres of economic

activity—such as macroeconomic policy coordination and others that will be touched upon later in this chapter—are other cases in point.

The second argument refers to the exceedingly unequal positions of the actors involved in global processes. In political terms, this means that within the global order, the smaller countries will be able to make their voice heard more clearly (or perhaps heard at all) only if they speak with a regional voice. This voice must be heard not only in the development of rules and standards, but also in the defense of their interests under existing rules and standards. In fact, the paradox is that such global rules are most important for small countries, which are, however, precisely the ones that have the least influence over their formulation and advocacy. Meanwhile, the most influential actors try to avoid making commitments or to compel other actors to accept their rules. These problems can be solved only if the smaller countries organize themselves.

The third argument, which is closely tied to the first two, is that regional and subregional institutions enjoy a greater sense of ownership. There are opponents to this view as well, of course, who contend that these institutions are less powerful than their individual members. The validity of these arguments will therefore depend on the depth of the corresponding regional and subregional agreements, which is what ultimately determines their effectiveness.

As the world becomes increasingly interdependent, the scope of autonomy has shifted to the subregional or regional level in some areas, as in the case of macroeconomic policy. It is also the case with the regulation of competition and of public utilities when transnational corporations enter the market. In all these fields, the regional arena is becoming the crucial sphere for the exercise of some degree of true autonomy, and it is possible that this may increasingly become the case as time goes on.

The main conclusion to be drawn from this analysis is that global public goods should be provided by a network of world and regional institutions, rather than by one or a few international institutions. A system of this type can be made to function efficiently and may prove to be more balanced in terms of power relations. In fact, this is the most advantageous system for the less powerful countries within the global order.

The construction of a truly new international architecture is founded upon the overall effect of global and regional institutional reforms. Unfortunately, many of the reform proposals put forward in recent years regarding the financial and, above all, social aspects of the international architecture focus almost entirely on adapting national structures to the global era. In other words, these proposals are looking at the national rather than the international architecture, and therein lies their main weakness.

Equitable Participation and Appropriate Rules of Governance

The insufficient degree to which developing countries participate in international economic institutions has been a controversial issue in recent years. In some cases—in the formulation of financial rules and standards, for example—they play little or no role at all, and even when they do have some role, their involvement is not commensurate with the size of their economies, much less with that of their populations. In other instances, even though decisions are understood to be made by consensus, in practice agreements are reached on a different basis, as happens in the world trading system. In addition, the cost of active participation in a complex world order may be prohibitive for the poorest and smallest countries.

These circumstances demonstrate the importance of ensuring adequate participation in decisionmaking at the international level. Achieving adequate participation will require affirmative action in favor of poor and small countries on the part of the international community. As discussed in the preceding section, it will also require an effort on the part of the smaller countries to organize themselves at the regional or subregional level.

Another point to be made is that preference should be given to institutional schemes having the largest possible number of active participants. Although groups formed by countries that share a particular interest or specific purpose may contribute to consensus building, such groups should channel their views through established multilateral mechanisms rather than taking their place.[4]

The adoption of appropriate rules of governance is another essential element. Principles developed at the national level in relation to democratic and corporate governance can serve as the foundations for building and improving international institutions (Marfán 2002). There is no single formula for accomplishing this, because constitutions, laws, rules and regulations, and traditions differ in each historical context and evolve over time. It can be said, however, that the most effective and legitimate forms of governance are based on shared principles. These principles do not, moreover, develop spontaneously, and an explicit effort must therefore be made to institutionalize them.

Four basic principles of good governance can be outlined here. The first is that government functions should be carried out by a body with executive powers rather than by an assembly. The second is that the rights of the governed take precedence over rules and regulations established by the various levels of government. Consequently, the rights of minorities should be clearly established, while bearing in mind that their identification and recognition as fundamental rights are the end result of a learning process. The third principle is that the authorities should regularly give an accounting of what they have done to safeguard the interests of the community and uphold the rights of all its members. Transparency, timely disclosure, and, more generally, accountability are essential components of this community process. The fourth principle is that the authorities should submit to the scrutiny of independent bodies and to outside audits that will build confidence among minority groups. These groups do not govern, but they do have the right to oversee the actions of those who hold power. Furthermore, the bodies in charge of enforcing individual rights should have the power to penalize wrongdoing.

A good example of the application of these principles is provided by political governance in a representative democracy, where executive power is exercised by representatives who have been elected by the majority. It is the duty of this branch of government to uphold the fundamental rights of citizens as set down in the constitution and other laws that apply equally to all citizens and to provide a regular accounting of the ends and means of government action. Oversight of its acts and its enforcement of citizens' rights and of the law are carried out by independent agencies. An important part of this function is the watchdog role performed by the principal parliamentary minority (the opposition).

Another example can be found in corporate governance. In this case, majority shareholders control the firm's board of directors and management. The dispersion and varying interests of minority stakeholders, on the other hand, make it difficult for them to organize themselves effectively. Good corporate governance seeks to prevent the shareholders that have a controlling interest from obtaining a disproportionate share of profits or other benefits relative to the size of their holdings. To achieve this, executives and members of the board are required to comply with certain rules concerning transparency and timely disclosure and with regulations that set out their responsibilities. In addition, there are independent oversight agencies (including outside auditors) and in-house auditing committees (usually formed by members of the board elected by minority shareholders). These bodies complement the work of regulatory agencies and the judiciary, which have the power to penalize wrongdoing. Recent major corporate scandals in the United States (ENRON and others) are dramatic evidence of the consequences of evading full compliance with these principles.

The governance of the globalization process could be substantially improved by adherence to these same principles. The most powerful nations are obviously the leaders of the globalization process and occupy a dominant position in the major international financial institutions, in which voting power—and, in a few cases, veto power—is based on capital contributions. The resemblance ends there, however, because the other principles of governance are not clearly established. For example, it is not certain that the more powerful nations' control over the process is legitimized by their respect for the rights of all countries, nor is there a universally accepted institutional structure for upholding the rights of less powerful nations. In fact, quite often there is not even a clear idea of what those rights are.

The application of these principles to improve the governance of the globalization process will therefore entail according priority to the fundamental rights of developing countries (especially the smaller ones), institutionalizing accountability, and increasing oversight by bodies that will inspire confidence in all the parties concerned. This approach involves placing certain limits on the power of the most influential countries, as this is the only way to improve the governance of the globalization process. It will also lead to a greater commitment to the global institutional structure on the part of developing countries by increasing their sense of ownership.

National Strategies for Dealing with Globalization

After reviewing the appropriate national context for applying strategies capable of dealing with globalization, this section examines some major policy components: macroeconomic management, the dynamic transformation of production structures, environmental sustainability, and social cohesion.

The Role and Basic Components of National Strategies

As has been discussed at length in the literature on institution building in recent years, in today's global era, any development strategy must be founded upon a solid, democratic social covenant to ensure its political stability; nondiscretionary local systems and modes of behavior that provide security of contract performance; and the formation of an impartial, efficient state bureaucracy. These are also, of course, basic components of a proinvestment environment.

These general sorts of institutional elements are not sufficient in themselves, however. They are the backdrop for the development process, but they do not account for the specific forces that drive growth in developing countries or, in many cases, lead to the depletion of growth impulses.[5] National strategies for today's global era should incorporate at least four additional elements: (a) macroeconomic policies designed to reduce vulnerability and facilitate productive investment; (b) strategies for developing systemic competitiveness; (c) a keen awareness of the priorities of the environmental agenda, which, by its very nature, is essentially global in scope; and (d) highly active social policies, especially in the fields of education, employment, and social protection (ECLAC 2000a 2000b, 2001a; ECLAC and U.N. Environment Programme [UNEP] 2001).

There are no universally valid models in any of these areas. Thus, the institutional learning process and, most importantly, the exercise of democracy have a broad sphere of action in which to function. One of the most serious mistakes made in the last quarter of the 20th century was the promotion of a single "solution" in each of these fields based on the principle of full market liberalization. The tendency to equate successful integration into the globalized world with economic liberalization overlooks the fact that many strategies have not been based on all-out market liberalization but instead on various ways of forming virtuous circle linkages between the state and the market. It would be just as mistaken, however, to take the opposite approach and try to resuscitate models that were successful when the world economy was less integrated but that are suited only to stages in the development of the world economy that are now clearly a thing of the past.

Macroeconomic Strategy

The experiences of Latin America and the Caribbean in the final quarter of the 20th century demonstrate that all forms of macroeconomic disequilibrium are economically and socially costly. This recognition implies, first of all, that macroeconomic discipline is essential, but it should be defined in a much broader sense than it generally has been in economic discourse in recent decades, which has focused on fiscal balances and low inflation. This narrower view overlooks other equally important dimensions of macroeconomic stability: balance-of-payments sustainability, the soundness of national financial systems, and the stability of real variables such as economic growth and employment. Macroeconomic management should be directed toward avoiding unsustainable public or private deficits, guarding against financial imbalances in all institutions (in terms of both flows and the way balances are structured), controlling inflation, and curbing any instability in real economic variables (ECLAC 2000a, 2001a; Ffrench-Davis 2000).

Achieving these objectives will entail some quite complex policy decisions, and, for these purposes, there is no simple way of defining stability or any universally valid system of macroeconomic management. In a volatile international environment, some degree of flexibility in macroeconomic management should be combined with suitable regulations. Recent events leave no doubt that, in the long run, macroeconomic authorities' credibility can be strengthened more effectively through prudently managed flexibility than through the adoption of overly rigid rules.[6]

Within this framework, one of the authorities' aims should be to lengthen the time horizon for macroeconomic policy management in order to take in the whole of the business cycle and support dynamic long-term growth. Encompassing the entire cycle will provide the necessary scope for the adoption of countercyclical macroeconomic policies that can help forestall unsustainable booms and afford sufficient flexibility in dealing with external crises (ECLAC 2000a; Ocampo 2002a). The option of using countercyclical policies is quite limited without the support of international institutions, however, and this has consequently become one of these institutions' basic functions in the current stage of the globalization process. The short- and long-term objectives of macroeconomic policy are, to a great extent, complementary—because more stable economic growth is one of the strongest incentives for fixed capital investment—but they can also confront policy makers with some difficult choices (ECLAC 2001a; Ocampo 2002b).

Based on these principles, fiscal policy should be designed using a pluriannual horizon. It should also be based on long-term guidelines for ensuring a structural fiscal balance. These guidelines should either make allowance for the use of moderate, temporary surpluses or deficits for countercyclical purposes or, alternatively, set an explicit target for the ratio between the public debt and GDP. The active use of stabilization funds (or equivalent instruments) can be the most effective way to build up surpluses during booms that can then be used to contend with crisis situations. The desirable level and structure of public revenues and expenditures will, in the long run, depend on what kinds of demands each society's fiscal covenant places on the state (ECLAC 1998c). In countries with very low tax burdens (as is true of a number of Latin American nations), taxes can be increased to finance the basic functions of the state, especially in social sectors. In fact, as recently stated by the World Bank (2002b), the tax burden and levels of public expenditure in the developing world tend to be low in comparison to those of industrial countries.

Monetary and exchange rate management are, of course, closely related. Some degree of flexibility in the exchange regime is necessary for countercyclical monetary management (i.e., the application of restrictive policies during booms and expansionary ones during the downswing in the cycle). The desirable degree of flexibility will be greater in the larger economies that have well-developed capital and exchange markets. It may be wise to allow the exchange rate to appreciate in order to soak up excess foreign exchange during booms, whereas a depreciation may be needed to spur the production of tradables during economic busts and to provide enough breathing room for reactivation-oriented fiscal and monetary policies.

In financially open economies, the prudential regulation of capital flows, either through the use of reserve requirements or taxes on external borrowing or by means of direct regulation,[7] is an extremely useful supplementary tool for avoiding excessive external borrowing during booms and preventing liability structures from becoming skewed toward short-term obligations. In more closed economies, caution should be used in opening up the capital account. In fact, if a country does not have a solid financial system, there is really no convincing argument for opening the capital account up at all. Strengthened prudential regulation and supervision are one of the pillars of any sound macroeconomic policy; their core function is to prevent unsustainable financial structures from being spawned during economic booms.

From a macro viewpoint, economic growth in the long run hinges on a combination of sound fiscal systems that provide the necessary resources for the public sector to do its job, a competitive exchange rate, moderate real interest rates, and the development of a deep financial market. Macroeconomic policy should be focused on ensuring the first three elements. The last is a very important complementary process.

The main objective of financial deepening is to provide suitably priced investment finance with sufficiently long maturities. In the absence of a well-developed financial market, many investors (particularly the larger ones) will turn to international lenders, thereby substituting exchange risk for maturity risk. Use of this escape valve therefore entails serious hazards, as well as being beyond the reach of smaller firms. The liberalization of financial systems in Latin America and the Caribbean has not deepened financial markets or reduced the region's high intermediation costs as much as had been expected. Consequently, the public sector still has an important role to play in promoting the emergence of new intermediaries and financing mechanisms (e.g., pension and investment funds, bond and mortgage markets, and hedging systems) or in arranging for the direct provision of such facilities by well-run development banks.

The existence of this unsatisfied demand for investment finance is compounded by the absence of suitable financial services for micro- and small enterprises and for the poorest households. This situation creates a greater demand for direct or indirect public intervention. Low national savings rates are another constraint on investment financing in Latin America and the Caribbean. Efforts to increase public-sector saving, the creation of corporate saving incentives (especially to encourage firms to retain profits), and special mechanisms to foster household saving (for retirement, in particular) may be useful means of raising national savings rates (ECLAC 2001a).

Building Systemic Competitiveness

A dynamic transformation of production structures should not be viewed as a reactive phenomenon or as an automatic result of good macroeconomic management, but rather as an active and essential component of any development strategy, even at this juncture in the globalization process (ECLAC 2000a; Rodrik 1999). The core objective of these strategies should be to build systemic competitiveness. This concept, whose first formulations date back to work done by ECLAC over a decade ago (ECLAC 1990; Fajnzylber 1990),[8] is based on three elements. The first is the role of knowledge as the foundation for competitiveness, because it is the only factor that enables countries to produce goods and services capable of "making the grade" on international markets while protecting and increasing their citizens' real incomes. The second is the idea that competitiveness depends less on individual firms than on the performance of each sector as a whole, its interaction with suppliers, and ultimately the smooth operation of the entire economic system. In sum, it is essentially a systemic phenomenon. The third is that given the serious imperfections existing in technology markets and strong externalities among economic agents associated with the systemic nature of competitiveness, the development of sound technology markets and production linkages is in large part the outcome of the deliberate efforts of the state and business associations and, particularly, of collaborative initiatives undertaken by the state and the private sector to create a virtuous circle that will bolster the system's competitiveness.

The three basic components of this strategy are (a) the creation of innovation systems to speed up the accumulation of technological capacity, (b) support for changes in production structures and the formation of production linkages, and (c) provision of quality infrastructure services. The creation of adequate social safety nets and sustainable environmental management are important complements to this effort. These elements concern other spheres of activity, however, and will be considered later on in this chapter.

Given the key role of knowledge, any competitiveness strategy must be based on increased investment in education, vocational and business training, and science and technology (ECLAC and U.N. Educational, Scientific and Cultural Organization [UNESCO] 1992). This process, whose aim is the creation of dynamic innovation systems, should be led by the state, but the private sector should also be actively involved. These efforts should focus on increasing the capacity of all actors to absorb knowledge and on developing appropriate mechanisms for the adaptation of technology and business skills, especially for medium-size and small firms. Business associations and incentives for various forms of collaboration between these associations and providers of educational and vocational training play a fundamental role in this effort. Innovation systems should be strengthened at all levels (i.e., local, national, and to a growing extent regional).

In view of the intrinsic importance and crosscutting nature of new information and communications technologies, efforts to promote their active use throughout the economic, social, and even political (e-government) systems are of vital importance. Access to a quality telecommunications network and to competitively priced information and communications equipment is one of the pillars of this endeavor. Other mainstays include the production of software, incorporation of technology into production and trade, and formation of business networks that make effective use of new technologies. The incorporation of such technologies into educational and health care systems requires special state support and community mechanisms to give low-income sectors access to them, because the emergence of a "domestic digital divide" (produced by disparities between different social sectors' access to new technologies) is a much more serious threat in Latin America and the Caribbean than the international digital divide.

Economic growth necessarily entails an ongoing process of changing production patterns in which some branches of production function as growth leaders and others lag behind. This process is not necessarily automatic or harmonious; the expansion of new sectors involves the development of a complementary set of activities based on a technological learning process, the establishment of commercial networks, and significant coordination costs (Chang 1994; Hirschman 1958; Ocampo 2002c). The diversification of the production structure must therefore be an explicit priority of any competitiveness strategy. This idea has been expressly recognized in the industrial world, where the process has become virtually synonymous with the development of cutting-edge technologies. It also enjoyed wide acceptance in the past as a component of state-driven industrialization strategies in developing countries, and today it is an essential tenet in the most successful

developing economies, especially those of East Asia. In contrast, diversification strategies have been discarded by most countries of the
region.

Within the context of the globalization process, the diversification
of production is guided by three priorities. The first is to diversify the
export base and target markets, which calls for a very active form of
commercial diplomacy aimed at securing stable access to external markets and the development of a competitive, high-quality service infrastructure—in the areas of finance, insurance, promotion, and certification—to back up exports of goods and services (ECLAC 1998a). In
this endeavor, one obvious priority is to increase the region's share of
world trade in technology-intensive goods and services.

The second priority is to develop programs to broaden the linkages
of activities oriented toward the international market or dominated by
transnational corporations. The weakening of such linkages is one of
the most problematic aspects of recent trends in the region. For this
reason, linkage policies designed to increase value added in export sectors and sectors with a high proportion of foreign direct investment
(FDI) should be adopted as a forward-looking priority. Among these
linkages, those associated with the provision of technology-intensive
services are of special importance. These policies would, in practice,
amount to a shift away from a policy aimed at maximizing the quantity of exports and FDI to a policy aimed at improving their quality.

A final priority in this regard is to support the formation of production clusters in particular locations. This process is a response to
the growing dynamism of local spheres of economic activity in the
global era. It is particularly important in steering small and medium-
size enterprises (SMEs) toward production for the international market or linkage with export sectors (ECLAC 2000a).

The other core aspect of competitiveness policy is the provision of
quality infrastructure services. In a number of countries, various public-private partnerships have succeeded in making significant progress
in this regard, particularly in telecommunications, port services, and
maritime transport, and—to a lesser extent and with some differences
from one country to another—in energy services (electricity and gas;
ECLAC 2001b). It must be acknowledged, however, that private participation in these sectors has been accompanied by serious regulatory
gaps and, in some cases, has burdened the state with contingent liabilities that do not always have a sound rationale (ECLAC 1998c,
2000a). The main problems in terms of infrastructure continue to be
found in land transport, including both railways and roads. Shortcomings in both the quantity and the quality of road networks are particularly severe. Accordingly, priority should be given to substantially

improving road infrastructure, correcting regulatory gaps, and rationalizing the management of contingent liabilities, while also improving the efficiency of state enterprises in areas where the state continues to provide services directly.

Progress on all these fronts will require major institutional and organizational efforts to formulate and implement active competitiveness policies, because the pre-existing systems of government intervention in productive development were dismantled or severely curtailed in most of the countries of the region during the economic liberalization phase. Such systems would, in any case, be ill-suited to the new environment. In this area, as in others, it is necessary to "invent" new institutions, whose management will no doubt require an intensive learning process.

The possible models for these institutions are certainly not uniform, as they depend on the specific characteristics of each situation. A public-private partnership is essential to fill the information gaps found in each of these sectors (i.e., the former's limited microeconomic information and the latter's insufficient familiarity with global and cross-sectoral processes). In other words, institutional design must take into account both the forest and the trees. The instruments to be developed for this purpose should be based on checks and balances that establish a clear link between incentives and results (Amsden 2001) and thereby preclude rent-seeking behavior on the part of beneficiary firms.

This endeavor should comprise various combinations of horizontal and selective instruments, depending on each country's institutional context, to be chosen on the basis of shared strategic visions of the directions to be emphasized in joint public-private efforts. This choice is less an exercise in picking winners, as it is commonly called, than an effort to identify opportunities and direct the actions needed to ensure that some of them bear fruit. This type of strategic exercise is one in which all private investors engage on a routine basis. It is hard to understand why some schools of economic thought consider it illegitimate to carry out such an exercise in relation to a particular territory, whether it be a town, a country, or even a subregion or region.

Environmental Sustainability

The agenda for environmental sustainability has gradually made its way into the institutions, public policies, and business practices of the Latin American and Caribbean countries. Although it is not yet, in the fullest sense, an integral part of the development process, the progress achieved thus far constitutes a much better institutional and social foundation than the one available 10 years ago when the U.N.

Conference on Environment and Development was held in Rio de Janeiro. The concept of sustainable development has also been gradually incorporated into educational systems, and the change in society's perception of environmental issues has strengthened citizens' awareness and commitment. The primary hurdles that remain in this area have to do with institutional and financial considerations and with the perception within business circles in the region of environmental sustainability as a cost rather than an opportunity (ECLAC and UNEP 2001).

With respect to institutional mechanisms, steps should be taken to set up clear and consistent regulatory frameworks and to achieve a stable level of public expenditure with a view to generating significant synergies with international financing and private investment. On the basis of existing management methods, the time has come to develop a new generation of more effective and prevention-oriented instruments for the integration of economic and environmental considerations. This process should primarily involve the use of economic instruments to provide adequate incentives to meet sustainability goals and to promote a greater use of clean production technologies by SMEs. One of the most promising lines of action in this area is the creation of genuine domestic (and regional) markets for environmental services, following the pioneering example of the Kyoto Protocol's clean development mechanism. Such instruments have the dual purpose of generating incentives to minimize environmental costs (the central objective of economic instruments), while at the same time channeling resources to the actors that are best able to provide environmental services most efficiently (ECLAC and U.N. Development Programme [UNDP] 2002).

A more active sustainable development strategy will require the allocation of more government resources. One option is to introduce "green taxes," as has been done in some industrial countries. Although great strides have already been made in reducing government subsidies for polluting industries, further reductions are needed.

In addition, current frameworks must be adapted to integrate explicit environmental policies with the implicit ones associated with sectoral economic policies and the patterns of structural change they entail. In view of the regressive trend in energy efficiency taking shape in the region, such integration and the use of this array of instruments should give priority to the reversal of that trend (ECLAC and UNEP 2001).

The formation of effective linkages between economic and environmental issues also requires a shift from a reactive agenda to one that takes a proactive approach to the relationship between environmental sustainability and economic development. This involves, first of all, identifying the opportunities offered by the international environmental agenda, in particular in regard to the supply of global public goods and the possibility of becoming net providers of environmental services, primarily in connection with the climate change and biodiversity agendas. The opportunities afforded by the Kyoto Protocol's clean development mechanism are particularly noteworthy in this regard. This proactive approach also entails taking advantage of opportunities to expedite scientific and technological development through the sustainable use of biotic resources, a better understanding of the region's natural resources, and the development of its own technologies for tapping these resources in sustainable ways (ECLAC 2000a).

In addition, this approach involves the active use of foreign investment as a potential channel for the transfer of clean technologies, the exportation of goods and services having a high environmental content (e.g., organic agricultural products and ecological or environmentally certified tourism), and the promotion of the international certification mechanisms increasingly demanded by industrial-country consumers. In fact, foreign investment and export activities in the region are turning out to be the areas in which the most progress is being made in incorporating clean technologies.

Types of production that rely on an abundant supply of natural resources but are slow in leading to the diffusion of technical progress are being eclipsed by economies that are successfully developing knowledge-based forms of production. It is therefore necessary to redirect the region's model of competitiveness toward new activities and toward an increase in the value added of natural resource-intensive activities. This shift requires the promotion of industrial activities and complementary services, including those that will increase the sustainability of primary activities.

Because of the territorial specificity of environmental management functions, strong operational links with local authorities need to be forged. Solving high-priority environmental problems in such areas as water resources management, solid waste disposal, ecological land use, and urban management requires the decentralization of environmental policies and instruments and a more balanced distribution of public expenditure and private investment. It is at the local level that the commitment between the state and the citizenry is expressed most clearly. Hence the importance of continuing to promote social consensus building in relation to the environmental agenda, particularly within the context of provincial and municipal sustainable development councils and the local Agenda 21 framework (United Nations 2002). Forums of this sort can become powerful tools for organizing public affairs and mobilizing additional resources to promote environmental sustainability at the subnational level (ECLAC 2000a).

Social Strategies in an Era of Globalization

Globalization has made it all the more urgent to achieve greater international competitiveness. Owing to the interrelationship between competitiveness and employment, however, competitiveness also entails new social risks. National globalization strategies should therefore focus on three areas within the social sector: education, employment, and social protection. Progress in these three areas is a prerequisite for equitable participation in the global era. Moreover, such progress is essential for the implementation of a rights-based international agenda at the national level.

Advances in these three areas are mutually reinforcing. Education is the primary means of halting the intergenerational reproduction of poverty and inequality. At the same time, globalization has increased the need for human resources capable of engaging in new modes of production, competition, and coexistence. Employment is at the heart of social integration, as an aspect of social fulfillment and as a source of income, and it therefore determines individuals' ability to gain access to basic consumer goods and thus avail themselves of their basic rights. Such access is crucial in the absence of societywide safety nets. Among the risks faced by the population are those associated with macroeconomic volatility, the adaptation of new technologies and ways of organizing work, and the elimination of jobs in many sectors in response to international competition (ECLAC 1997, 2000b).

In education, national efforts should focus on reducing disparities in attendance and achievement between income levels and between rural and urban areas at all levels of schooling (preschool, elementary, technical, university). Efforts to achieve greater equity should therefore focus on achieving universal coverage, preferably up to the end of secondary school, and reducing socioeconomically based differences in the quality of the education that is provided.

In developing their educational systems, the Latin American and Caribbean countries face both traditional challenges and challenges related to new technologies. Meeting them will require a diversified package of policies, which each country must tailor to fit its own characteristics and objectives. Public education expenditure must also be increased, of course, with the general objective being to reach levels similar to those found in OECD countries: around 5 percent of GDP. To improve educational continuity, governments must give priority to increasing the coverage of preschool education, which is still comparatively limited; expanding secondary education coverage and completion rates; increasing the availability and range of technical and professional educational options; and achieving greater consistency between technical-vocational and higher education, on the one hand, and the requirements of the job market and competitiveness, on the other. These efforts should be supplemented by targeted compensatory measures designed to have long-lasting effects in areas in which educational performance is poor, as well as more relevant curricula, use of new technological resources on a mass scale, and the empowerment of communities to assist in furthering educational goals.

Achieving social inclusiveness requires the development of new approaches to learning based on access to knowledge, networking, and the use of information and communication technologies (ICTs). Educators need to make better use of the cultural and educational audiovisual industry by merging cultural programming in the media with schooling so that the two will reinforce each other. Urgent steps should be taken to ensure that students in poor rural and urban areas can learn to use interactive media that are not available to them at home, because school is the ideal environment for ensuring, distributing, and democratizing their use. The modernization of educational tools is not enough, however. It is even more important, in conjunction with these new tools, to develop higher cognitive functions by orienting the learning process toward problem identification and problem solving, an increased capacity for reflection, creativity, the ability to distinguish between what is relevant and what is not, and planning and research skills. All these functions are vital in an information-saturated world. Progress also has to be made in the design and use of portals (educational content) and in the training of educators (teachers, administrators, and families).

In this era of globalization, the primary challenge in the area of employment is to prevent the expansion of world trade from resulting in the violation of workers' basic rights or in the downward convergence of wages and working conditions in countries at different levels of development. The Declaration on Fundamental Principles and Rights at Work and its follow-up (ILO 1998) reaffirm the member countries' commitment to such fundamental rights as freedom of association and the right to collective bargaining, the prohibition of forced or slave labor, the progressive abolition of child labor, and nondiscrimination.

The creation of new jobs is sustainable only when the economic activities concerned are competitive in the long term. This means that productivity must be enhanced and, therefore, that comprehensive strategies must be devised to increase investment in human resources and ensure that gains in competitiveness are not based on the reduction of labor costs or the concentration of wage increases in the most dynamic or well-organized sectors. Productive restructuring and increased labor mobility make it necessary to give workers opportunities to learn how to adapt to new conditions and thus increase their employability. Countries will therefore have to invest in worker retraining based on a new approach and, possibly, a different institutional framework. The development of basic competencies, rather than specific skills, will give workers a knowledge base that will enable them to adapt more easily to the demands of new jobs. Because informal activities, microenterprises, and small businesses play a major role in job creation, they should be given access to factors of production (capital and land) and to the tools they need to modernize their operations (managerial and technological know-how), and programs should be set up to help them gain access to dynamic industrial networks (ECLAC and UNESCO 1992).

To these ends, ministries of labor should adopt labor policies that place more emphasis on self-regulation by social actors (social dialogue) and that focus on the large groups of workers who remain outside modern sectors (unemployed and informal-sector workers). In addition, they should be repositioned in political and administrative terms so as to give them a place in economic cabinets and to restore, in many cases, their role in setting the direction for labor policy.

The development of social safety nets should be guided by the principles of universality, solidarity, efficiency, and integrality (ECLAC 2000a). Progress cannot be made toward universality unless the sharp inequities in access to services and in their quality are corrected. Solidarity should be ensured through a combination of compulsory contributions, public transfers, and cross-subsidies between different income strata and risk groups.

Social safety nets are seriously flawed in terms of both coverage and the new risk structure associated with globalization. The countries of the region, with their chronic shortcomings in the coverage of traditional risks (illness, old age, disability, and death, as well as those existing in the areas of nutrition, housing, and education), now face the additional burden of protecting their populations from the effects of such risks as employment and income vulnerability.

Sharp business cycles and the rigidity of real wages—which have been heightened by the steps taken to curb inflation—have made wage earners more vulnerable to changes in those cycles. Because many of the existing social safety nets were designed to serve wage earners, it has now become necessary to develop a system of social protection whose coverage extends to persons who do not hold formal-sector jobs and to create more comprehensive unemployment insurance schemes. Job creation policies will continue to be of crucial importance in this context, of course. As the experience of some European countries demonstrates, social protection policies should focus on boosting employment as a means of helping to ensure universal social protection. In emergency situations, it is necessary to develop special employment and poverty alleviation programs for vulnerable sectors based on permanent institutional arrangements that allow such measures to be implemented quickly and that link them to other objectives such as job training, infrastructure provision, and territorial development (ECLAC 2001d).

Given the current scope of informal-sector employment and unemployment, the potential for providing comprehensive coverage through traditional social safety nets is quite limited, as is the usefulness of wage-based taxes and levies as a source of funding. Accordingly, emphasis should be placed on the implementation of systems based on citizenship rather than on employment. Reforms in general, and reforms in the social security system in particular, should therefore introduce combined and complementary insurance mechanisms that reflect the diverse forms of employment now in use. These types of arrangements will also promote labor mobility and provide protection in times of externally generated adversity.

The quantity and quality of the social safety nets that can be funded by mandatory contributions, general taxes, or a combination of the two depend on each country's current level of economic development and on the nature of its fiscal covenant, which embodies political and social agreements about the level of well-being that should be guaranteed to citizens. A country's fiscal situation is not static, of course, and a fiscal covenant for the protection of citizens' rights should therefore include an element of progressivity whereby public contributions for social protection and poverty reduction can be increased at the margin. Moreover, an inclusive system of social protection must place special emphasis on the views of target groups and provide for a constant flow of information to the public regarding opportunities for and means of accessing social safety nets and for taking part in decision-making (ECLAC 2000a).

The Key Role of Action at the Regional Level

Latin America and the Caribbean have progressed further in terms of regional integration than any other developing region, and these countries' experiences may therefore be instructive for other regions. Progress in this area was sparked by the political impetus that built up around the issue of integration in the late 1980s and early 1990s.

Unfortunately, this momentum has waned in the last few years. In addition, the institutional structure for integration remains fragile, and the convergence of existing agreements toward the formation of larger areas and the consolidation of customs unions are tasks yet to be accomplished. It is therefore imperative for the countries to renew their political commitment to regional integration. Such a commitment would not necessarily be incompatible with global negotiations or broader trade negotiations, such as those directed toward the formation of the Free Trade Area of the Americas. Nonetheless, if regional integration processes are to remain relevant within the context of a hemispheric free trade area or the globalization process, they will need to be deepened further.

The momentum displayed by the regional integration process in the late 1980s was a paradoxical phenomenon inasmuch as, according to the more orthodox doctrines, integration was (and still is) a force that distorts trade flows. Empirical evidence indicates, however, that integration actually tends to create rather than divert trade flows. Moreover, the flows it generates tend to be of high quality (ECLAC 1998b), demonstrated by the tendency of regional flows to have greater technological content and to create more production linkages. One of the main advantages of these processes is that countries with similar levels of development can take advantage of specialization economies for intraindustry trade. Another advantage is that lower transaction costs allow smaller firms to participate in intraregional trade, especially between neighboring countries, helping to counter the traditional tendency for external trade operations to be monopolized by larger firms within each sector of production or trade.[9]

In consequence, regional markets can provide an excellent training ground for firms—especially smaller enterprises—to learn how to deal with external markets and can therefore help new firms and sectors to venture into export activity. A further benefit of such integration processes is that they provide an opportunity to harmonize a wide range of differing rules and thus reduce the associated transaction costs, thanks not only to geographic proximity but also to the similarity of institutional traditions.

This positive vision of integration is borne out by the increase recorded in intraregional trade, especially within South America, between 1990 and 1997, when the augmented flows consisted primarily of manufactures, particularly technology-intensive ones. Recently, however, these trade flows have been hurt by macroeconomic instability in the region. In fact, they have proved to be highly elastic in response to abrupt business cycles in a number of the countries, especially in South America (ECLAC 2001c).

Macroeconomic cooperation has thus become a pivotal element in efforts to consolidate trade integration processes. In this respect, progress has been made in all the existing subregional schemes, and these initiatives should continue to move forward from the discussion and exchange of information and the adoption of common macroeconomic rules toward the institutionalization of peer review for preventive purposes and the design of stricter forms of macroeconomic coordination. Such mechanisms may eventually lead, in some cases, to monetary unions. In tandem with these efforts, the prudential regulation and supervision of national financial systems also stand to benefit from progress in the exchange of information, peer reviews, and the development of common standards.

ECLAC (2001a) has also argued that efforts must be made to develop regional and subregional financial institutions. Latin America and the Caribbean already have valuable assets of this type, including a wide network of multilateral development banks made up of the Inter-American Development Bank, the Andean Development Corporation, the Central American Bank for Economic Integration, the Caribbean Development Bank, and the Financial Fund for the Development of the River Plate Basin. The experience gained by the Latin American Reserve Fund points to the possibility of providing regional resources to augment the exceptional financing furnished to distressed countries. This could be accomplished either by significantly increasing the Latin American Reserve Fund's resources and membership or by means of mutual support agreements (specifically, foreign exchange swaps) between central banks.

In addition, the expansion of trade makes it all the more necessary to harmonize the different regulatory schemes. These include technical standards and phytosanitary requirements, customs codes, and government procurement and servicing regulations. Several of these areas have already seen some progress. It is important to move forward in other areas, however, most notably in relation to rules on competition and on the regulation of public utilities. With respect to rules on competition, the European Union's experience provides grounds for the belief that as common markets and an active process of intraregional investment are consolidated, agreements on competition issues and, eventually, the adoption of a common policy on competition clearly have distinct advantages over rules on unfair competition that apply solely to external trade. A framework of this nature would, among other things, make it possible to deal more effectively with potentially unfair practices on the part of transnational corporations.

Because high-technology goods account for such a sizeable percentage of intraregional trade, it is important to take joint action to promote the development of the corresponding sectors in ways that will avoid the rigidities of the old (and largely unsuccessful) sectoral complementarity agreements. The aim of such measures should be to generate regional and subregional innovation systems and to pave the way for the development of broader schemes for cooperation in education and in research and development (R&D). They could also provide a suitable framework for strategic R&D alliances or for the formation of new production clusters made up either of domestic firms in countries that are members of a regional or subregional agreement or of these firms together with transnational corporations. A key element in this process would be the establishment of regional funds. Funds of this type should also serve to accelerate the transfer of technology to developing countries.

In the area of physical infrastructure, in addition to harmonized standards on transport, energy, and telecommunications, infrastructural and regulatory networks need to be geared to the demands of regional integration. This kind of approach necessarily entails action at a supranational level. An interesting example in this respect was the creation of the Association of Caribbean States in 1994 to promote greater cooperation in the subregion. The physical integration plans agreed upon at the South American Summit of 2000 and the Puebla–Panama Plan are other indications of progress in this area. A number of border-area development plans are also under way that represent a further example of the major shift in spatial perception brought about by integration. This type of approach is also gradually being introduced in initiatives for the promotion of sustainable development in the management of shared ecosystems (e.g., the Amazon, the Andean ecosystem, the Caribbean Sea, and the Mesoamerican corridor) and shared river basins.

The uniqueness of the Latin American and Caribbean region stems not only from its generous endowment of natural resources and the global importance of the environmental services that these resources enable it to provide, but also from the global hazards inherent in the region's rapid environmental deterioration. It is extremely important for the countries at the forefront of the negotiations regarding the region's contributions to the two most significant issues on the global sustainable development agenda—climate change and biodiversity— to continue to play that leadership role. A clear example of this is the support that has been shown for the sustainable development agenda adopted by the region within the context of the international negotiations on the clean development mechanism provided for in the Kyoto Protocol, which could, in addition, generate income for the region.

Special mention should be made of the potential valuation of the environmental services provided by the region's ecosystems. Drawing attention to the region's unique position in this respect, consolidating regionwide efforts to protect strategic ecosystems and garnering worldwide support for this initiative represent the starting point for a regional agenda oriented toward safeguarding the stability of those of its ecosystems that are most important and valuable from a global standpoint.

The existing structure of the region's environmental institutions needs to be gradually reformed, beginning with the consolidation of the role of the Forum of Environment Ministers and the environmental programs associated with subregional integration schemes, such as the Central American Environment and Development Committee, the Amazon Cooperation Treaty, the environmental agreement of the Andean Community, and the Programme of Action for the Sustainable Development of Small Island Developing States in the Caribbean. Efforts must be made to increase the economic, social, and environmental coherence of these programs and to develop an agenda that integrates relevant sectoral policies and brings about a convergence of regional and subregional stances in global debates on sustainable development.

In the social sphere, numerous agreements have been reached by the different subregional integration schemes, as well as a number of broader instruments,[10] but the implementation of these provisions is very limited (Di Filippo and Franco 2000). In this respect it appears preferable to set more limited and concrete objectives whose attainment will have a more thorough-going impact. Two areas are particularly important in this respect. The first is support for intraregional labor migration. To facilitate the migration of workers and to ensure adequate protection for them and their families, it will be essential to devise means of transferring social security coverage, particularly in the case of health and retirement benefits, from one country to another.

The second is the area of education. Progress can be achieved in this domain by generating regional exchanges and creating networks of experts, governments, and organizations that can operate either via electronic communication or in face-to-face meetings. These contacts would allow experts to discuss and share best practices, successful and imaginative experiences, the strengths and weaknesses of reforms, teaching modalities, school computerization programs, and so forth. It is also important to undertake joint measures to generate educational content, software, portals, and textbooks; compare educational achievements; set standards by levels; establish criteria for assessing professional qualifications; and implement in-service teacher training programs. In addition to contributing to the development of the region's education systems, these initiatives would facilitate the establishment of regional accreditation systems and contribute to the reciprocal recognition of professional qualifications. It is also important to "educate for regional integration" and thus increase people's awareness of the fact that they belong to a region that shares a culture, a history, and perhaps a common fate. Basic education is the ideal sphere in which to instill an awareness of regional identity and put an end to xenophobia.

A final point to be made is that the "democratic clauses" included in integration agreements, the various forums for the region's heads of state, and the nascent subregional and Latin American parliaments together provide the cornerstone for a broad agenda of political integration that is as yet in its infancy.

The Global Agenda

Globalization is a multidimensional process. A detailed examination of some of its dimensions—such as its political or cultural aspects, for example—goes beyond the bounds of this analysis, however. The following examination of the global agenda is not, therefore, intended to provide a comprehensive treatment of the subject. As a case in point, the discussion on global public goods focuses on just two—the international macroeconomic order and sustainable development—out of a wide range of subjects referred to in the introductory portion of this chapter. The importance that ECLAC places on the correction of international asymmetries, on the other hand, justifies a more detailed consideration of this issue's three main dimensions: financial and macroeconomic considerations, production and technology, and international labor mobility. The chapter concludes with a series of observations regarding the development of a rights-based international social agenda.

The Provision of Global Public Goods in the Macroeconomic Sphere

In recent years there has been growing awareness of the fact that international financial and macroeconomic stability is a global public good that generates positive externalities for all international market participants and forestalls negative externalities associated with contagion, whether from "irrational exuberance" (to use the term coined by Alan Greenspan, chairman of the U.S. Federal Reserve Board) or from financial panics and recessionary impulses in general.

Hence the importance of taking global action on a number of fronts. The first is to build institutions capable of ensuring the global coherence of the major economies' macroeconomic policies. The lack of mechanisms for fully internalizing the effects that those policies have on the rest of the world is one of the main defects of the existing international order. When policy inconsistencies are manifested in the volatility of exchange rates for the major currencies, they generate additional adverse spillovers for developing countries. The IMF should play a central role in efforts to coordinate the major economies' macroeconomic policies. The scope of such an initiative will extend beyond the bounds of the dialogues being conducted in more restricted arenas, such as the Group of Seven forum.

The second front is macroeconomic surveillance of all economies with a view to prevention and the formulation of codes of good practice for macroeconomic management (in particular with regard to fiscal and monetary policy, public and external debt management, and management of international reserves). A great deal of headway has been made in recent years, and this is reflected in the greater emphasis that the IMF is placing on prevention in its article IV consultation process, on monitoring financial markets, and on constructing vulnerability indicators or early warning systems.

Work on the formulation of international standards for the prudential regulation and supervision of financial markets and on the provision of market information has also been moving ahead. Although this is clearly a third line of action for ensuring international macroeconomic stability, efforts in this area have received criticism on at least five counts: (a) the lack of participation by developing countries in the formulation of such standards; (b) the tendency to standardize such regulations without taking into account differences in the individual countries' regulatory traditions and absorption capacities; (c) the attempts made to tie IMF financial assistance to compliance with codes and standards on which no international consensus has been reached; (d) the limited attention devoted to such topics as the regulation of institutional investors operating in developing countries, direct regulation of highly leveraged activities, and operations in derivatives markets; and (e) the failure to devote sufficient attention to the regulation of rating agencies, whose evaluations have proved to be procyclical and have been severely criticized. Thus, as the process of designing international standards proceeds, steps must be taken to rectify these situations.

An even more complex issue is the lack of initiatives for the design of international standards in respect of capital flows to developing countries. Because of the residual nature of these markets in global terms, they are not a central regulatory concern for the industrial countries. Their regulation therefore tends to be covered by general standards that could have the effect of drastically reducing flows or raising borrowing costs unduly. The idea of giving rating agencies a major role in the industrial countries' regulatory systems by extending the application of a rule now used for institutional investors to include commercial banks could create similar difficulties, given the procyclical nature of risk ratings. These issues have been widely debated as part of the discussion of the Basel Committee banking reforms. Care should therefore be taken to ensure that any new regulatory measures that are adopted do not exacerbate the existing system's discrimination against capital flows to developing countries (Griffith-Jones and Spraat 2001; Reisen 2001).

Although international cooperation in the area of taxation cannot, strictly speaking, be termed a global public good, it is of growing importance, because the tax system is necessarily involved in obtaining a sufficient volume of public resources to finance the provision of national, regional, and global public and merit goods (FitzGerald 2001; Zedillo and others, 2001). Competition for footloose investment has tended to result in the reduction of capital taxes, and this, in turn, has either diminished the public sector's ability to generate resources or driven up the direct or indirect tax burden for less mobile factors of production, especially labor. Given these circumstances, steps should be taken to promote information-exchange agreements among tax authorities and double taxation agreements, as well as other, broader agreements aimed at avoiding tax competition, coordinating measures to combat tax evasion, and eventually harmonizing tax systems. The treatment of offshore centers warrants particular attention in this respect.

The international institutional structure in this field is virtually nonexistent. Consequently, in addition to new agreements, it may be necessary to create a new organization to foster international tax cooperation. Subregional or hemispheric agreements and the expansion of cooperation activities already being pursued by OECD with nonmember countries are intermediate options that should also be explored.

Sustainable Development as a Global Public Good

The 1992 U.N. Conference on Environment and Development was clearly a milestone in the formulation of a global agenda for sustainable development; it marked the birth of a political consensus of the highest level. This was the beginning of the transition toward a new international environmental regime based on a new generation of environmental conventions and a global program of action.[11] Agreement was also reached at that time on innovative principles that would provide a more equitable foundation for international coóperation. Indeed, the conference marked a turning point in the negotiation of multilateral agreements by offering a broader vision of development that acknowledges the importance of reconciling the aims of economic growth and international trade with the sustainable use of natural resources and environmental protection. Many of these agreements and their protocols include innovative financing mechanisms and instruments for facilitating developing countries' access to new technologies. After the conference, further progress was made with the conclusion of multilateral agreements highlighting environmental hazards that, in the light of advances in scientific knowledge, have resurfaced as important issues. What is essentially new in these agreements is that they spell out the linkages between the environment, human health, and production and consumption patterns, on the one hand, and economic, trade, and social policies, on the other.[12] This global awareness of countries' interdependence with regard to worldwide environmental problems helped ensure that the legally binding instruments discussed at the Rio Conference were adopted and ratified faster than similar instruments in earlier decades and that virtually all countries became parties to them.

Although the international community took up these agreements enthusiastically, this initial momentum began to wane as the decade wore on. Indeed, 10 years after the U.N. Conference on Environment and Development, it is clear that the persistence of a piecemeal approach to sustainable development has considerably delayed the implementation of the conference's outcome. Much remains to be done in terms of putting consistent policies into practice in the areas of finance, trade, investment, technology, and sustainable development. Furthermore, the financial resources needed to implement the series of agreements concluded since the Rio Conference have not been forthcoming, nor have steps been taken to improve the technology transfer mechanisms they envisage. At the World Summit on Sustainable Development, held in Johannesburg in August and September 2002, the participants reaffirmed the political commitments laid down in the Rio Declaration, particularly principle 7 on common but differentiated responsibilities and principle 15, which deals with the precautionary approach. In addition, the 34 goals agreed upon in the Plan of Implementation of the Summit build upon the Agenda 21 commitments and the development goals set out in the U.N. Millennium Declaration. For the first time, countries expressly recognized the importance of region-specific initiatives and of cooperation among various public, private, and civil society stakeholders through voluntary partnerships.

Some of the most critical items for inclusion on the global agenda that are now being discussed at the international level (ECLAC and UNEP 2001; United Nations 2002) include the need to modify unsustainable consumption and production patterns in both industrial and developing countries. In this connection, energy efficiency is certainly one of the core issues on the agenda. Clearly, one of the goals in this regard has to be the formation of a world alliance for the use of renewable energy sources and clean, energy-efficient conventional technologies. The Kyoto Protocol is the ideal multilateral instrument for driving this strategy forward. The recent agreements reached at Bonn and Marrakesh, which elaborate upon the protocol, provide grounds for cautious optimism regarding the implementation of the clean development mechanism, which, with some conspicuous exceptions, has received the support of the international community. This mechanism represents the first material expression of a market for global environmental services, which should be expanded upon in this and other fields in the future. The negotiation of energy agreements should form part of a broader range of activities designed to promote ecoefficiency and the use of clean technologies at the global level. Progress in this area can be furthered by commitments on the part of transnational corporations to help work toward these goals, the extension of voluntary international standards (ISO 14000), technology transfers to developing countries, and assistance for SMEs. Individual firms should take on greater responsibilities in this regard, and technological development programs should be carried out to enhance the productivity and competitiveness of developing-country industries. Further efforts should also be made to promote the design of environmentally friendly products; the corresponding labeling system; and other transparent, verifiable, and nondiscriminatory means of providing information to consumers, while taking care not to let these initiatives be used as hidden trade barriers.

Another important sphere of action is the sustainable management of ecosystems and biodiversity. In this case the idea would be to form a global partnership to build a stronger worldwide commitment to the *in situ* conservation of biodiversity and the relevant ecosystems and to prevent their degradation. Such a partnership should operate within a framework that combines the principles underlying the global stewardship of terrestrial and marine environments with quantitative targets and specified means for achieving those aims and should be guided by the core objectives of the Convention on Biological Diversity, the International Convention to Combat Desertification, and the Global Programme for the Protection of the Marine Environment. In order to ensure the effective implementation of these initiatives, a multinational clearing house and fund should be set up to finance the conservation and restoration of ecosystems and to identify the global environmental services generated by high-priority natural marine and terrestrial ecosystems. This will also entail generating synergies among multinational and regional instruments and conventions dealing with the protection and sustainable use of biodiversity and ecosystems, including the Collaborative Partnership on Forests.[13]

In relation to the issue of genetic resources, the Cartagena Protocol on Biosafety should be ratified, and approved mechanisms for assessing the possible risk to biodiversity posed by the introduction of genetically engineered living organisms should be implemented. Over the past decade, biotechnology has become a major industry that plays a strategic role in enhancing competitiveness. However, innovations in this field have been the preserve of the private sector in industrial countries and are protected by intellectual property rights. This means that the vast majority of developing countries have limited access to these innovations, whose potential risks are an additional source of growing concern. The Cartagena Protocol provides an international regulatory framework in this area that reconciles trade protection with environmental protection. It is also the first multilateral treaty to institutionalize the precautionary principle and establish an advance informed agreement procedure to ensure that countries have the information they need to decide whether to import modern biotechnology products. Nonetheless, equitable technology-transfer mechanisms designed to enable developing countries, particularly megadiversity countries, to participate actively in this emerging market have yet to be established.

Such mechanisms can be developed only if adequate financing for sustainable development can be ensured. To this end, operational strategies are needed for mobilizing global resources to address global problems based on the principle of common but differentiated responsibilities. The possibility of imposing international levies on environmentally harmful activities should be explored; the revenues obtained from such levies could be paid into special funds that could then be used to find multilateral solutions for those problems. One possible means of achieving this would be to apply instruments similar to the clean development mechanism in other fields of activity. This approach could be used to develop genuine global markets for environmental services based on a flexible interpretation of principle 16 of the Rio Declaration on Environment and Development (the "polluter pays" principle) that would permit mitigation actions to be carried out in geographic locations other than the pollution site.

Education, research, development, technology transfer and adaptation, and information access will play an increasingly vital role in the achievement of sustainability. Given the existing evidence of the world's increasing ecological fragility owing to cumulative environmental damage on a variety of scales, the precautionary principle is taking on new meaning. Environmental protection efforts are no longer enough; the need for adaptation and mitigation and, above all, for scientific and technological developments to meet new challenges is constantly on the rise. Within this context, mechanisms for protecting intellectual property—including both formal knowledge and informal traditional knowledge—are of particular importance.

The foregoing considerations underscore the need for greater coherence and compatibility between the international trading system (including the protection of intellectual property) and the cause of sustainable development. The declaration issued at the fourth World Trade Organization (WTO) Ministerial Meeting at Doha (November 2001) represents a major stride forward in this respect, as it explicitly acknowledges the need to analyze the interrelationship between WTO rules and multilateral environmental agreements. It states in no uncertain terms that countries that wish to adopt measures to protect human, animal, or plant health and the environment may do so provided that such provisions do not constitute discriminatory trade practices or hidden protectionism. In addition, it identifies priority issues for consideration by the WTO Committee on Trade and Environment, including the effect of environmental measures on market access, especially in relation to developing countries; the relevant provisions of the Agreement on Trade-Related Aspects of Intellectual Property Rights; and labeling requirements for environmental purposes.

Lastly, globalization is giving rise to new imperatives in the area of global environmental management and, consequently, international cooperation. On the one hand, it prompts governments to adopt a proactive stance at the international level that provides for the use of innovative multilateral arrangements to protect global environmental goods and services. On the other, it encourages the private sector to take the lead in this effort, especially in relation to certain multilateral environmental agreements and their protocols. The issue of governance for sustainable development is of tremendous international interest in this connection. In particular, urgent action is needed to bolster the U.N. system's capacity to meet the challenges of sustainable development on the basis of coordination agreements and joint programming mechanisms that will enable the system to move beyond piecemeal approaches and forge close links with regional and subregional organizations, as well as multilateral credit institutions.

The Correction of Financial and Macroeconomic Asymmetries

Apart from the systemic issues relating to global macroeconomic and financial stability that have been discussed in earlier sections, international financial reform efforts should focus on correcting basic financial and macroeconomic asymmetries in the global economic system. This task should be addressed on a comprehensive basis that includes macroeconomic surveillance, the regulation of capital flows, the provision of liquidity during crises, the design of multilateral schemes for dealing with debt overhangs, measures for strengthening multilateral development banks, and the achievement of a new consensus regarding the scope of conditionality. The aims of this comprehensive effort should be to reduce the segmentation and volatility of developing countries' access to international financial resources and to provide greater scope for the adoption of countercyclical macroeconomic policies by developing countries.

A comprehensive approach of this nature suggests that macroeconomic surveillance actions taken by the IMF and complementary regional institutions should be oriented toward prevention—that is, toward preventing the accumulation of imbalances and high-risk debt profiles during economic booms. Programs undertaken by the IMF in conjunction with multilateral banks and with the Bank for International Settlements to support the formation of more solid financial systems in developing countries are a key component of this task. Clear incentives should also be provided for compliance with strict, prevention-oriented macroeconomic and financial standards, particularly with regard to automatic access to IMF contingent credit lines during crises. For development banks, this approach will entail the design of credit lines for the express purpose of encouraging developing countries to adopt countercyclical forms of economic management.[14]

From the regulatory standpoint of the industrial countries, the main objective should be to reduce the risk associated with operations involving countries whose net borrowings (especially of short-term resources) are disproportionate to the size of their economies and financial sectors. The objective is to discourage high-risk financing at its source. This effort may require the application of special standards to financial operations with developing countries, rather than the general types of standards that have been developed with industrial markets in mind. More specifically, rating agencies' risk assessments should not be used for regulatory purposes; on the contrary, these agencies should themselves be regulated and should be required to rate sovereign risk on the basis of objective, publicly known criteria.

Developing countries should, for their part, maintain full autonomy in the management of their capital accounts. International financial institutions should analyze regulatory experiences in this area very carefully and should encourage countries to take steps to constrain external borrowing during booms whenever it becomes apparent that such booms or the countries' current account deficits are unsustainable.

Meanwhile, the IMF should gradually evolve into a quasi-lender of last resort at the international level. This entails the use of special drawing rights (SDRs) as the main instrument for financing its operations. The additional demand for Fund resources during crises should be met with temporary issues of SDRs rather than by means of the existing arrangements to borrow, which are made available at the discretion of a handful of industrial countries. In the long run, SDRs should be used as a multilateral tool for meeting additional liquidity requirements associated with the growth of the world economy.

In implementing adjustment programs during crises, the authorities should take account of how they will affect the most vulnerable sectors of the population. The application of this principle, which has gained growing international acceptance in recent years, should extend beyond the creation of social safety nets to include the design of macroeconomic adjustment policies themselves. This approach will help ensure a policy mix having the least possible social impact on the poorer sectors of the population (United Nations 2001).

In order to deal with problems of moral hazard, preventive macroeconomic surveillance and a sound regulatory scheme will be needed. An additional element that is not yet part of the international order would be a suitable mechanism for handling debt overhangs. Although such schemes may be used to manage liquidity problems, there are other, more effective tools that have been used in the past for this purpose. One approach is for the regulatory authorities in industrial countries to bring pressure to bear on banks to keep the relevant countries' lines of short-term credit open. This should, in any case, be the aim of IMF emergency financing. In fact, in the absence of a good emergency financing scheme, problems of liquidity may turn into problems of insolvency. This is why debt workout mechanisms, whose main purpose is the management of solvency problems, should be seen as a supplement rather than as a substitute for emergency financing.

The chief components of this new mechanism should be the following:

• collective action clauses to facilitate negotiations with creditors; these clauses should be universally applied to avoid creating a new factor of discrimination against developing countries.
• an internationally sanctioned (perhaps by the IMF) standstill mechanism.
• voluntary negotiations among the parties regarding public and private external liabilities. These negotiations could be backed up by mediation—and perhaps international arbitration—mechanisms administered either by a new agency or by a panel of experts convened by the IMF.
• preference in the restructuring process for private financing extended during crisis periods and, in some cases, a requirement that additional resources be provided.
• credit from multilateral lending agencies during renegotiations and the period immediately following their conclusion. The focus should be on expediting the countries' re-entry into private capital markets; the most suitable instrument for this purpose may be a system of guarantees backed up by a special fund to be managed by the major development banks.[15]

Maintaining a strong multilateral development banking system is another component of this strategy. These banks have proved to be very important not only in guaranteeing financing to countries lacking access to financial markets, especially the poorer nations, but also in providing long-term financing to middle-income countries when credit on private markets dries up. The countercyclical role played by multilateral lenders—which includes support for programs to protect the most vulnerable sectors of the population during crises—should not be confused with the provision of liquidity, which is the central objective of IMF actions. A more active use of guarantees to leverage private resources during these periods may be the appropriate instrument in this context. Multilateral banks perform a number of other functions as well: the promotion of innovative activities, especially in relation to social development and private participation in infrastructure projects; support for financial deepening in developing countries and for national development banks' efforts to promote that process; technical assistance in general; and support for the provision of global public goods in coordination with U.N. bodies.

The final element in this integral approach is a new international agreement as to the scope of conditionality. The aim here is to provide a strong foundation in international practices for macroeconomic and development policy ownership. Some progress has been made in this respect, as indicated by the analysis and discussion of this question that occurred within the IMF in 2001. As noted earlier, however, new forms of conditionality sometimes lurk behind words of support for the concept of ownership; hence the importance of an explicit international agreement on this question. Given the tendency for homogeneous views to predominate within international lending agencies, a public debate regarding their visions of development is an essential control mechanism and an important exercise in order to make the diverse range of development options a reality (Stiglitz 1999). Even with such a debate, however, a greater plurality of views within these institutions may well be necessary in order to counter the strong inclination toward institutional homogenization exhibited by these agencies over the past two decades.

Overcoming Production and Technological Asymmetries

The transmission of production and technological impulses from the industrial world to developing countries involves two basic processes: (a) the gradual transference of raw material production, mature industries, and demand for standardized services to developing countries and (b) technology transfer and developing countries' increasing participation in its generation and in higher-technology branches and activities of production. The international trade agenda should be directed toward the first of these aims, but in the long run, it is the second type of process that will lead to the actual elimination of international asymmetries.

The main items on the trade agenda are well known (Third World Network 2001; UNCTAD 1999; World Bank 2002a). The first is a broad liberalization of world agricultural trade that includes a phaseout of export subsidies, a substantial reduction in the sizeable production subsidies provided in industrial countries, the lowering of tariffs on these products, and the gradual elimination of the tariff-quota system (which, in practice, amounts to a system of quantitative restrictions). The second is the successful dismantling of the Multifibre Arrangement provided for in the Uruguay Round agreements, together with the reduction of tariff peaks and tariff escalation based on processing levels. The third is the industrial countries' liberalization of the supply of labor-intensive services (e.g., construction and tourism) in order to permit temporary migration by all categories of labor for the provision of those services. The fourth is the establishment of stricter multilateral antidumping disciplines and guarantees of full observance of the ban on voluntary export restrictions agreed upon in the Uruguay Round.

In addition to these priority objectives, steps need to be taken to ensure broader participation by developing countries in the design of technical standards of all sorts and to facilitate a wider use of WTO dispute settlement mechanisms, whose development was one of the most important improvements made in the multilateral order in the 1990s. Because of the high cost of maintaining negotiating teams and of using the institutional mechanisms that have been established, all of this depends on the proper organization of the smaller and poorer countries' technical teams, on the existence of legal instruments to backstop dispute settlement procedures involving these countries, and on the provision of multilateral resources to finance these procedures.

Above and beyond all these considerations, the international community must realize that strategies for creating systemic competitiveness are a key component of development processes. To this end, the Uruguay Round maintained certain degrees of freedom for import substitution (by means of specified levels of protection and the infant industry principle) and for adjustments in such industries to cope with competition (safeguards), but it significantly reduced the scope of action for middle-income countries' export promotion policies. Disciplines were established for export subsidies, and trade-related investment measures were prohibited (performance agreements and local content rules), which reduced the degree of discretionality in the active promotion of "infant export industries" and export diversification in general. As in other fields, as a general rule the agreements tend to allow the types of subsidies most commonly used by industrial countries (subsidies for technology, regional development, environmental protection) while restricting those most frequently used by developing countries (free trade zones, direct subsidies for export activities, performance agreements). Although the conversion of incentives to bring them into line with the results of the Uruguay Round should continue to be a priority for developing countries, the discussion of policy options available to the countries, especially for diversifying their exportable supply, should be accorded a high priority in the Development Round that began in Doha in late 2001.[16]

Multilateral talks on trade in goods and services are being pursued in Latin America and the Caribbean concurrently with a number of other negotiation processes that are being conducted with industrial countries by the region as a whole, by subregional blocs, and on a bilateral basis. Negotiations with the United States and Canada and the talks being held with the European Union are cases in point. These processes are particularly important because they aim to move beyond the bounds of the preferential schemes existing for various subregions (which, by definition, do not constitute permanent commitments) in order to ensure untrammeled access to the major industrial markets. These negotiations also cover other issues, most notably the protection of investment and intellectual property.

In line with the above considerations, the respective agreements should guarantee the achievement of the priority trade objectives discussed here, while also maintaining the developing countries' autonomy in the adoption of active competition policies focusing, in particular, on the diversification of the export base. Issues relating to the protection of intellectual property will be discussed in a later section.

The Free Trade Area of the Americas is the most ambitious initiative in this area; its goal is to create the world's largest zone of this type. In addition, it will encompass countries of widely varying levels of development and size. From a strictly commercial standpoint, because average tariff levels in the United States are already quite low (under 2 percent as of 2000) and nearly three-fourths of the region's exports enter the U.S. market duty free (ECLAC 2002b), the greatest potential gains for the Latin American and Caribbean countries would be the rollback of tariffs on some heavily protected products (agricultural products, textiles, and apparel, in particular) and, most importantly, the elimination of nontariff barriers, such as the discretionary use of antidumping provisions.

It will be important to make sure that this agreement includes special provisions to accommodate the widely varying levels of development and sizes of the signatory countries' economies, both during the transition period and once it is fully implemented. In the first phase, a decisive element will be the provision of technical assistance and funding for the re-engineering of production activities so that they can meet the challenges posed by the agreement. In the second, it is important for the countries of the region to maintain the necessary autonomy to adopt active competition policies.

The evidence presented in the preceding chapters indicates that free trade is not in itself enough to guarantee convergence of the countries' levels of development. Past experience suggests that at least two other types of policies are also necessary. Both, it should be said, have played a significant role in the past in bringing about the convergence of income levels in industrial countries and in the most comprehensive integration process undertaken by the United States with a Latin American economy (i.e., the case of Puerto Rico; see box 5.1). The first type of policy would facilitate greater international mobility for labor, which will be discussed later in this chapter. The second is a policy of transferring resources from the more advanced regions to the less

Box 5.1 Economic Links between Puerto Rico and the United States

The Puerto Rican and U.S. economies are closely integrated. Puerto Rico shares a common citizenship, defense force, currency, and market with the United States, and there is free movement of goods and factors of production between the two.

The basic pillars of the development strategy known as Operation Bootstrap that Puerto Rico launched in the 1940s were tax incentives, federal tax credits on income earned by U.S. corporations on the island (section 936 of the U.S. Internal Revenue Code, which is now being phased out), and free trade. Encouraged by these tax incentives, many corporations operating in Puerto Rico chose to retain their profits and deposit them with financial institutions on the island, thereby providing an important source of liquidity for financial intermediaries. A decade ago, these resources were deposited in 936 funds amounting to about US$10 billion and represented around one-third of total commercial bank deposits. By 2000 these funds made up less than 6 percent of total deposits.

Federal transfers have also played a key role in Puerto Rico's economy, although their relative size has been declining over time. In 2000 total federal transfers were equivalent to 20 percent of GDP. Transfers to individuals amounted to US$5.5 billion, or 14.3 percent of personal income (down from 22 percent in 1990). About 60 percent of these transfers to individuals were earned benefits, including veteran's pensions, Medicare, and social security payments. Grants, which consist primarily of payments made under the food stamp program, amounted to 39 percent of transfers to individuals.

In addition to trade and capital flows, labor also moves freely between Puerto Rico and the United States. In 1950, Puerto Rico's resident population amounted to 2.2 million, and 226,000 Puerto Ricans who had been born on the island were living in U.S. cities. By 2000 these figures had risen to 3.8 million and 1.2 million, respectively.

Operation Bootstrap spurred robust industrial growth that transformed Puerto Rico from an agriculture-driven economy into a manufacturing- and services-driven economy. Between 1950 and 1990, the island's GDP grew by 4.4 percent a year, and the manufacturing sector's share of total output expanded from 22 percent to 39 percent. Convergence of living standards has, nonetheless, moved ahead at no more than a moderate pace. By 1990, per capita income in Puerto Rico (US$6,000) was almost half that of Mississippi, which was then the state with the lowest income; this was, nevertheless, an improvement over 1950, when Puerto Rico's per capita income had been 39 percent of that of the lowest-ranking state. As of 2000, however, per capita income in Puerto Rico (US$10,150) was still around half that of Mississippi.

developed ones for the express purpose of bringing about a convergence of development levels. In the case of Puerto Rico, this policy also
included generous tax incentives for investment on the island,
although the results of this measure have been modest.

The European Union has clearly been the international arena in
which this principle has been upheld most forcefully, thanks to the
Union's social cohesion policy. It is symptomatic of the political phi-
losophy underlying these accords that the deepening of economic integration processes seen during the final decade of the 20th century was
accompanied by the increased use of an explicit policy of cohesion
(Marín 1999). What is more, this policy now also embraces the Central European countries that hope to join the European Union. The
possibility of setting up a cohesion or integration fund to provide the
necessary backing for hemispheric agreements was put forward by
a number of heads of state at the Summit of the Americas held in
Quebec in April 2001[17] and therefore warrants special attention.

The expansion of the WTO negotiating agenda to include new issues
has been the subject of a great deal of debate. ECLAC fully acknowledges the need for the region to make a firm commitment to the international environmental agenda, the enforcement of fundamental labor
rights and principles, and the International Covenant on Economic,
Social and Cultural Rights. It also, however, shares the view that such
commitments pertain to other spheres of international action and
should not be linked to commitments relating to international trade.

A multilateral investment agreement could help to simplify the complex network of bilateral and regional accords that have been signed
in the past few years, but it would need to meet three basic requirements: (a) its scope would have to be confined to protecting investment; (b) it would have to preserve the developing countries' autonomy in regulating their capital accounts for macroeconomic purposes;
and (c) it would have to maintain their autonomy in adopting active
policies on FDI, including policies designed to improve the linkages
between FDI and national production. Another useful step would be the
conclusion of a global competition agreement that would rein in the
strong trend toward international concentration in certain activities
and branches of production, as well as the anticompetitive practices of
some large transnational corporations.[18] A mechanism of this type
might also serve as a framework for the development of substitutes for
more discretionary forms of intervention (such as antidumping provisions). It is not certain, however, that WTO would be the most suitable framework for the negotiation of multilateral investment or competition agreements, and it is even more debatable whether it would be
the appropriate agency to implement agreements in these fields. It may
well be preferable to create a new international organization that, in

addition to agreements in these two areas, could also be responsible for implementing agreements on intellectual property and trade-related investment. WTO could then focus exclusively on the regulation of trade in goods and services.

Another controversial aspect of the Uruguay Round agreements has been the application of multilateral intellectual property disciplines to all WTO members. Although this agreement may appear to be essential to ensure the provision of a global public good (the creation of technological knowledge), the fact remains that this can only be accomplished through the concession of a temporary monopoly—that is, by defining, for a specific period, what is potentially a public good as a private good. Because technological development is the activity that is most highly concentrated in industrial countries, this form of protection—and the redistribution of income that it entails—reinforces one of the basic asymmetries existing in the international economy.

Given the high cost that this mechanism may have for developing countries, the World Bank (2002a) recently stated that its benefits for low-income countries are not clear and that the agreement should therefore be implemented gradually and in accordance with each country's level of development. Middle-income countries derive benefits from greater protection of intellectual property for appellations of origin, for intraindustry trade that relies on trademark protection, for cinematographic and television productions, for software, and in a number of other cases. This type of protection is also important in providing guarantees for foreign investment and in ensuring that consumers will have secure access to a wide range of quality products. At the same time, however, the protection of intellectual property raises the cost of technology and may block technology transfers if the country affording such protection does not produce the good or use the technology in question.

The agreements reached at the fourth WTO Ministerial Conference represent a major stride forward in the definition of one of the cases—public health—in which the net effects of the protection of intellectual property can be quite harmful. The main problem in this case is that protection can drive up consumer prices so much that large sectors of the population cannot afford the goods or services in question. This case serves to illustrate a broader principle: that the definition of knowledge as a public good should, under certain circumstances, prevail over its definition as a private good for the purpose of intellectual property protection.

This observation opens the door for a broader discussion of fields in which the public good represented by knowledge should predominate. Some of the most obvious cases are those in which potentially patentable knowledge is scientific knowledge in a strict sense (certain types of knowledge about genetics, in particular) or in which access to certain types of knowledge is the basis for the acquisition of new knowledge (this principle is recognized, for example, in the International Convention for the Protection of New Varieties of Plants, which guarantees access to protected varieties for use as breeding stock for the development of other new varieties). Actually, inasmuch as technological development is the result of a cumulative learning process and relies heavily on acquired experience in the production domain, this last case is part of a larger set of instances that include secondary innovations derived from the adaptation of technology and reverse engineering.

The problem that arises in such cases is all the more serious when a country's priorities for diversifying its production activities conflict with the protection of intellectual property owned by firms that do not produce the protected good or that do not use the protected technology in that country. In such instances, this type of protection is a real obstacle. In these cases, as in that of public health, either a new consensus has to be reached regarding limitations on the protection of intellectual property, or else more comprehensive regulations will have to be designed concerning the use of compulsory licenses or the expiration of intellectual property rights.

Another series of problems is related to particular aspects of the intellectual property rights agenda that are of special interest to developing countries but that have not been properly applied or set down in agreements. One such problem is raised by the need for effective technology transfer mechanisms and means of ensuring greater participation by developing countries in the generation of new knowledge. WTO should accord priority to devising these kinds of mechanisms and instruments, because they are needed to counterbalance the adverse distributive effects produced at the global level by the protection of intellectual property. Another problem refers to the relationship between the protection of intellectual property and the Convention on Biological Diversity and to the protection of traditional knowledge, including folklore. These considerations also draw attention to the pressing need for the countries of the region to take an inventory of the resources they wish to protect at the international level in order to defend their cultural, intellectual, genetic, and geographic heritage.

The Full Inclusion of Migration on the International Agenda

The full incorporation of the issue of migration on the international agenda is another important element in the formation of an international system capable of overcoming the asymmetries of the global order. There is no theoretical justification whatsoever for liberalizing goods, services, and capital markets while continuing to apply stringent restrictions to the international mobility of labor. Moreover, asymmetric market liberalization has a regressive impact at the global level, because it works to the benefit of the more mobile factors of production (capital and skilled labor) and to the detriment of the less mobile factors (unskilled labor). This constraint also nullifies one of the mechanisms that historical studies identify as having played a fundamental role in the convergence of income levels in today's industrial countries (see chapter 4). In addition, placing greater restrictions on the mobility of unskilled labor selectively siphons off human capital from developing countries, tends to accentuate skills-based income inequalities, and sets the stage for one of the most harmful industries in the world of today: the smuggling of migrants and other persons. Apart from its significance as an economic factor, migration is a very important source of mutual cultural enrichment and contributes to the formation of a cosmopolitan society.

One of the priority items on the international agenda should therefore be to forge agreements that will increase labor mobility and strengthen the governance of international migration. The main objective should be the conclusion of a global agreement on migration policy. The scope of existing instruments is, for the most part, quite limited. The broadest instrument of this type is the International Convention on the Protection of the Rights of Migrant Workers and Members of Their Families, which was adopted by the United Nations General Assembly in 1990. After more than a decade, the condition for its entry into force was met on March 14, 2003, with the deposit of the twentieth instrument of ratification by Guatemala. Six other Latin American and Caribbean countries had previously ratified the Convention (Belize, Bolivia, Colombia, Ecuador, Mexico, and Uruguay). The importance of this Convention, which entered into force on July 1, 2003, lies in its reaffirmation of the fundamental human rights of migrant workers and their families, including those who lack proper documentation. It also provides states with a legal instrument that facilitates the standardization of national legislation.

A closely related element is the reduction of the risks associated with discrimination and xenophobia through ratification of the relevant international instruments and compliance with the plan of action signed at the World Conference against Racism, Racial Discrimination, Xenophobia and Related Intolerance, held in Durban, South Africa, in 2001.

Broadening the commitments made in regard to the temporary mobility of workers within the framework of the WTO General Agreement on Trade in Services is another important objective. As stated earlier, one of the priorities in this area is to secure greater commitments on the part of industrial countries with respect to services that are intensive in low-skilled labor, in which developing countries may have comparative advantages.

There is no question that migration issues should be included on the hemispheric agenda, in multilateral agreements reached between the Latin American and Caribbean region and the European Union, and in regional integration processes. There are also a wide range of bilateral conventions and negotiations that can help to increase opportunities for international migration. One promising example is the recent opening of a dialogue between Mexico and the United States on this subject. All of these multilateral and bilateral agreements should seek to increase temporary and permanent labor mobility and to move forward on issues closely related to migration, such as social security and the accreditation of individuals' academic and professional or vocational qualifications.

In addition to their efforts to do away with xenophobia and discrimination and to guarantee immigrants' rights, host-country governments should take steps to help migrants become fully integrated into society. This is, in fact, essential in order to ensure the social cohesion of societies in which there are a large number of immigrants. To this end, states should set up mechanisms in such areas as public education and social services to facilitate immigrants' integration into society and thus help them to exercise their economic and social rights. The other side of the coin is that immigrants should respect and embrace their host culture and should fully comply with the host country's laws.

The home countries of migrants can also benefit from this process in various ways. First of all, they receive remittances, which have become an important source of capital flows for many countries of the region. Reducing remittance transfer costs, promoting programs that provide emigrants with means of contributing to their home communities, and using these resources in productive ways are some of the types of action that could be taken on this front. Links with emigrants can also be used to give their home countries the benefit of their scientific, professional, and entrepreneurial skills, as well as to create a market for idiosyncratic products. The countries of the region should also recognize the right of emigrants to take part in their home countries' political processes.

Finally, it is the responsibility of home and host countries to work together to combat the smuggling of migrants. Their efforts in this area should include communication programs in communities of origin to warn the population of the dangers of such practices.

Economic, Social, and Cultural Rights: The Foundations for Global Citizenship

One of the main advances associated with the globalization process in recent decades has been the worldwide propagation of values or principles such as respect for human rights, equity, democracy, respect for ethnic and cultural diversity, and environmental protection. Some of the most important principles relating specifically to social development are those set forth in the International Covenant on Economic, Social and Cultural Rights, whose signatories are committed to guaranteeing their citizens a set of goods and services regarded as essential in order for them to lead decent lives. The Covenant identifies the formulation of an international social agenda with the recognition of all members of global society as citizens and, hence, as possessing certain rights. Viewed from another vantage point, the goods and services required to obtain a basic level of well-being are both rights and commodities—"merit goods," to use the terminology of welfare economics. Accordingly, the provision of such goods should be subject to regulation, the actual level of supply should be made public, and claims on such goods should be enforceable (ECLAC 2000a). This process should be regarded as the core element of a holistic poverty reduction program.

Economic, social, and cultural rights, together with civil and political rights, form an indivisible, interdependent whole. It is recognized, however, that the exercise of economic, social, and cultural rights is not automatic and that their progressive enforcement will require a determined economic and political effort. Such efforts should match those actions required under national democratic processes to determine what level of nutrition, health care, education, housing, and other rights or merit goods can be supplied on a sustainable basis to all citizens; what (public, private, or mixed) schemes should be used to deliver them; and what level of public resources will be needed to do so.

This necessarily entails a political process leading to the formation of national—but increasingly global—social and fiscal covenants in which access to such goods is seen as the result of a political decision regarding the allocation of resources for guaranteeing citizens' economic, social, and cultural rights. These covenants should be shaped by a political debate on the role of the state and the relationship between economic policy and social development—a debate that can ultimately result in a consensus on the relevant priorities and what pace of progress toward the gradual achievement of those rights is feasible.[19]

Upholding these rights continues to be an essentially national responsibility, however. No clearly defined, stable international policies or mechanisms have yet been devised that would allow countries' aspirations or accomplishments to transcend their national boundaries. Moreover, guaranteeing such rights is the job of the state and does not explicitly involve other important agents, such as business enterprises. Finally, there is thus far no clear incentive for the enforcement of these rights or methods to ensure their application.

Consequently, the enforceability of economic, social, and cultural rights needs to be gradually shifted from regional and national evaluations to a much more clearly defined political enforceability within the context of international forums and, most importantly, representative national forums where international assessments of the countries' fulfillment of their commitments can be discussed. This type of evaluation should be a comprehensive one that includes not only these rights, but also other internationally recognized social rights (the Fundamental Principles and Rights at Work agreed upon within the framework of the International Labour Organization and the rights of children, women, and ethnic groups) and the commitments made at world summits dealing with closely related issues. This political enforceability may gradually lead, under certain conditions, to a legal enforceability in the context of the relevant national and international courts. The commitments undertaken and their enforceability must at all times be commensurate with each country's level of development and, in particular, its ability to achieve target levels that can be effectively guaranteed for all its citizens, thus avoiding the emergence of voluntarism or populism.

Given the sharp inequalities and asymmetries of the global order, an essential element in the material expression of such rights is the fulfillment of the ODA commitments made within the framework of the United Nations (0.7 percent of industrial countries' GDP, with a minimum of 0.15–0.20 percent of GDP going to the least developed countries) and adherence to the basic guidelines agreed upon by the international community (i.e., the importance of placing priority on the effort to combat poverty and ownership of economic and social development strategies). Within this context, development cooperation should be regarded as a means of supporting rights-based efforts to build democracy, promote civil and political rights, and eliminate poverty. International undertakings such as the "20/20 initiative" are an important step in this direction.[20] Because a global effort of this magnitude will clearly take quite some time to complete, regional or subregional integration programs can serve as a much-needed intermediate stage in the process.

The responsibility for upholding rights and for their development and application transcends national boundaries and the purview of the state, however. Partnerships will therefore have to be formed with many different actors. Awareness of this fact within the United Nations has led to the formulation of the Global Compact, which calls upon the entrepreneurial sector in all countries to uphold human rights in business practices and to support suitable public policies on human rights, basic labor rights, and environmental protection.[21] This type of initiative, together with other undertakings on the part of civil society, can contribute to the consolidation of a genuine rights-based culture, which is the very essence of global citizenship.

Notes

1. The dividing line between public goods, which are nonexcludable in consumption, and those with strong externalities is somewhat blurred, and this list therefore includes some goods (e.g., public spaces, many forms of cultural expression and human knowledge) that do not fit the classic definition of public goods.

2. The right to development was enshrined in U.N. General Assembly resolution 41/128 of December 4, 1986. This resolution defines development as "a comprehensive economic, social, cultural and political process, which aims at the constant improvement of the well-being of the entire population and of all individuals on the basis of their active, free and meaningful participation in development and in the fair distribution of benefits resulting therefrom." Sengupta (2001) focused on the components of justice and equity inherent in this concept and on the importance of making sure that countries' growth rates are not only reasonable but also sustainable and are not achieved at the cost of human rights or a decline in opportunities for personal fulfillment. See, in this regard, Artigas (2001).

3. Kant (1795) called for the formation—based on a covenant among states—of a cosmopolitan society. Kant was one of the first philosophers to propose that the social contract be extended to include states, provided that they complied with the "republican clause" by guaranteeing individual rights and freedoms, the division of power, the supremacy of the law, and a representative system of government.

4. See, for example, Culpeper (2000) regarding the proliferation of groups or associations dealing with financial issues.

5. To use the terms Maddison (1991) used, these factors are associated with the "ultimate causality" rather than the "proximate causality" of economic growth. See also Ocampo (2002c).

6. This may, in fact, be the major lesson to be learned from Argentina's experiences over the past decade.

7. Direct regulatory tools include rules on borrowing by public-sector agencies at all levels and direct restrictions on certain types of private flows (short-term borrowing, portfolio flows, or external borrowing by nontradable sectors).

8. These concepts also contain elements developed concurrently by other authors; see, in particular, Porter (1990).

9. See Berry (1992) for a discussion of this topic.

10. There are, in fact, agreements on individual and collective guarantees for migrants, modalities of representation of corporate interests (businesspeople, workers, professionals, consumers), labor mobility and provision of health services in border areas, standardization of educational and professional credentials, and validation of pensions.

11. The participants in the conference adopted Agenda 21, the Rio Declaration on Environment and Development; the Non-Legally Binding Authoritative Statement of Principles for a Global Consensus on the Management, Conservation and Sustainable Development of All Types of Forests; the Convention on Biological Diversity; and the Framework Convention on Climate Change.

12. This is particularly evident in the Kyoto and Cartagena Protocols and in the Rotterdam and Stockholm Conventions.

13. See the report of the Secretary General to the Commission on Sustainable Development acting as the preparatory committee for the World Summit on Sustainable Development (E/CN.17/2002/PC.2/7), December 19, 2001.

14. One of the possible options would be lines of credit incorporating accelerated amortization clauses based on specified macroeconomic variables, in which national counterpart funds are "saved" in the banks during booms and are then disbursed, together with the development banks' contributions, during crises.

15. For a more exhaustive discussion of this topic, see Krueger (2001), Machinea (2002), and UNCTAD (1998, 2001a).

16. In paragraph 10.2 of the Doha decision on implementation-related issues and concerns, the Ministerial Conference "takes note of the proposal to treat measures implemented by developing countries with a view to achieving legitimate development goals, such as regional growth, technology research and development funding, production diversification and development and implementation of environmentally sound methods of production as non-actionable subsidies." Strictly speaking, the only major restriction in the Uruguay Round agreements is the provision relating to the diversification of production and, more specifically, of exportable supply, because subsidies for the other purposes identified therein are broadly authorized in the Marrakesh Agreement.

17. The president of Mexico made particular reference to the possibility of a cohesion fund, and a number of prime ministers from the Caribbean drew attention to the importance of having an integration fund. The government of Ecuador, which was responsible for coordinating the negotiations until October 2002, later proposed that a fund should be established to promote competitiveness.

18. A *de minimis* clause could be introduced to stipulate that the relevant agreement applies only to firms that have international market shares above a given percentage.

19. One of the priority courses of action in this regard is the compilation, dissemination, and analysis of information on the status of economic, social, cultural, and other rights and the fulfillment of goals agreed upon at world summits with a view to setting priorities, creating a culture of responsibility, and bringing about policy changes.

20. For an evaluation of this initiative as it relates to the countries of the region, see Ganuza, León, and Sauma (2000).

21. For more information, see www.unglobalcompact.org.

References

The word "processed" describes informally reproduced works that may not be commonly available through libraries.

Abreu, Marcelo de Paiva. 1993. "Trade Policies and Bargaining in a Heavily Indebted Economy: Brazil." In Diana Tussie and Davis Glover, eds., *The Developing Countries in World Trade: Policies and Bargaining Strategies*. Boulder, Colo.: Lynne Rienner Publishers.

Aceña, Pablo Martín, and Jaime Reis, eds. 2000. *Monetary Standards in the Periphery: Paper, Silver and Gold, 1854–1933*. New York: St. Martin's Press.

Aghion, Philippe, Eve Caroli, and Cecilia García-Peñalosa. 1999. "Inequality and Economic Growth: The Perspective of the New Growth Theories." *Journal of Economic Literature* 37(4): 1615–60.

Akyüz, Yilmaz. 1998. "The East Asian Financial Crisis: Back to the Future?" In Jomo Kwame Sundaram, ed., *Tigers in Trouble: Financial Governance, Liberalisation and Crises in East Asia*. Hong Kong: Hong Kong University Press.

Albert, Michel. 1993. *Capitalism against Capitalism*. London: Whurr Publishers.

Amsden, Alice. 1989. *Asia's Next Giant: South Korea and Late Industrialization*. New York: Oxford University Press.

———. 2001. *The Rise of "The Rest": Challenges to the West from Late Industrializing Countries*. New York: Oxford University Press.

Annan, Kofi A. 2000. *We the Peoples: The Role of the United Nations in the Twenty-First Century*. A/54/2000. New York: Department of Public Information.

————. 2001. *The Nobel Lecture*. Press Release L/53/2001. December 10, Oslo, Norway.

Artigas, Carmen. 2001. *The U.N. Contribution to the Globalization of Ethical Values: Examining Some Opportunities*. Políticas Sociales series No. 54, LC/L.1597-P. U.N. Publication Sales No. S.01.II.G.138. Santiago, Chile: Economic Commission for Latin America and the Caribbean.

Atkinson, Anthony Barnes. 1996. "Income Distribution in Europe and the United States." *Oxford Review of Economic Policy* 12(1): 15–28.

————. 1999. *Is Rising Income Inequality Inevitable? A Critique of the Transatlantic Consensus*. Helsinki, Finland: United Nations University and World Institute for Development Economics Research.

Bairoch, Paul. 1981. "The Main Trends in National Economic Disparities since the Industrial Revolution." In Paul Bairoch and Maurice Lévy-Leboyer, eds., *Disparities in Economic Development since the Industrial Revolution*. London: Macmillan Press.

————. 1993. *Economics and World History: Myths and Paradoxes*. Chicago: University of Chicago Press.

Baldwin, Richard, and Philippe Martin. 1999. "Two Waves of Globalization: Superficial Similarities, Fundamental Differences." Working Paper 6904. Cambridge, Mass.: National Bureau of Economic Research.

Bank for International Settlements (BIS). 2001. *71st Annual Report*. Basel, Switzerland.

————. 2003. *Quarterly Review*. Several issues.

Barro, Robert J. 1997. *Determinants of Economic Growth: A Cross-Country Empirical Study*. Cambridge, Mass.: MIT Press.

Barro, Robert J., and Xavier Sala-i-Martin. 1995. *Economic Growth*. New York: McGraw-Hill.

Bartlett, Christopher, and Sumantra Goshal. 1989. *Managing across Borders: The Transnational Solution*. New York: McGraw-Hill.

Berry, Albert. 1992. "Firm (or Plant) Size in the Analysis of Trade and Development." In Gerald K. Helleiner, ed., *Trade Policy, Industrialization and Development: New Perspectives*. New York: United Nations University, World Institute for Development Economics Research, and Oxford University Press.

————, ed. 1998. *Poverty, Economic Reform, and Income Distribution in Latin America*. London: Lynne Rienner Publishers.

Berry, Albert, François Bourguignon, and Christian Morrison. 1983. "Changes in the World Distribution of Income between 1950 and 1977." *Economic Journal* 93: 331–50.

———. 1991. "Global Economic Inequality and Its Trends since 1950." In Lars Osberg, ed., *Economic Inequality and Poverty: International Perspectives.* New York: Sharpe.

Bielschowsky, Ricardo. 1998. "Cincuenta años de pensamiento de la CEPAL: Una reseña." In *Fifty Years of ECLAC Thought.* Santiago, Chile: Economic Commission for Latin America and the Caribbean and Fondo de Cultura Económica.

Blommestein, Hans. J. 1995. "Structural Changes in Financial Markets: Overview of Trends and Prospects." In *The New Financial Landscape: Forces Shaping the Revolution in Banking, Risk Management and Capital Markets.* Paris: Organisation for Economic Co-operation and Development.

Bourguignon, François, and Christian Morrison. 2002. "Inequality among World Citizens: 1820–1990." *The American Economic Review* 92(4): 727–44.

Braudel, Fernand. 1994. *The Dynamics of Capitalism.* Mexico City, Mexico: Fondo de Cultura Económica.

Bulmer-Thomas, Victor. 1994. *The Economic History of Latin America since Independence.* Cambridge Latin American Studies 77. New York: Cambridge University Press.

Burda, Michael C., and Barbara Dulosch. 2000. *Fragmentation, Globalization and Labor Markets.* Working Paper Series 352. Munich: CESifo.

Bustillo, Inés, and Helvia Velloso. 2002. "The U.S. Interest Rates, Latinoamerican Debt, and Financial Contagion." *Revista de la CEPAL* 78(December): 87–104.

Cairncross, Francis. 1997. *The Death of Distance: How the Communications Revolution Will Change Our Lives.* Cambridge, Mass.: Harvard Business School Press.

Calvo, Guillermo, Eduardo Fernando Arias, Carmen Reinhart, and Ernesto Talvi. 2001. "Growth and External Financing in Latin America." Paper presented at the 42nd Annual Meeting of the Board of Governors of the Inter-American Development Bank, March, Santiago, Chile.

Calvo, Guillermo, Leonardo Leideman, and Carmen Reinhart. 1992. "Capital Inflows and Real Exchange Rate Appreciation in Latin

America: The Role of External Factors." IMF Working Paper 92/62. Washington, D.C.

Cárdenas, Enrique, José Antonio Ocampo, and Rosemary Thorp, eds. 2000a. *An Economic History of Twentieth Century Latin America.* Vol. 1: *The Export Age: The Latin American Economies in the Late Nineteenth and Early Twentieth Centuries.* New York: Palgrave Press and St. Martin's Press.

———, eds. 2000b. *An Economic History of Twentieth Century Latin America.* Vol. 3: *Industrialisation and the State in Latin America: The Post War Years.* New York: Palgrave Press and St. Martin's Press.

Castles, Stephen, and Mark J. Miller. 1993. *The Age of Migration: International Population Movements in the Modern World.* New York: Guilford Press.

Chang, Ha-Joon. 1994. *The Political Economy of Industrial Policy.* London: Macmillan and St. Martin's Press.

———. 2001. "Infant Industry Promotion in Historical Perspective: A Rope to Hang Oneself or a Ladder to Climb With?" Paper presented at the conference on Development Theory at the Threshold of the Twenty-First Century," August, Economic Commission for Latin America and the Caribbean (ECLAC), Santiago, Chile.

———. 2002. "Pulling Up the Ladder? Policies and Institutions for Development in Historical Perspective." Cambridge, U.K.: Cambridge University.

Chenery, Hollis, Sherman Robinson, and Moshé Syrquin. 1986. *Industrialization and Growth: A Comparative Study.* New York: Oxford University Press.

Chesnais, François. 1993. "Globalisation, World Oligopoly and Some of Their Implications." In Marc Humbert, ed., *The Impact of Globalisation on Europe's Firms and Industries.* London: Pinter Publishers.

Cimoli, Mario, and Nelson Correa. 2002. "Trade Openness and Technological Gaps in Latin America: A Low Growth Trap." Paper presented at the conference on Innovation and Growth: New Challenges for the Regions, January 18–19, Sophia Antipolis, France.

Cimoli, Mario, and Giovanni Dosi. 1995. "Technological Paradigms, Patterns of Learning and Development: An Introductory Roadmap." *Journal of Evolutionary Economics* 5(3): 243–68.

Coatsworth, John H., and Jeffrey G. Williamson. 2002. "The Roots of Latin American Protectionism: Looking before the Great

Depression." NBER Working Paper 8999. Cambridge, Mass.: National Bureau of Economic Research.

Cornia, Giovanni Andrea. 1999. "Liberalization, Globalization and Income Distribution." Working Paper 157. Helsinki, Finland: United Nations University and World Institute for Development Economics Research.

Culpeper, Roy. 1995. "The Return of Private Capital Flows to Latin America: The Role of U.S. Investors." In Ricardo Ffrench-Davis and Stephany Griffith-Jones, eds., *The New Financial Flows to Latin America: Sources, Effects, and Policies*. Mexico City, Mexico: Fondo de Cultura Económica.

————. 2000. "The Evolution of Global Financial Governance." In Roy Culpeper and Devesh Kapur, eds., *Global Financial Reform: How? Why? When?* Ottawa, Ontario, Canada: North–South Institute.

Dam, Kenneth W. 1970. *The GATT: Law and International Organization*. Chicago: Chicago University Press.

D'Arista, Jane W., and Stephany Griffith-Jones. 2001. "The Boom of Portfolio Flows to 'Emerging Markets' and Its Regulatory Duplications." In Stephany Griffith-Jones, Manuel F. Montes, and Anwar Nasution, eds., *Short-Term Capital Flows and Economic Crises*. Oxford, U.K.: Oxford University Press.

Deininger, Klaus, and Lyn Squire. 1996. "A New Data Set Measuring Inequality." *World Bank Economic Review* 10(3): 565–91.

Demirgüç-Kunt, A., and Vokislav Maksimovic. 1998. "Law, Finance, and Firm Growth." *Journal of Finance* 53(6): 2107–37.

Di Filippo, Armando, and Rolando Franco. 2000. *Regional Integration, Development and Equity*. Mexico City, Mexico: Siglo Veintiuno Editores and Economic Commission for Latin America and the Caribbean.

Dodd, Randall. 2003. "Derivatives, the Shape of International Capital Flows and the Virtues of Prudential Regulation." In Ricardo Ffrench-Davis and Stephany Griffith-Jones, eds., *From Capital Surges to Drought: Seeking Stability for Emerging Economies*. New York: Palgrave Macmillan/UNU-WIDER.

Dosi, Giovanni. 1999. "Some Notes on National Systems of Innovation and Production, and Their Implications for Economic Analysis." In Daniele Archibugi, Jeremy Howells, and Jonathan Michie, eds., *Innovation Policy in a Global Economy*. Cambridge, U.K.: Cambridge University Press.

Dowrich, Steve, and J. Bradford DeLong. 2001. "Globalisation and Convergence." Paper presented at the National Bureau of Economic Research conference on Globalization in Historical Perspective, May 3–6, Santa Barbara, Calif.

Dunning, John H. 1993. *Multinational Enterprises and the Global Economy*. New York: Addison-Wesley.

Dussel Peters, Enrique. 2000. *Polarizing Mexico: The Impact of Liberalization Strategy*. Boulder, Colo.: Lynne Rienner Publishers.

Easterly, William. 2001a. *The Elusive Quest for Growth: Economists' Adventures and Misadventures in the Tropics*. Cambridge, Mass.: MIT Press.

———. 2001b. "The Lost Decades: Developing Countries' Stagnation in Spite of Policy Reform 1980–1998." *Journal of Economic Growth* 6(2): 135–57.

Eatwell, John, and Lance Taylor. 2000. *Global Finance at Risk: The Case for International Regulation*. New York: New Press.

ECLAC (Economic Commission for Latin America and the Caribbean). 1990. *Changing Production Patterns with Social Equity: The Prime Task of Latin America and the Caribbean Development in the 1990s*. Libros de la CEPAL series No. 25. LC/G.1601-P. U.N. Publication Sales No. E.90.II.G.6. Santiago, Chile.

———. 1992a. *Preliminary Overview of the Latin American Economy, 1992*. LC/G.1751. Santiago, Chile.

———. 1992b. *Social Equity and Changing Production Patterns: An Integrated Approach*. Libros de la CEPAL series No. 32. LC/G.1701/Rev.1-P; LC/G.1701(SES.24/3). U.N. Publication Sales No. E.92.II.G.5. Santiago, Chile.

———. 1994. *Open Regionalism in Latin America and the Caribbean: Economic Integration as a Contribution to Changing Production Patterns with Social Equity*. Libros de la CEPAL series No. 39. LC/G.1801/Rev.1-P. U.N. Publication Sales No. E.94.II.G.3. Santiago, Chile.

———. 1996a. *The Economic Experience of the Last Fifteen Years: Latin America and the Caribbean, 1980–1995*. Libros de la CEPAL series No. 43. LC/G.1925/Rev.1-P. U.N. Publication Sales No. E.96.II.G.3. Santiago, Chile.

———. 1996b. *Strengthening Development: The Interplay of Macro- and Microeconomics*. LC/G.1898/Rev.1-P. U.N. Publication Sales No. E.96.II.G.2. Santiago, Chile.

———. 1997. *The Equity Gap: Latin America, the Caribbean and the Social Summit*. Libros de la CEPAL series No. 44. LC/G.1954/Rev.1-P. U.N. Publication Sales No. E.97.II.G.11. Santiago, Chile.

———. 1998a. *Latin America and the Caribbean: Policies to Improve Linkages with Global Economy*. 2nd ed. Santiago, Chile: Fondo de Cultura Económica.

———. 1998b. *Economic Survey of Latin America and the Caribbean, 1997–1998*. LC/G.2032-P. U.N. Publication Sales No. S/E.98.II.G.2. Santiago, Chile.

———. 1998c. *The Fiscal Covenant: Strengths, Weaknesses, Challenges*. Libros de la CEPAL series No. 47. LC/G.1997/Rev.1-P. U.N. Publication Sales No. E.98.II.G.5. Santiago, Chile.

———. 2000a. *Equity, Development and Citizenship*. LC/G.2071/ Rev.1-P. U.N. Publication Sales No. E.00.II.G.81. Santiago, Chile.

———. 2000b. "The Equity Gap: A Second Assessment." LC/G.2096. Santiago, Chile.

———. 2001a. *Growth with Stability: Financing for Development in the New International Context*. Bogotá, Colombia: Economic Commission for Latin America and the Caribbean and Alfaomega.

———. 2001b. *A Decade of Lights and Shadows*. Bogotá, Colombia, and Washington, D.C.: Economic Commission for Latin America and the Caribbean and Alfaomega.

———. 2001c. *Latin America and the Caribbean in the World Economy, 1999–2000*. LC/G.2085-P. U.N. Publication Sales No. E.01.II.G.17. Santiago, Chile.

———. 2001d. *Social Panorama of Latin America and the Caribbean, 2000–2001*. LC/G.2138-P. U.N. Publication Sales No. E.01.II.G.141. Santiago, Chile.

———. 2002a. *Globalization and Development*. LC/G.2157(SES 29/3). April. Santiago, Chile.

———. 2002b. *Latin America and the Caribbean in the World Economy: 2000–2001*. LC/G.2149-P. U.N. Publication Sales No. S.02.II.G.6. Santiago, Chile.

ECLAC and United Nations Development Programme. 2002. *Financing for Sustainable Development in Latin America and the Caribbean: From Monterrey to Johannesburg*. LC/R.2098. Santiago, Chile.

ECLAC and United Nations Environment Programme. 2001. *The Sustainability of Development in Latin America and the Caribbean:*

Challenges and Opportunities. LC/G.2145(CONF.90/3). Santiago, Chile.

ECLAC and UNESCO (United Nations Educational, Scientific, and Cultural Organization). 1992. *Education and Knowledge: Basic Pillars of Changing Production Patterns with Social Equity.* LC/G.1702/Rev.1-P. Libros de la CEPAL series No. 33. U.N. Publication Sales No. E.92.II.G.6. Santiago, Chile.

The Economist. 2002. "Latin America's Politics: A Backlash Against the Free Market?" Print edition, August 15, 29–30.

Eichengreen, Barry. 1996. *Globalizing Capital: A History of the International Monetary System.* Princeton, N.J.: Princeton University Press.

Emmerij, Louis, Richard Jolly, and Thomas G. Weiss. 2001. *Ahead of the Curve? UN Ideas and Global Challenges.* Bloomington, Ind.: Indiana University Press.

Escaith, Hubert, and Samuel Morley. 2001. "The Effect of Structural Reforms on Growth in Latin America and the Caribbean: An Empirical Approach." *El Trimestre Económico* 68(4): 469–513.

Fajnzylber, Fernando. 1990. *Industrialization in Latin America: From the "Black Box" to the "Empty Box": A Comparison of Contemporary Industrialization Patterns.* Cuadernos de la CEPAL series No. 60. LC/G.1534/Rev.1-P. U.N. Publication Sales No. E.89.II.G.5. Santiago, Chile.

Feeney, Paul. W. 1994. *Securitization: Redefining the Bank.* New York: St. Martin's Press.

Feenstra, Robert C. 1998. "Integration of Trade and Disintegration of Production in the Global Economy." *Journal of Economic Perspectives* 12(4): 31–50.

Feenstra, Robert C., and Gordon H. Hanson. 2001. "Global Production Sharing and Rising Inequality: A Survey of Trade and Wages." Working Paper 8372. Cambridge, Mass.: National Bureau of Economic Research. http://www.nber.org/papers/w8372

Ffrench-Davis, Ricardo. 2000. *Reforming the Reforms in Latin America: Macroeconomics, Trade and Finance.* London: Macmillan and St. Antony's College.

Ffrench-Davis, Ricardo, and José Antonio Ocampo. 2001. "The Globalization of Financial Volatility: Challenges for Emerging Economies." In Ricardo Ffrench-Davis, ed., *Financial Crises in "Successful" Emerging Economies.* Washington, D.C.: Brookings Institution Press and Economic Commission for Latin America and the Caribbean.

Finger, J. Michael, and Ludger Schuknecht. 1999. "Market Access Advances and Retreats: The Uruguay Round and Beyond." Policy Research Working Paper 2232. Washington, D.C.: World Bank.

FitzGerald, Valpy. 2001. "International Tax Cooperation and Capital Mobility." Paper prepared for the 29th session of the Economic Commission for Latin America and the Caribbean. Processed.

Fornari, Fabio, and Aviram Levy. 1999. "Global Liquidity in the 1990s: Geographical Allocation and Long-Run Determinants." *BIS Conference Papers* 8. Available from http://www.bis.org/pub1/confer08.htm

François, Joseph F., Bradley McDonald, and Hakan Nordström. 1996. "A User's Guide to Uruguay Round Assessments." Staff Working Paper RD-96-003. Geneva: Economic Research and Analysis Division, World Trade Organization.

Franklin, R. Edwards. 1993. "Financial Markets in Transition, or the Decline of Commercial Banking." *Changing Capital Markets: Implications for Monetary Policy*. Proceedings of a conference, August 19–21, Jackson Hole, Wyoming. Kansas City, Mo.: Federal Reserve Bank of Kansas.

Freeman, Christopher. 1987. *Technology Policy and Economic Performance: Lessons from Japan*. London: Pinter Publishers.

Fujita, Masahisa, Paul Krugman, and Anthony J. Venables. 1999. *The Spatial Economy: Cities, Regions and International Trade*. Cambridge, Mass.: MIT Press.

Ganuza, Enrique, Arturo B. León, and Pablo F. Sauma. 2000. "Gasto público en servicios sociales básicos: La situación regional." *Papeles de Población* 6(24): 175–225.

GATT (General Agreement on Tariffs and Trade). 1958. "Trends in International Trade" (Haberler Report). Geneva: GATT Secretariat.

———. 1994. *The Outcomes of the Uruguay Round: The Legal Texts*. Geneva.

Gereffi, Gary. 1994. "The Organization of Buyer-Driven Global Commodity Chains: How U.S. Retailers Shape Overseas Production Networks." In Gary Gereffi and Miguel Korzeniewicz, eds., *Commodity Chains and Global Capitalism*. Westport, Conn.: Praeger.

———. 2000. *The Transformation of the North American Apparel Industry: Is NAFTA a Curse or a Blessing?* Desarrollo Productivo series No. 84. LC/L.1420-P. U.N. Publication Sales No. E.00.II.G.103. Santiago, Chile: Economic Commission for Latin America and the Caribbean.

Gerschenkron, Alexander. 1962. *Economic Backwardness in Historical Perspective: A Book of Essays*. Cambridge, Mass.: Belknap Press of Harvard University Press.

Giarini, Orio. 1999. "From the Value of Material Products to the Value of Performance." *Progress Newsletter* 29(July): 16–18.

Greenspan, Alan. 1998. "The Structure of the International Financial System." Remarks presented at the Annual Meeting of the Securities Industry Association, November 5, Boca Raton, Fla.

Griffith-Jones, Stephany, and Stephen Spratt. 2001. "The Pro-cyclical Effects of the New Basel Accord." In Jan Joost Teunissen, ed., *New Challenges of Crisis Prevention: Addressing Economic Imbalances in the North and Boom–Bust Cycles in the South*. Proceedings of the Forum on Debt and Development, December, The Hague, Netherlands.

Grossman, Gene M., and Elhanan Helpman. 1991. *Innovation and Growth in the Global Economy*. Cambridge, Mass.: MIT Press.

Group of Ten. 2001. "Report on Consolidation in the Financial Sector." Basel, Switzerland. http://www.bis.org

Grunwald, Joseph, and Kenneth Flamm. 1985. *Global Factory: Foreign Assembly in International Trade*. Washington, D.C.: Brookings Institution.

Hamel, Gary, and C. K. Prahalad. 1985. "Do You Really Have a Global Strategy?" *Harvard Business Review* 4: 139–48.

Hatton, Timothy J., and Jeffrey G. Williamson. 1998. *The Age of Mass Migration*. Oxford, U.K.: Oxford University Press.

Hawkins, Jeff. 2001. "Quality Shipping in the Asia Pacific Region." *International Journal of Maritime Economics* 3(1): 79–101.

Helleiner, Gerald K., ed. 1994. *Trade Policy and Industrialization in Turbulent Times*. New York: Routledge.

———. 2000a. "Markets, Politics and Globalization: Can the Global Economy Be Civilized?" Presented at the 10th Raúl Prebisch Lecture, December 11, Geneva.

———. 2000b. "External Conditionality, Local Ownership and Development." In Jim Freedman, ed., *Transforming Development*. Toronto: University of Toronto Press.

Hernández, Isabel. 2002. "Comprehensive Regional Strategy for Reducing Poverty and Ethnic Discrimination among Indigenous Groups." Report of the Economic Commission for Latin America and the Caribbean and the Government of Italy. Siena, Italy: Centro Interdipartimentale di Studi sull'America Indígena Università degli Studi.

Hilbert, Martin, and Jorge Katz. 2002. *Building an Information Society: A Perspective from Latin America and the Caribbean*. Santiago, Chile: Division of Production, Productivity and Management, Economic Commission for Latin America and the Caribbean.

Hirschman, Albert O. 1958. *The Strategy of Economic Development*. New Haven, Conn.: Yale University Press.

Hofman, André. 2000. "Standardised Capital Stock Estimates in Latin America: A 1950–94 Update." *Cambridge Journal of Economics* 24(1): 45–86.

Hotelling, Harold. 1929. "Stability in Competition." *Economic Journal* 39: 41–57.

Howells, Jeremy. 2000. *Innovation & Services: New Conceptual Frameworks*. CRIC Discussion Paper 38. Manchester, U.K.: Centre of Research on Innovation and Competition, University of Manchester.

ILO (International Labour Organization). 1998. *Declaration on Fundamental Principles and Rights at Work and Its Follow-up*. Adopted by the General Conference of the ILO, 86th Session, June 18, Geneva.

IMF (International Monetary Fund). 1998. *World Economic Outlook*. Washington, D.C.

————. 2001a. *Conditionality in Fund-Supported Programs: Policy Issues*. Washington, D.C.: Policy Development and Review Department.

————. 2001b. *International Financial Statistics* CD/ROM version. Washington, D.C.

Jara, Alejandro. 1993. "Bargaining Strategies of Developing Countries in the Uruguay Round." In Diana Tussie and Davis Glover, eds., *Countries in World Trade Policies and Bargaining Strategies*. Boulder, Colo.: Lynne Rienner Publishers.

J.P. Morgan Chase. 2002. *Emerging Markets Outlook*. Several issues.

Kamin, Steven B., and Karsten von Kleist. 1999. "The Evolution and Determinants of Emerging Market Credit Spreads in the 1990s." BIS Working Paper 68. Basel, Switzerland: Bank for International Settlements.

Kant, Immanuel. 1795. "Perpetual Peace: A Philosophical Sketch." In "Kant on the Web/English Translation of Secondary Writings."

Katz, Jorge. 2001. *Structural Reforms, Productivity and Technological Change in Latin* America. LC-G.2129-P. U.N. Publication Sales No. E.01.II.G.22. Santiago, Chile: Economic Commission for Latin America and the Caribbean.

Katz, Jorge, and Martin Hilbert. 2002. "América Latina en su transición a la era digital." Paper presented at the III Encuentro de Ciudades Digitales, April 29–30, Valencia, Spain.

Kaul, Inge, Isabelle Grunberg, and Marc A. Stern. 1999. *Global Public Goods*. New York: Oxford University Press.

Kenny, Charles, and David Williams. 2000. "What Do We Know about Economic Growth? Or, Why Don't We Know Very Much?" *World Development* 29(1): 1–22.

Keynes, John M. 1936. *The General Theory of Employment, Interest and Money*. Cambridge, U.K.: Cambridge University Press.

Kindleberger, Charles P. 1978. *Manias, Panics and Crashes: A History of Financial Crisis*. New York: Basic Books.

———. 1984. *Financial History of Western Europe*. London: George Allen and Unwin.

King, Robert G., and Ross Levine. 1993. "Finance and Growth: Schumpeter Might Be Right." *Quarterly Journal of Economics* 108(3): 717–37.

Knetter, Michael M., and Matthew J. Slaughter. 1999. "Measuring Product-Market Integration." NBER Working Paper 6969. Cambridge, Mass.: National Bureau of Economic Research. http://www.nber.org

Krueger, Anne. 2001. "International Financial Architecture for 2002: A New Approach to Sovereign Debt Restructuring." Paper presented at the National Economists' Club Annual Members' Dinner, American Enterprise Institute, November 26, Washington, D.C.

Krueger, Anne O., and Sarath Rajapatirana. 1999. "The World Bank Policies towards Trade and Trade Policy Reform." *World Economy* 22(6): 717–40.

Krugman, Paul. 1990. *Rethinking International Trade*. Cambridge, Mass.: MIT Press.

———. 1995. *Development, Geography and Economic Theory*. Cambridge, Mass.: MIT Press.

———. 1999. "The Return of Depression Economics Returns." *Foreign Affairs* 78(1): 56–74.

Kuczynski, Pedro-Pablo, and John Williamson. 2003. *After the Washington Consensus: Restarting Growth and Reform in Latin America*. Washington, D.C.: Institute for International Economics.

La Fuente, Mario, and Pedro Sáinz. 2001. "Participation by the Poor in the Fruits of Growth." *CEPAL Review* No. 75. LC/G.2150-P. Santiago, Chile.

Lahera, Eugenio. 2002. *Introduction to Public Policies.* Santiago, Chile: Breviarios, Fondo de Cultura Económica.

Levitt, Theodore. 1983. "The Globalization of Markets." *Harvard Business Review* 83(3): 92–102.

Lewis, William Arthur. 1978. *Growth and Fluctuations 1870–1913.* London: George Allen and Unwin.

Lindert, P. H., and Jeffrey G. Williamson. 2001. "Does Globalization Make the World More Unequal?" Paper presented at the National Bureau of Economic Research conference on Globalization in Historical Perspective, May 3–6, Santa Barbara, Calif.

Lucas, Robert E., Jr. 1988. "On the Mechanics of Economic Development." *Journal of Monetary Economics* 22(1): 3–42.

Machinea, José Luis. 2002. *Debt Crisis, International Financing, and the Role of the Private Sector.* Financiamiento del Desarrollo series No. 117. LC/L.1713-P. U.N. Publication Sales No. S.02.II.G.23. Santiago, Chile: Economic Commission for Latin America and the Caribbean.

Maddison, Angus. 1989. *The World Economy in the 20th Century.* Paris: OECD Development Centre.

———. 1991. *Dynamic Forces in Capitalist Development: A Long-Run Comparative View.* New York: Oxford University Press.

———. 1995. *Monitoring the World Economy 1820–1992.* Paris: OECD Development Centre.

———. 2001. *The World Economy: A Millennial Perspective.* Paris: OECD Development Centre.

Marfán, Manuel. 2002. "Globalization and Governability." Santiago, Chile: Economic Commission for Latin America and the Caribbean.

Marglin, Stephen A., and Juliet Schor. 1990. *The Golden Age of Capitalism.* Oxford, U.K.: Oxford University Press.

Marín, Manuel. 1999. "Integration and Cohesion: The European Experience." Paper prepared for the Sixth Meeting of the Montevideo Circle, November 12–13, Santo Domingo, Dominican Republic.

Mariti, Paolo. 1993. "Small and Medium-Sized Firms in Markets with Substantial Scale and Scope Economies." In Marc Humbert, ed., *The Impact of Globalisation on Europe's Firms and Industries.* London: Pinter Publishers.

Michalopoulos, Constantine. 2000. "Trade and Development in the GATT and WTO: The Role of Special and Differential Treatment for Developing Countries." Paper presented at the World Trade Organization Seminar on Special and Differential Treatment for Developing Countries, March 7, Geneva.

Milanovic, Branko. 1999. "True World Income Distribution, 1988 and 1993: First Calculation Based on Household Surveys Alone." World Bank Policy Research Working Paper 2244. Washington, D.C.

———. 2002. "Worlds Apart: International and World Inequality, 1950–2000." Washington, D.C.: World Bank.

Morley, Samuel. 2000. *Income Distribution in Latin America and the Caribbean.* Santiago, Chile: Economic Commission for Latin America and the Caribbean and Fondo de Cultura Económica.

Mortimore, Michael, and Wilson Peres. 2001. "Corporate Competitiveness in Latin America and the Caribbean." *CEPAL Review* No. 74. LC/G.2135-P. Santiago, Chile.

Myrdal, Gunnar. 1957. *Economic Theory and Underdeveloped Regions.* London: Duckworth.

Nelson, Richard. 1988. "National Systems of Innovation." In Giovanni Dosi, Christopher Freeman, Richard Nelson, Gerald Silverberg, and Luc Soete, eds., *Technical Change and Economic Theory.* London: Pinter Publishers.

———. ed. 1993. *National Innovation Systems: A Comparative Analysis.* New York: Oxford University Press.

Nurkse, Ragnar. 1953. *Problems of Capital Formation in Underdeveloped Countries.* New York: Oxford University Press.

Ocampo, José Antonio. 1999. *Reforming the International Financial System: A Debate in Progress.* Santiago, Chile: Economic Commission for Latin America and the Caribbean and Fondo de Cultura Económica.

———. 2001a. "A New Look at the Development Agenda." *CEPAL Review* No. 74. LC/G.2135-P. Santiago, Chile.

———. 2001b. "Raúl Prebisch and the Development Agenda at the Dawn of the Twenty-First Century." *CEPAL Review* No. 75. LC/G.2150-P. Santiago, Chile.

———. 2002a. "Developing Countries' Anti-Cyclical Policies in a Globalized World." In Amitava Dutt and Jaime Ros, eds., *Development Economics and Structuralist Macroeconomics: Essays in Honour of Lance Taylor.* Aldershot, U.K.: Edward Elgar.

———. 2002b. "Recasting the International Financial Agenda." In John Eatwell and Lance Taylor, eds., *International Capital Markets: Systems in Transition.* New York: Oxford University Press.

———. 2002c. "Structural Dynamics and Economic Development." In Valpy FitzGerald, ed., *Social Institutions and Economic Development: A Tribute to Kurt Martin.* Dordrecht, Netherlands: Kluwer.

Ocampo, José Antonio, and María Ángela Parra. 2003. "Returning to an Eternal Debate: The Terms of Trade for Commodities in the Twentieth Century." Economic Commission for Latin America and the Caribbean, Serie Informes y Estudios Especiales, No. 5. *CEPAL Review* No 79. Santiago, Chile.

OECD (Organisation for Economic Co-operation and Development). 1996. *Globalization of Industry (Overview and Sector Reports).* Paris.

————. 2000a. "The Service Economy." *Business and Industry Policy Forum Series.* Paris.

————. 2000b. *Trends in International Migration, Annual Report.* 2000 Edition. Paris.

————. 2001a. *Institutional Investors Statistical Yearbook, 2001.* Paris.

————. 2001b. *Trends in International Migration.* SOPEMI 2001 Edition. Paris.

Ohmae, Kenichi. 1985. *Triad Power: The Coming Shape of Global Competition.* New York: Free Press.

Oman, Charles. 1994. *Globalisation and Regionalisation: The Challenge for Developing Countries.* Paris: OECD Development Centre.

O'Rourke, Kevin H. 2001. "Globalization and Inequality: Historical Trends." Paper presented at the Annual Bank Conference on Development Economics, World Bank, May 1–2, Washington, D.C.

O'Rourke, Kevin H., and Jeffrey G. Williamson. 1999. *Globalization and History: The Evolution of a Nineteenth-Century Atlantic Economy.* Cambridge, Mass.: MIT Press.

Palma, Gabriel. 2001. "Recent Changes in Latin American Income Distribution: On Changing Property Rights, Distributional Coalitions and Institutional Settlements." Cambridge Mass. Processed.

————. 2002. "De-Industrialization: Its Sources and Dynamics, Towards a New Concept of the Dutch Disease." Cambridge, U.K.: Cambridge University. Processed.

Pérez, Carlota. 2001. "Technological Change and Opportunities for Development as a Moving Target." *CEPAL Review* No. 75. LC/G.2150-P. Santiago, Chile.

Persaud, Avinash. 2000. "Sending the Herd off the Cliff Edge: The Disturbing Interaction between Herding and Market-Sensitive Risk Management Practices." London: State Street.

Piore, Michael J., and Charles Sabel. 1984. *The Second Industrial Divide: Possibilities for Prosperity.* New York: Basic Books.

Polanyi, Karl. 1957. *The Great Transformation: The Political and Economic Origins of Our Time.* Boston: Beacon Press.

Porter, Michael, ed. 1986. *Competition in Global Industries.* Cambridge, Mass.: Harvard University Press.

———. 1990. *The Competitive Advantage of Nations.* New York: Free Press.

Prebisch, Raúl. 1951. "Growth, Disequilibrium and Disparities: Interpretation of the Process of Economic Development." In *Economic Survey of Latin America, 1949.* E/CN.12/164/Rev.1. U.N. Publication Sales No. 51.I.G.1. New York.

———. 1984. "Five Stages in My Thinking on Development. In Gerald M. Meier and Dudley Seers, eds., *Pioneers in Development.* New York: Oxford University Press.

Pritchett, Lant. 1997. "Divergence, Big Time." *Journal of Economic Perspectives* 11(3): 3–18.

Quah, Danny. 1995. "Empirics for Economic Growth and Convergence." Centre for Economic Policy Research Discussion Paper 1140. London.

Rajan, Raghuram G., and Luigi Zingales. 2001. "The Great Reversals: The Politics of Financial Development in the 20th Century." NBER Working Paper 8178. Cambridge, Mass.: National Bureau of Economic Research.

Rayment, Paul. 1983. "Intra 'Industry' Specialisation and the Foreign Trade of Industrial Countries." In Stephen Frowen, ed., *Controlling Industrial Economies.* London: Macmillan.

Reisen, Helmut. 2001. "Will Basel II Contribute to Convergence International Capital Flows?" Paper prepared for the Oesterreichische Nationalbank 29th Economics Conference, May 31 and June 1, Vienna, Austria.

———. 2002. "Ratings since the Asian Crisis." In Ricardo Ffrench-Davis and Stephany Griffith-Jones, eds., *Capital Flows to Emerging Markets since the Asian Crisis.* United Nations University, World Institute for Development Economics Research, and Economic Commission for Latin America and the Caribbean.

Rodríguez, Francisco, and Dani Rodrik. 2001. "Trade Policy and Economic Growth: A Skeptic's Guide to the Cross-National Evidence." In Ben S. Bernanke and Kenneth Rogoff, eds., *NBER Macroeconomics Annual 2000.* Vol. 15. Cambridge, Mass.: MIT Press.

Rodrik, Dani. 1997. *Has Globalization Gone Too Far?* Washington, D.C.: Institute for International Economics.

———. 1999. *The New Global Economy and the Developing Countries: Making Openness Work*. Policy Essay 24. Washington, D.C.: Overseas Development Council.

———. 2001a. "Development Strategies for the Next Century." Paper prepared for the conference on Development Theory at the Threshold of the Twenty-First Century, August 28–29. Santiago, Chile: Economic Commission for Latin America and the Caribbean.

———. 2001b. "The Global Governance of Trade As If Development Really Mattered." Paper prepared for the United Nations Development Programme, April, New York.

Romer, Paul. 1990. "Are Nonconvexities Important for Understanding Growth?" NBER Working Paper 3271. Cambridge, Mass.: National Bureau of Economics Research.

Ros, Jaime. 2000. *Development Theory and the Economics of Growth*. Ann Arbor, Mich.: University of Michigan Press.

Rosenstein-Rodan, Paul N. 1943. "Problems of Industrialization of Eastern and South-Eastern Europe." *Economic Journal* 53: 202–11.

Rosenthal, Gert. 2001. "The Contribution of the Economic Commission for Latin America and the Caribbean to the United Nations' Intellectual Legacy." In *United Nations Intellectual History Project: Vol. 12. Views from the Regional Commissions: ECLAC*. New York.

Rowthorn, Robert E. 1999. "Unemployment, Wage Bargaining and Capital-Labour Substitution." *Cambridge Journal of Economics* 23(4): 413–25.

Sáez, Sebastián. 1999. *Strategy and Bargaining in the Multilateral System of Commerce: Applied International Economics*. Santiago, Chile: Dolmen Ediciones.

Salt, John. 1999. "Current Trends in International Migration in Europe." Geneva: Council of Europe.

Schumpeter, Joseph. 1939. *Business Cycles: A Theoretical, Historical and Statistical Analysis of the Capitalist Process*. New York: McGraw-Hill.

Sen, Amartya. 1999. *Development as Freedom*. New York: Alfred A. Knopf.

Sengupta, Arjun. 2001. *Third Report of the Independent Expert on the Right to Development, Mr. Arjun Sengupta, Submitted in Accordance with Commission Resolution 2000/5*. E/CN.4/2001/WG.18/2. Paper presented to the Economic and Social Council, United Nations, January 2, Geneva.

Singer, Hans W. 1950. "The Distribution of Gains Between Investing and Borrowing Countries." *American Economic Review* 40(2): 473–85.

Solimano, Andrés. 2001. *The Evolution of World Income Inequality: Assessing the Impact of Globalization.* Macroeconomía del Desarrollo series No. 11. LC/L.1686-P. U.N. Publication Sales No. E.01.II.G.124. Santiago, Chile: Economic Commission for Latin America and the Caribbean.

———. 2002. "Globalizing Talent and Human Capital: Implications for Developing Countries." Paper prepared for the World Bank Fourth Annual Conference on Development Economics in Europe, June 24–26, Oslo.

SOPEMI (Continuous Reporting System on Migration). 2001. *Annual Report, 2001, statistical annex.* Paris.

Srinivasan, T. N. 1996. *Developing Countries and the Multilateral Trading System: From GATT (1947) to the Uruguay Round and the Future Beyond.* Washington, D.C.: Economic Development Institute, World Bank.

Stallings, Barbara, and Wilson Peres. 2000. *Growth, Employment and Equity: The Impact of the Economic Reforms in Latin America.* New York: Brookings Institution Press and Economic Commission for Latin America and the Caribbean.

Stewart, Frances. 2000. "Income Distribution and Development." Paper prepared for the 10th United Nations Conference on Trade and Development, February 12, Bangkok, Thailand.

Stiglitz, Joseph A. 1994. "The Role of the State in Financial Markets." In *Proceedings of the World Bank Annual Conference on Development Economics, 1993.* Washington, D.C.: World Bank.

———. 1999. "The World Bank at the Millennium." *Economic Journal* 109: 577–97.

Studart, Rogério. 1995. *Investment Finance in Economic Development.* London: Routledge.

———. 1996. "The Efficiency of the Financial System, Liberalization and Economic Development." *Journal of Post Keynesian Economics* 18(2): 269–92.

Sutton, John. 1991. *Sunk Costs and Market Structure.* Cambridge, Mass.: MIT Press.

———. 1998. *Technology and Market Structure, Theory and History.* Cambridge, Mass.: MIT Press.

Sylos Labini, Paolo. 1957. *Oligopoly and Technical Progress.* Cambridge, Mass.: Harvard University Press.

Third World Network. 2001. "The Multilateral Trading System: A Development Perspective." Paper prepared for the United Nations Development Programme, December, New York.

Thomas, Harmon, and John Whalley, eds. 1998. *Uruguay Round Results and the Emerging Trade Agenda: Quantitative-Based Analyses from the Development Perspective* Publ/98/23. U.N. Publication Sales No. GV.E.98.0.26. Geneva.

Thorp, Rosemary. 1998. *Progress, Poverty and Exclusion: An Economic History of Latin America in the 20th Century.* Baltimore: Johns Hopkins University Press.

Triffin, Robert. 1968. *Our International Monetary System: Yesterday, Today and Tomorrow.* New York: Random House.

Turner, Louis, and Michael Hodges. 1992. *Global Shakeout, World Market Competition: The Challenges for Business and Government.* London: Century Business.

Tussie, Diana. 1987. "The Less Developed Countries and the World Trading System: A Challenge to the GATT." In *Studies in International Political Economy.* London: Pinter Publishers.

———. 1988. "Latin America Debtor Coordination: Which Is the Logic of Action?" In Stephany Griffith-Jones, ed., *External Debt, Bargaining, and Adjustment in Latin America.* Mexico City, Mexico: Fondo de Cultura Económica.

———. 1993. "The Uruguayan Round and the Trading System in the Balance: Dilemmas for Developing Countries." In Manuel R. Agosin and Diana Tussie, eds., *Trade and Growth: New Dilemmas in Trade Policy.* London: Macmillan.

UNCTAD (United Nations Conference on Trade and Development). 1995. *World Investment Report 1995: Transnational Corporations and Competitiveness. Overview.* UNCTAD/DTCI/26. New York.

———. 1997. *Trade and Development Report, 1997.* UNCTAD/TDR/1997. U.N. Publication Sales No. E.97.II.D.8. Geneva.

———. 1998. *Trade and Development Report, 1998.* UNCTAD/TDR/1998. U.N. Publication Sales No. E.98.II.D.6. Geneva.

———. 1999. *Trade and Development Report, 1999.* UNCTAD/TDR/1999. U.N. Publication Sales No. E.99.II.D.1. Geneva.

———. 2000. *World Investment Report, 2000: Cross-Border Mergers and Acquisitions and Development.* UNCTAD/WIR/2000. U.N. Publication Sales No. E.00.II.20. Geneva.

———. 2001a. *Trade and Development Report, 2001.* UNCTAD/TDR/2001. U.N. Publication Sales No. E.00.II.D.10. Geneva.

————. 2001b. *World Investment Report, 2001.* UNCTAD/ WIR/(2001). U.N. Publication Sales No. E.01.II.D.12. Geneva.

————. 2002a. *Trade and Development Report, 2002: Developing Countries in World Trade.* UNCTAD/TDR/(2002). U.N. Publication Sales No. E.02.II.D.10. New York.

————. 2002b. *World Investment Report, 2002: Transnational Corporations and Export Competitiveness.* U.N. Publication Sales No. E.02.II.D.4. New York.

UNCTAD and World Trade Organization. 1996. *Strengthening the Participation of Developing Countries in World Trade and the Multilateral Trading System.* TD/375/Rev.1. Geneva.

UNDP (United Nations Development Programme). 1999a. *Human Development Report, 1999.* New York.

————. 1999b. *Human Development Report for Central and Eastern Europe and the CIS 1999: The Human Cost of Transition.* New York.

UNESCO (United Nations Educational, Scientific, and Cultural Organization). 2001. *The State of Science and Technology in the World, 1996–1997.* Montreal, Quebec, Canada: Institute for Statistics.

United Nations. 1948. "Universal Declaration of Human Rights." Adopted by the General Assembly on December 1.

————. 1966. "International Covenant on Economic, Social and Cultural Rights." Adopted and opened for signature, ratification, and accession by the General Assembly on December 16.

————. 1999a. "Towards a New International Financial Architecture: Report of the Task Force of the Executive Committee on Economic and Social Affairs of the United Nations." LC/G.2054. Santiago, Chile: Economic Commission for Latin America and the Caribbean.

————. 1999b. *Treaty Series: Cumulative Index* No. 25. New York.

————. 2000. "United Nations Millennium Declaration." A/RES/55/2. Resolution adopted by the General Assembly at the Millennium Summit, September 6–8, New York.

————. 2001. *Social Dimensions of Macroeconomic Policy: Report of the Executive Committee on Economic and Social Affairs of the United Nations.* Informes y Estudios Especiales series No. 1. LC/L.1662-P. U.N. Publication Sales No. E.01.I.G.204. Santiago, Chile: Economic Commission for Latin America and the Caribbean.

————. 2002. *Report of the Secretary-General on Implementing Agenda 21.* E/CN.17/2002/PC.2/7. New York: Commission on Sustainable Development, Economic and Social Council.

UNSD (United Nations Statistical Division). 2002. Commodity Trade Statistics (COMTRADE), Electronic Database. New York: Department of Economic and Social Affairs, United Nations.

Wade, Robert. 1990. *Governing the Market: Economic Theory and the Role of Government in East Asian Industrialization.* Princeton, N.J.: Princeton University Press.

Winham, Gilbert R. 1986. *International Trade and the Tokyo Round Negotiation.* Princeton, N.J.: Princeton University Press.

Wood, Adrian. 1998. "Globalisation and the Rise in Labour Market Inequalities." *Economic Journal* 108(450): 1463–82.

World Bank. 1998. *Assessing Aid.* World Bank Policy Research Report. New York: Oxford University Press.

———. 1999. *World Development Indicators.* CD/ROM version. Washington, D.C.

———. 2001a. *Global Development Finance, 2001.* CD/ROM version. Washington, D.C.

———. 2001b. *World Development Indicators, 2001.* CD/ROM version. Washington, D.C.

———. 2002a. *Global Economic Prospects and the Developing Countries: Making Trade Work for the World's Poor 2002.* Washington, D.C.

———. 2002b. *Globalization, Growth and Poverty: Building an Inclusive World Economy.* New York: Oxford University Press.

Zedillo, Ernesto, Abdulatif Y. Al-Hamad, David Bryer, Mary Chinery-Hesse, Jacques Delors, Rebeca Grynspan, Alexander Y. Livshits, Abdul Magid Osman, Robert Rubin, Manmohan Singh, and Masayoshi Son. 2001. "Recommendations of the High-Level Panel on Financing for Development." Report prepared for the United Nations Secretary-General, June 22.

Index

Note: *b* indicates boxes, *f* indicates figures, *n* indicates notes (*nn* more than one note), and *t* indicates tables.